# ART
# ARGUMENT
# AND ADVOCACY

## MASTERING
## PALIAMENTARY
## DEBATE

# ART, ARGUMENT, AND ADVOCACY

## MASTERING PARLIAMENTARY DEBATE

JOHN MEANY AND
KATE SHUSTER

INTERNATIONAL DEBATE EDUCATION ASSOCIATION
NEW YORK • AMSTERDAM • BRUSSELS

Published in 2002 by
The International Debate Education Association
400 West 59th Street
New York, NY 10019

Library of Congress Cataloging-in-Publishing Data
Meany, John
    Art, argument and advocacy: mastering parliamentary debate /
John Meany & Kate Shuster. p.cm.
Includes index.
ISBN 0-9702130-7-7
 1. Deabates and debating. I. Shuster, Kate, 1974- II.Title
PN4181 .M38 2002
808.53--dc21

Printed in the United States of America

# TABLE OF CONTENTS

# PREFACE

Parliamentary debate is dynamic, entertaining and challenging. The world's most popular form of academic and contest debating, parliamentary debate is also the fastest growing debating format. This is because it is uniquely accessible. Parliamentary debate teaches sophisticated skills in extemporaneous speaking, critical listening, critical thinking, research, and presentation.

Parliamentary debate is different throughout the world. This book provides a comprehensive description of the American, or "two team," format and the British, or World Championship, "four team" format. Though not a comprehensive description of all parliamentary debate techniques and issues, the principles described in the text are relevant to any format.

The text is designed for novice and advanced competitors and debate coaches, and is suitable for classroom instruction. The parliamentary debate format is appropriate for public, non-competitive debating. We strongly believe in the value of classroom and public debates. Issues of controversy and concern for all individuals and communities demand that people be able to express themselves through voice and argument. The skill development in this text as well as the format information we provide will assist in staging public events for classes, community groups, non-profit organizations, government agencies, corporations, and activist groups on important matters of local, national, and international politics.

We have included all of the basic elements of public speaking, critical thinking, critical listening, and research skills for new debaters.

The text also contains sophisticated argument skills for experienced practitioners that include exercises, sample speeches, excerpts, and resources, as well as a glossary and more than 1,000 potential debate topics. All these resources are useful for novice and experienced debaters as well as debate trainers and coaches. The best way to learn how to debate is through constant practice. The exercises in each chapter are meant to help you learn how to use the vocabulary and concepts in parliamentary debate gradually, rather than all at once. Some exercises may be profitably repeated with different topics and in different groups of debaters.

The text presents some technical jargon associated with debate, but whenever jargon is used, a common or plain meaning description of the same concepts is also given. Our goal is to help debaters adapt their speeches from the information in the text for use before inexperienced or experienced judges or a diverse array of audiences. Jargon is not meant to substitute for elegant rhetoric in parliamentary debates. We have included some jargon associated with other debate formats including a policy or Lincoln-Douglas debate because many debaters learn their skills from textbooks or online sites that use those formats as models. Also, parliamentary debaters frequently participate in multiple formats – international or American and others – as part of their debating experience. Policy and Lincoln-Douglas formats are debated in several countries, so there is substantial overlap between debate communities. Debaters need to understand the jargon and techniques of other formats to effectively counter those students with that experience. We keep this information related to policy debate and Lincoln-Douglas debate to a minimum and always place it in the context of parliamentary debate.

This book is designed to be read and studied over a period of time, rather than absorbed in a single sitting. While you read the text, you may encounter vocabulary terms that you do not immediately understand. Take notes on these vocabulary words and closely examine their accompanying definitions or explanations.

We have included information on debate and argumentation theory and practice to allow practitioners to innovate the thinking, practice, and craft of parliamentary debate. No community can remain static for long. Debate is particularly dynamic. The norms and practices of debate are continuously reinvented by debaters and coaches alike. We hope that this book will aid, rather than hinder, this process of growth and change in the debate community. We encourage readers to use the text to develop their own exercises, and to adapt its precepts where necessary.

The authors wish to thank IDEA and Noel Selegzi for their support of debate and of this textbook's production in particular.

John Meany wishes to thank Robert Branham, the former director of debate at Bates College, an inspirational teacher of debate who introduced this author to parliamentary debate. Bob was a brilliant debate theorist with a commitment to debate education. John also wishes to thanks his son, Jake Meany, for his sacrifices, patience, and support during the production of this book and current and former members of the Claremont Colleges Debate Union, who have shared with him in learning the art and practice of parliamentary debating.

Kate Shuster wishes to thank her mother, Sandra Shuster, for her unwavering support and love. She has been an inspiration in times of trouble and prosperity alike; also her brothers, Matthew and Will; and her father, Don Shuster, who is missed. Kate also wishes to thank her dear friend Jon Brody, a former University of Texas debater, whose example and guidance taught her to be innovative and creative in thought as well as debate.

# FORMATS AND SPEAKER RESPONSIBILITIES

## FORMATS

Parliamentary debating formats vary among different countries, even within countries in different debate leagues or at specialized tournaments. Rules for debating are formally established and institutionally maintained; this chapter discusses two popular and distinct parliamentary formats—the American format and British format. In addition to formal rules (and it is important to note that there are few "official" rules of parliamentary debating, which is one of the more attractive features of the event, regardless of format), there are informal conventions. These latter guidelines are often understood, or misunderstood, as "rules" for contest debating. The rules of debating primarily address speaking times, number of teams and speakers, order of speeches, and decision making.

## THE AMERICAN FORMAT

A standard American competitive format for a parliamentary debate includes two debate teams, one on each side of a motion. Each team has two people. One team supports a motion for debate (the motion is also known as the topic, proposition or resolution). The team supporting the motion is known as the proposition team. (In the USA and some other countries, the proposition team is also known as the "government.") The proposition team has the burden to prove that the motion for debate is more probably true than false. In other words, the proposition team must convincingly demonstrate that it has successfully supported the motion.

The other team in the debate is known as the opposition. (They are not ever known as the anti-government, rebel alliance, revolutionary front or the oxymoronic Anarchists United.) The opposition team argues against the proposition's support for the motion.

For each debate, a motion is announced and the teams are given a period of time to prepare the debate. The typical preparation time period is fifteen minutes, although there are variations. The debate begins after preparation time has ended.

There are six speeches in the debate. The first four speeches, known as constructive speeches, form the foundation of the debate. The proposition and opposition constructive speeches establish the core arguments for each team's side of the motion.

The latter two speeches are rebuttal speeches, with each side getting one speech to summarize. Each rebuttal speaker uses her speech to identify the salient issues for her team and propose the reasons why her team has convincingly won the debate.

The debate proceeds as follows:
- First proposition constructive speech     7 minutes
- First opposition constructive speech     8 minutes
- Second proposition constructive speech     8 minutes
- Second opposition constructive speech     8 minutes

- Opposition rebuttal                      4 minutes
- Proposition rebuttal                    5 minutes

These speeches are also known by the following titles and abbreviations:

- Prime Minister Constructive               (PMC)
- Lead Opposition Constructive             (LOC)
- Member of Government                  (MG)
- Member of Opposition                  (MO)
- Lead Opposition Rebuttal                (LOR)
- Prime Minister Rebuttal                  (PMR)

The speakers for the proposition open and close the debate. The opening speaker for each side presents two speeches in the debate – the opening constructive speech and the rebuttal speech. The second person on each side delivers a single speech – the member speech for her team. There is no preparation time for speakers during the debate. Each speaker, in appropriate turn, immediately follows the previous speaker.

There is a judge for each debate. In many debates, particularly those directly determining the outcome of a tournament, there are panels of judges, typically three or five judges per panel, with individual deliberation and a majority decision to decide a contest.

In some cases, there may be a designated Speaker of the House (or "Chair") or presiding parliamentary officer. More commonly, however, the judge or designated individual on a panel of judges, functions as Speaker of the House, introducing debaters for their speeches and ruling on parliamentary points directed to the chair. There is no preparation time between speeches. After one speech is finished, the Speaker of the House calls upon the next debater to proceed.

A debate may have a designated timekeeper to track preparation time and speaking time. In the absence of a timekeeper, the judge usually keeps time. The timekeeper announces the end of preparation time. Technically, the debate officially begins immediately at the conclusion of the preparation time. The timekeeper signals time to the speakers during the debate with hand signals or a series of cards indicating remaining time. For example, if a speaker is delivering a seven minute speech and has used three minutes of her time, the timekeeper should signal "four," the remaining time for the speech. The timekeeper should never signal elapsed time in a speech. It is sufficiently challenging to deliver a winning debate speech without having to perform an arithmetic calculation to determine available speaking time. The person keeping time should signal the remaining time to the speakers at the passing of each full minute and at the half-minute mark of the final minute. The timekeeper should also note when the speaker has no remaining time.

The timekeeper announces available time for points of information during the constructive speeches. After the first minute and before the last minute of each constructive speech, the timekeeper will "knock;" that is, rap her knuckles on a desk or table, slap a table with a gavel or palm of her hand, ring a bell, fire a blast of an air horn, squeeze a duck unexpectedly, or perform some other brief, noisy gesture.

Each round of tournament debating has a different topic; the motion for debate is announced just before the debate begins. There are different approaches to the announcement of a motion. They are listed in the order of their popularity.

- A motion may be attached to the ballot presented to each judge to complete regarding the outcome of the debate. (See the chapter on judging for more on ballots and decision making. A sample parliamentary debate ballot is included in the resources appendix.) When the two teams and judge arrive at the assigned location for the debate, the judge announces the motion to the teams and begins preparation time.
- The tournament may have a central gathering place. At that site, a tournament representative will make a verbal announcement of the motion for all participants.
- A sheet of paper may be attached to the judge's ballot. The sheet will contain three potential motions for debate. The proposition team and opposition team each "strike" a debate topic, i.e., each remove a motion from the list. The remaining topic is the motion for the debate. The debaters then announce the topic to the judge and preparation time begins.

- Two motions are attached to the judge's ballot or announced at a central gathering place. One motion is "open" and the other is "closed." (Open and closed motions are discussed in the chapter on topic interpretation.) For example, one motion may be "open" – "Bury it," and other "closed" – "This House would eliminate the secret policy deliberations of the WTO." The proposition team selects either motion.

- A motion is attached to the judge's ballot. The motion contains opposing statements. For example, a motion might read "This House would/would not support NATO expansion into Russia." The proposition team then selects either possibility for the debate. In other words, the proposition team may defend either "This House would support NATO expansion into Russia," or "This House would not support NATO expansion into Russia." In some leagues or tournament competitions, it is appropriate for the proposition team to declare their selection before preparation time begins. On other occasions, the proposition does not announce the motion for debate until their opening speech.

## THE BRITISH FORMAT

A standard British intervarsity tournament substantially departs from the American parliamentary format. Each debate involves four teams, with two teams on each side of the motion. Each team has two people. As in the American format, the teams supporting the motion are known as the proposition and the teams opposing them are known as the opposition. This is one of many similarities between the American format and the British format. The language and argument style of all parliamentary debating is liberally borrowed from the British, Irish and Canadian formats. This might explain the use of the titles "Prime Minister" and "Leader of the Opposition" in American parliamentary debating. We believe this is a slightly better explanation for the use of these anachronistic, somewhat perplexing terms than the other popular claims regarding their use –collective madness for all things Anglo.

Of the two teams on the same side of the motion, one is designated first proposition and the other as second proposition. The same is the case for the opposition teams: teams are listed as first or second opposition. Each team has a different role described in detail below in the section on speaker responsibilities. Briefly, the first proposition teams function in the same way as American debaters do in the constructive speeches, establishing an argument for the motion and defending and disputing it. The second proposition team provides an extension of the original case of the first proposition team, expanding the debate to new areas of critical examination. The second opposition team refutes this new argument direction. The final speakers for each team in the debate are much like rebuttalists in the American format, effectively summarizing the winning points of the debate for their respective side.

The announcement of a motion for debate at a central gathering site is this format's preferred model. Preparation time is similar to American format event. The debate commences 15 or 20 minutes after the announcement of the motion.

There are eight speeches in the debate. Each speaker delivers a single speech. Each speech is the same duration, usually either five or seven minutes. There is no preparation time for speakers during the debate. Each speaker, in appropriate turn, immediately follows the previous speaker.

In the British format, a proposition team opens the debate and an opposition team closes the debate. Although arguments are integrated during a debate, it is also appropriate to consider and evaluate the debate format as if it constitutes two parallel debates, administered consecutively.

- First proposition, first speaker
- First opposition, first speaker
- First proposition, second speaker
- First opposition, second speaker
- Second proposition, first speaker
- Second opposition, first speaker
- Second proposition, second speaker
- Second opposition, second speaker

Points of information play a particularly important role in this format and are available after the first minute and before the final minute of each of the eight speeches. Because each speaker only has a single stand on the floor, it is important for each debater to make his or her presence known at other portions of the debate. For example, the opening speakers will not be heard for nearly 45 minutes if they do not successfully make points of information during their opponents' speeches. Likewise, the latter speakers will not play a role in establishing the debate's foundational issues if they fail to advance informational points at an early stage of the proceedings.

Managing points of information is a particular challenge in this format. Because of the importance of making points, debaters are more likely to make them in the British than the American format. In addition, a speaker holding the floor faces four respondents, rather than two, who are able to make points of information. With less speaking time to make winning claims, it is extraordinarily challenging to present organized, winning material and at the same time manage the distractions and interruptions from the other side.

There may be one or more than one judge for the debate. In the American format, each judge deliberates privately and makes a decision about the outcome of the debate. The judge decides a winner of the debate in a zero-sum game: The team that does not win the debate loses the debate. The judge also provides individual marks for each of the four debaters. Because there is private deliberation and voting by judges, it is necessary to have an odd number of judges for each debate. (This requirement is distinguished from the common complaint of debaters, namely, that there are a number of odd judges at each tournament.)

In the British format, judicial decision making is by consensus. This means that debates may be evaluated by an odd or even number of critics. After their deliberation at the conclusion of the debate, the judge or judging panel issues a single decision. The debate decision ranks the four teams in the round of debate from first to fourth place. Each judge also provides individual speaker marks for the participants.

In order to succeed, debate teams must not only defeat the two teams on the opposing side but must also outperform the debate team assigned to the same side of the motion. Teams do not coordinate information or otherwise work together during preparation time in these debates. Each team prepares individually and must show some loyalty to the team on its side and simultaneously demonstrate superiority to that team. Debaters are penalized for failing to support the debate team on its side of the motion.

There is likely to be a person designated Speaker of the House ("Chair") to announce each speaker in turn. Points of order and personal privilege are not available in the format and the chair is not called on to issue rulings on these parliamentary matters.

Parliamentary points, such as points of information, points of order, and points of personal privilege, are discussed at length in a later chapter. They should not be confused with speaker points, which are points on a fixed scale assigned by judges to individual competitors in the debate after the debate has transpired. Parliamentary points are an integral part of the process of debating, but their accumulation (or lack thereof) does not directly influence the outcome of a debate. For more on how debates are decided, please reference the section on judging in the "Skills" chapter.

## SPEAKER RESPONSIBILITIES

### THE AMERICAN FORMAT

Parliamentary debating is extemporaneous argument. Debaters are presented with a motion for debate and have a scant 15 minutes to prepare. They do not read published material or argument briefs gathered prior to preparation time during their presentations. Parliamentary debaters speak from notes they've made during the preparation time prior to or during the debate.

Each speaker position in parliamentary debate involves responsibilities for effective presentation, defense, and refutation of motions. In addition, parliamentary debaters are members of teams and some responsibilities of speakers involve shared efforts with a colleague.

Many parliamentary debaters, particularly in the USA, have developed an unfortunate habit of beginning each speech with a series of "thanks" to the Speaker of the House, opponents, partner, members of the audience, furniture, and any other carbon-based life-form or inorganic matter occupying space in the debating chamber. This affectation is apparently designed to instruct the assembled judges and audience that faux civility is back in fashion. The disingenuousness and mechanistic construction of thanking conventions is almost certain to bore or rankle any listener with critical thinking skills or even those with slight ripples of brain wave activity. Does the speaker genuinely believe that the opponent, a complete stranger, is "honorable"? Is the speaker truly "happy" that the proposition team has presented a powerful case for debate? Can the dermatologically challenged youth performing the role of erstwhile rent-a-partner be accurately described as either "lovely" or "brilliant"?

In a similar manner, speakers end their stand on the floor with a resoundingly obvious "I/We beg to propose" or the clever rejoinder, "I/We beg to oppose." Really? The proposition team wants the proposition team to win the debate and the opposition team wants the opposition team to win the debate? What an unexpected development in the proceedings! Want more advice? Stop begging. It is unseemly; it does not resonate with persuasive authority.

Debaters, all debaters, should begin and end speeches with proper introductions and conclusions. (This matter is discussed in the chapter on performance). This section on speaker responsibilities identifies the fundamental strategic and tactical roles of speakers. Subsequent chapters offer more complete commentary on preparing and delivering the full text of each speech in a debate.

Each speaker is known by one or more references to the speech she will deliver in the debate. The opening speaker for the proposition team is variously known as "Prime Minister," "first prop," or "PMC." The latter is a code for the title of the speech itself – it literally translates as "Prime Minister Constructive," but it has come to be used as a title for the speaker as much as a reference to the speech. The other speakers in the debate are known in a similar manner:

- First speaker, proposition: Prime Minister, first prop, PMC
- First speaker, opposition: Leader of the Opposition, Leader, Leader Opp, first opp, LOC
- Second speaker, proposition: Member of Government, member of gov, second prop, MG

- Second speaker, opposition: Member of Opposition, member opp, second prop, MO
- Opposition rebuttalist: Lead Opp rebuttal, LOR
- Proposition rebuttalist: Prime Minister rebuttal, PMR (for some debaters, this speaker is also known as "that lying, deceitful, manipulative &*%@#, always with a new argument in the final speech of the debate")

FIRST SPEAKER, PROPOSITION (A.K.A., "PRIME MINISTER CONSTRUCTIVE"). The opening speaker in the debate makes a case for the motion. To make a case, a speaker offers a logical proof, a demonstration that the motion is more probably true than false. The first speaker for the proposition interprets the motion for debate, defining any ambiguous terms or otherwise clarifying the foundation for the argument. The speaker may establish additional frameworks for the discussion, including decision making criteria or other evaluative tools to assist the judge.

The speaker is likely to offer a history of the debate's subject matter. Parliamentary debate topics are generated from all academic disciplines and subject fields: economics, philosophy, cultural studies, the sciences, the law, politics, social studies, women's studies, media studies, immigration, race relations, education, human rights, national defense and social welfare. It is not likely that judges have precisely the same knowledge base as opening speakers. A history of the issue in controversy helps debaters inform the judge in a way that might assist the judge's appreciation of subsequent argument claims from the proposition team.

After the opening speaker provides a clear foundation for the debate, she presents a case, that is, a detailed exposition of arguments in support of her interpretation of the motion. A succinct interpretation of the motion is also known as a case statement.. The case typically consists of three or four main arguments with corresponding examples or other forms of contemporary or historical evidence.

It is the obligation of the opening speaker to prove the motion. As Raymond Alden explained in his 1900 treatise on The Art of Debate,there is an "obligation resting upon one or other parties to a controversy to establish by proofs a given proposition, before being entitled to receive an answer from the other side." This responsibility rests, he concluded, "upon the side that would be assumed to be defeated if no progress at all were made in the consideration of the case."

The case will typically consist of three or four main arguments, with corresponding examples or other forms of contemporary or historical evidence. For example, on the motion, "This House would abolish affirmative action," an opening speaker might organize her main arguments in the following manner:

1. Affirmative action has failed to address race and gender issues over time.
2. Affirmative action policies undermine community reform by assimilating the best and brightest of marginalized communities into mainstream culture.
3. Alternatives to affirmative action are more likely to deal with the root causes of racism and sexism.

The opening speaker would have sufficient reasoning and examples to make concise, complete, and compelling arguments on each of these issues. The speaker would offer a summary of her speech to demonstrate the manner in which the arguments met the burden of proof for her interpretation for the motion.

**FIRST SPEAKER, OPPOSITION (A.K.A., "LEADER OF THE OPPOSITION").** The opposition team provides "clash" in the debate. Clash, one of the fundamental principles of any kind of debate, is simply what happens when arguments directly oppose each other. This idea is examined more in the chapter on argument theory. The opposition team provides clash when they attempt to undermine the logic of the proposition team's case. The opposition argues that the motion, as interpreted by the proposition, does not hold.

The first opposition speaker uses tactics of direct and indirect refutation to counter the proposition team's case. The opening speaker for the opposition may challenge the definition of the motion or the proposition's decision framework of the debate. (See the chapter on topic interpretation for more on arguing theses issues). The first opposition speaker may also challenge the main arguments of the proposition's case.

Refuting the main points of the case, that is, disputing the argument analysis or factual claims of the opening speaker, is called direct refutation. The opening speaker for the opposition should critically evaluate the first proposition speaker's arguments, pointing out inconsistencies, trivialities, logic gaps, argument fallacies, improper causal chains and exaggerated claims. This speaker might also offer counters to the examples presented in the proposition case.

The opposition could also promote clash with the proposition case through indirect argumentation. Indirect argumentation involves issues that are not formally included in the proposition team case (i.e., the issues not mentioned in the opening speech by the first proposition speaker) but are, nonetheless, intimately related to consideration of the matter. These material arguments, including disadvantages, counterplans and critiques, are discussed in detail in subsequent chapters.

The optimal opposition strategy in the opening speech is to present some combination of direct and indirect refutation, carefully selecting from among all available opposition arguments the more salient and potentially effective ones for presentation in the debate.

The opposition is not obliged to disagree with every argument of the proposition team's case. It is wearying and ineffectual to engage in this sort of reactionary gainsaying of each of the proposition's main arguments. It may be, in fact, to the advantage of the opposition to agree with a proposition argument. Agreement may focus the discussion on those points in genuine controversy or may support a different and more powerful position for the opposition team.

Opposition debaters, particularly in the opening speech, should at least account for all the main arguments of the proposition case. The opening opposition speaker should do this in a forthright and formal manner, making it apparent to the judge that all major elements of the proposition case have been addressed. By this, we mean that the first opposition speaker should say something about each of the major issues of the case, either by identifying points of agreement and relocating the core issues of the debate to other matters or by directly or indirectly disputing the proposition claims.

This approach does not necessarily limit the options of the opposition speaker, nor does it involve a mechanical rejoinder to each of the proposition team's major issues. It is possible for the opening opposition speaker to identify two or three main lines of argument, for example, one to address the issues of the case (direct refutation) and two new initiatives that could undermine the proposition position in the debate but, at the same time, are not ideas articulated in the opening speech (indirect refutation). The opposition speaker might then let the judge know that these three issues are of greater import than the other matters in the opening speech, i.e., the other major arguments for the proposition team are trivial distractions and not fundamental to a proper evaluation of the motion.

**SECOND SPEAKER, PROPOSITION (A.K.A., "MEMBER OF GOVERNMENT").** The second constructive speech for the proposition team is that team's last opportunity to introduce new arguments and issues. The only stand on the floor for the proposition, after this constructive speech, is the final rebuttal speech in the debate. This is a particularly important speech for the proposition, as it immediately precedes two consecutive opposition speeches – the second opposition constructive speech (or "Member of the Opposition" speech) and the opposition rebuttal speech (or "Leader of the Opposition rebuttal.")

The opposition speeches give that side of the debate 12 consecutive minutes to advance arguments. The second proposition speaker must convincingly prove her side's case to withstand the serious forthcoming opposition assault.

The second speaker for the proposition refutes all the major objections to the case as offered by the opening speaker for the opposition. In addition, this speaker reestablishes the principles of the case, initially presented by her colleague in the first proposition speech. In doing so, she might supplement her colleague's reasoning, offer additional examples or otherwise amplify the opening presentation.

**SECOND SPEAKER, OPPOSITION (A.K.A., "MEMBER OF OPPOSITION").** This is the final constructive speech in the debate for the opposition team. No new arguments or issues may be introduced after this speech by the side opposing the motion.

The second speaker for the opposition has several options for her speech. She may continue the objections of the first opposition speaker to the proposition team's case; present new arguments against the proposition team (these arguments may be either direct or indirect refutation); defend and expand the opposition's counterplan, disadvantages, critiques and other indirect argumentation if they have been presented; and evaluate inconsistencies between the arguments of the first and second proposition speakers.

Although the speech is known as a constructive speech and a proposition team may make points of information during "unprotected" speaking time, debaters should be cautious about presenting information as if the second opposition speech was a constructive speech. It should function as an opposition rebuttal speech.

The second opposition speaker, like any constructive speaker in the debate, may introduce new arguments, but this is an unwise tactic because this speaker will be immediately followed by the opposition's last speech in the debate, its sole rebuttal speech. If the second opposition speaker introduces new arguments into the debate, the opposition rebuttalist will be able to repeat that information in her speech but will not be able to expand or amplify the points. There is no foundation to do so as the proposition team has not yet had an opportunity to dispute any of the claims from the second opposition constructive speaker.

In fact, the only opportunity for the proposition team to answer these issues is in their next stand on the floor, the proposition rebuttal, which also happens to be the last speech in the debate. This means that any positions advanced by the second speaker of the opposition are, essentially, "naked" arguments. The opposition debaters are unable to explain, defend, or extend the arguments. Virtually any argument in the proposition rebuttal will defeat these newly entered issues and a clever proposition speaker might try to capture new arguments or turn them to her advantage, employing them as winning strategies for the her side. Paradoxically, new arguments presented in the second opposition speech might be the key to victory for the proposition.

It is vital to expand the arguments from the first opposition speaker. It is equally important to answer or account for the key issues of the second proposition speaker. The opposition team, in their second speech, should be careful about introducing new arguments or unnecessarily expanding arguments in the debate.

If the second opposition speech functions as a rebuttal, then the opposition offers an integrated front of 12 minutes of argumentation, an effective tactic to overwhelm a final proposition rebuttalist's five-minute speech. The second opposition speaker should effectively summarize issues, explaining carefully the impact of each argument (i.e., the manner in which the argument plays a decisive role in the outcome of the debate). Opposition speakers should share rebuttal responsibilities, with each speaker managing a section of the debate.

OPPOSITION REBUTTALIST (A.K.A., "LEADER OF THE OPPO-SITION REBUTTAL"). This part of the debate is the summary speech for the opposition team, the last opportunity this side will have to explain winning arguments. Rebuttals are an opportunity to contrast the main lines of argument of the proposition and opposition. The speaker should select from among the issues of the debate. It is not possible to cover every argument in the debate. There are likely to be too many argument points from the constructive speeches in the debate, and, to compound difficulties, the rebuttalist has approximately one-half the allotted time of the constructive speakers. (The opposition rebuttalist has four minutes for the speech, in contrast to the proposition constructive speakers who have, respectively, seven- and eight-minute speeches.)

The opposition rebuttal speaker should focus attention on the salient two to four major issues that might tip the debate to the opposition side. The opposition should select more than one issue. Multiple, independent winning arguments may increase the probability that the opposition will succeed in the debate.

These arguments must have a foundation in the constructive speeches. New arguments may not be introduced in the opposition rebuttal. The opposition rebuttalist should carry through important issues from her opening speech in the debate, as well as her partner's constructive speech. The speaker should be cautious to avoid rote repetition of the second opposition speech. Too many opposition rebuttalists merely repeat the issues from their partner's speech Bad idea. Simple repetition is hardly the most effective explanatory, argumentative or persuasive presentation. Simple repetition is hardly the most effective explanatory, argumentative or persuasive presentation. Simple repetition is hardly the most effective explanatory, argumentative or persuasive presentation. (That last bit should just about settle the matter.)

Rebuttal repetition does not advance the opposition's agenda in the debate. It retards it. It suspends it for four minutes. It also provides the proposition rebuttalist with time to prepare her speech. The proposition speaker has already heard the opposition's potentially winning arguments in the final opposition constructive speech. There is no reason for her to listen to the issues again. By repeating the arguments in the opposition rebuttal, the opposition merely sets free the proposition rebuttalist. There is no reason to pay attention to the opposition rebuttal speaker. She is on to more important tasks. With four minutes to craft her five-minute speech, the final rebuttalist is almost certain to offer effective rejoinders to the opposition's claims. Paradoxically, the conventional opposition rebuttal, a restatement of the issues of the second opposition speaker, works best for the opposing side.

PROPOSITION REBUTTALIST (A.K.A., "PRIME MINISTER REBUTTAL"). The proposition has the final speech in the debate. This speech should effectively summarize the entire debate. The proposition rebuttalist has similar goals as the final opposition speaker. The final rebuttalist should extend the arguments from the constructive speeches, taking care to answer the major arguments from the opposition speakers, particularly the final opposition stand on the floor. The proposition rebuttalist should offer multiple, independent proofs of the motion to increase the probability that any single idea will be sufficient for a victory.

For this speaker, there may be an exception to the "no new arguments in the rebuttal" rule. The proposition rebuttalist is entitled to answer new arguments made in the second opposition constructive speech, because the final rebuttal is the first opportunity in the debate that the proposition team has to refute these issues. Although the answers to the new arguments of the second opposition speaker may appear to be "new," they are not new arguments in the debate. They have their foundation in a constructive speech.

## THE BRITISH FORMAT

There are subtle and dramatic differences in speaker roles between the American and British debate formats. Many of the roles, particularly for speakers opening and closing the debate, are nearly identical to speaker roles in the American form. As in the American format, after the opening proposition case, British format debaters advance new issues and challenge the ideas of their opponents.

FIRST SPEAKER, FIRST PROPOSITION. The first speaker in the British debate format has a nearly identical role to the first speaker for the proposition in the American format. The speaker interprets the motion and makes a convincing case for it. The case should provide opportunities for serious debate and for argument extension. (See the role of the first speaker, second proposition, above.)

FIRST SPEAKER, FIRST OPPOSITION. Same as the first speaker, opposition, in the American format.

SECOND SPEAKER, FIRST PROPOSITION. This is extraordinarily similar to the second speaker, proposition, in the American format. This speaker should amplify the arguments of her partner and initiate at least one new argument in the debate.

SECOND SPEAKER, FIRST OPPOSITION. Same as the second speaker, opposition, in the American format. This speaker should amplify the arguments of her partner and initiate at least one new argument in the debate.

FIRST SPEAKER, SECOND PROPOSITION. At last, a serious point of departure between the British and American formats. The second proposition team's first speaker must establish an extension of the case presented by the first proposition team's opening speaker. The case extension may not simply repeat the ideas of the opening speaker of the debate, nor may the speaker offer yet another example for the same argument. While showing loyalty to the opening proposition team, the first speaker of the second proposition team must subtly shift the discussion to new area of investigation or amplify an opening team's symbols, themes or underlying assumptions. This speaker then follows the form of the opening speaker, establishing a case for modifying the motion. The case includes three or four main lines of argument constituting a logical proof for the second proposition team's interpretation of the motion.

Because the second proposition team shares a side of the motion with the first proposition team, it is important for the second team to offer a position that is consistent with the initial argument claims. To do otherwise, that is, to undermine the arguments of the opening proposition team, is to figuratively stab colleagues in the back. (At least the authors hope that it is only figurative knife play.) When this undermining occurs, the second proposition team is said to "knife" the first team. "Knifing" is almost always held against a second proposition team. It is so disfavored by judges that it is difficult for a team engaging in the practice to receive a rank higher than fourth place. Consider that parliamentary debate's roots lie in governing bodies, which frequently involve coalition governments of more than one party. When one party rejects the claims of their supposed partner, they are in effect disbanding the coalition.

**FIRST SPEAKER, SECOND OPPOSITION.** Same as the first speaker, opposition, in the American format. This speaker must rebut the case presented by the second proposition team's first speaker.

**SECOND SPEAKER, SECOND PROPOSITION** This speech is very much like a rebuttal in the American format. The speaker summarizes the debate, making the necessary points for a winning conclusion for her team.

**SECOND SPEAKER, SECOND OPPOSITION.** Same as the second speaker, opposition, in the American format, or second speaker, proposition, in the British format.

## CONCLUDING THOUGHTS ON FORMATS

Although there are substantial differences between parliamentary debate formats, the major styles are quite similar in substance. The process of argumentation and refutation to determine winners and losers of debates varies little from debate to debate. The proposition team will, invariably, make a case for the topic. The opposition team will refute or otherwise undermine the proposition team's case. As the debate progresses, both teams will develop lines of argument to prove why their side wins the debate. At the end, both sides have a chance to summarize their arguments and refute the major issues raised by their opponents. Finally, the judge or judges will render a decision about the debate, assigning either ranks or a winner and a loser. They will assign speaker points on a fixed scale to individual debaters. After these decisions are made, the judge will offer oral and written critiques of the debate.

Regardless of the specific format used for debate, good debate requires ethical practice. We advise you to consider the seriousness of the event when you practice debate. Do not, through your behavior or arguments, make the event a joke. This is a waste of money and time for your organization and for your opponents and critics.

As a debater, critic, or trainer, you shoulder an obligation to know and follow the policies of tournaments and leagues in which you participate. At tournaments, the rules often dictate the format and other procedures, including judge behavior. At the league level, policies usually regulate behavior, including harassing behavior, between debaters and other tournament participants. In the USA, the National Parliamentary Debate Association has the following harassment policies in their by-laws (updated July 2001):

"Academic debate provides a forum for the expression, criticism, and discussion (and for the tolerance) of a wide range of opinions. Participants are encouraged to develop skills in reasoned and supported argument while avoiding the pitfalls of faulty argument. Academic debate does not provide a license for demeaning actions and it does not tolerate sexual harassment. Any participant who suffers discrimination or harassment as part of the activity is denied the guarantee of an equal opportunity to work, learn, and grow in the area of academic debate and may be harmed in mind, body, and performance."

"Sexual harassment is a form of discrimination and consists of verbal or physical conduct of a sexual nature, imposed on the basis of sex, that has the effect of denying or limiting one's right to participate in the activity, or creates a hostile, intimidating, or offensive environment that places the victim in an untenable situation and/or diminishes the victim's opportunity to participate fairly. Sexual conduct can become discriminatory and harassing when the nature of the interaction is unwelcome, or when a pattern of behavior that is offensive to a "reasonable woman" (or man, as the case may be) exists. These definitions, which comply with the EEOC and other legal definitions, rely strongly on the perceptions of the complainant and it is important to recognize that differences in social position between the complainant and the accused can compound the degree of threat or potential harm perceived in a situation."

It is important that leagues work to develop policies regarding harassment and other exclusionary behaviors that might occur at tournaments or other league events. As you become involved in debate, you should investigate the relevant policies of your league to ensure that your behavior is in compliance with the norms of the organizations in which you participate. Regardless of policies and procedures, however, debaters, trainers, and judges have an obligation to behave in a civil and respectful manner towards other participants in the activity.

In the interest of pursuing open debate and discussion, all participants must respect each other and create an environment free of intimidation. All debate formats create space for dynamic, engaged, and informed discussion. One of the only major variables to change from debate to debate in parliamentary debating is the topic. Teams should expect to debate a different topic in each debate. In the next chapter, we discuss the types of topics and explain the process of topic analysis that debaters should employ.

# TOPICS AND TOPIC INTERPRETATION

Parliamentary debates are usually extemporaneous events, with the announcement of a motion for debate approximately 15 minutes prior to each debate. It is also possible to have set topics for debating. Some debate tournaments announce topics hours or weeks in advance of a competition. Specialized debate events, for example, a public debate in a parliamentary format conducted between two schools or on the Internet, may have its topics announced in advance, usually to attract an audience.

Most motions begin with the phrase, "This House would..." or "This House believes..." or "This House should..." The expression "This House" refers to the decision makers in a deliberative parliament. In most cases, the decision maker is the judge or panel of judges for the debate. Proposition debaters will advance a case that is designed to convince the decision makers that the motion is more likely to be true than false. If the decision makers agree with the proposition team, the motion is affirmed. This agreement demonstrates that the "House" supports the ideas expressed by the proposition team. In other circumstances, the "House" includes the audience, as a substitute for or in addition to designated judges. It may be the case that the first proposition speaker interprets "This House" for the purpose of advancing her arguments in the debate, providing an altogether different understanding of the phrase.

Topics are fact statements, policy or value comparisons or national or international policy directives. The proposition in a parliamentary debate is also known as the **topic, resolution**, or **motion**. Motions are categorized by their language, and fall into several loose categories.

In one typology, motions are identified as resolutions of fact, value and policy. A resolution of fact proposes a factual claim that is subsequently subject to debate:

- This House believes that the economy of the USA is recovering from recession.
- Jury nullification in drug trials is an increasingly serious problem.

A resolution of value compares value claims or postulates an expression of a "good" that is subject to debate:

- It is appropriate to sacrifice freedom to promote security.
- This House prefers the local to the global

A policy resolution calls for an action to be taken.

- The United Nations should prosecute international terrorists.
- The federal government of the USA should increase regulation of industries in its borders to substantially reduce their production and/or emission of environmental pollutants.

Although the topic's language might tip participants off as to the type of motion proposed for debate, the act of correctly categorizing the motion as a fact, value, or policy motion has little to do with the debate's actual argumentation. After all, debate argumentation includes elements of fact, value, and policy. Debaters inevitably offer expressions of the "good." (That is the reason debaters are convinced that others will listen to them. Debaters advocate sound or favorable ideas, proper opinions, expressions of the good and legitimate value claims, and an audience is subsequently willing to engage the speaker.)

Debaters understand value claims in the context of human and institutional behaviors (i.e., policy). It is nearly impossible to intelligently discuss "values" in the abstract. (As a thought-experiment, try to explore any value claim – life, liberty, equality, justice, privacy, aesthetics – without due consideration of government, corporate or personal behavior.) For example, an advocate for liberty does not necessarily support the value of liberty in every conceivable context. A speaker defending the value of liberty is unlikely to support the freedom of individuals to kill or steal. Few debaters would argue for a liberty interest to sexually exploit children or marry neighbors' pets. Contextual understanding, the appreciation of specific individual or institutional policy choices, is necessary to give meaning to the concept of liberty.

Of course, debaters use factual material in all their debates. In other words, fact, value and policy issues are all available to debaters on each fact, value or policy resolution. It is, in fact, largely impossible to separate issues of fact, value, and policy. In a debate, you cannot really discuss values in the abstract. When confronted with a topic such as "This House opposes discrimination against minorities," a proposition team must do more than merely argue that discrimination in the abstract is bad. Pragmatically, this argument puts them in a weak position. To oppose this sort of case for the motion, the opposition team would merely have to provide some examples of cases in which it is appropriate to pursue a policy of limited discrimination. The opposition could, for example, argue that discriminatory affirmative action or the imposition of representative quotas achieves important benefits in the long-term pursuit of equal representation and opportunity.

It is important to remember that parliamentary debate comes from roots in the processes of governmental and other decision-making bodies. In parliamentary convocations worldwide, advocates are called on to do more than simply argue that discrimination (or inflation, or toxic waste) is bad in the abstract. They are expected to offer a proposal to deal with existing situations of concern. This does not mean that all proposition teams are therefore expected to offer a specific plan for action. Proposition teams must offer specific examples of the problem identified in the motion, but may refrain from offering a plan per se.

In addition to resolutions of fact, value and policy, resolutions are understood as **open** or **closed**. A closed motion is sometimes called a **straight** resolution. An open motion is also known as a **linkable** resolution. A closed or straight resolution is meant to be taken literally. For example, on the motion, "This House would send peacekeeping troops to the Middle East," it is expected that the proposition team would offer a relatively conservative interpretation of the motion, establishing reasons for military force intervention in the nations bordering the eastern Mediterranean Sea.

An open or linkable motion is more abstract. "Bury it." "There should be a new song for America." "Don't fear the reaper." The proposition team may define the terms of these open or linkable motions in most any way they choose, generally linking the abstract motion to a public policy controversy. For example, a defense of the topic "Bury it" might have the proposition team call for an end to national missile defense plans in the USA, "burying" the plan for the defense program for reasons of technical and political unfeasibility. The link between the motion and case can be tenuous, although some leagues and tournaments insist upon a closer relationship between the two, even for open motions.

There are some motions that can be characterized as **relatively open** or **relatively closed**. These motions provide for a range of proposition cases within a tightly constrained range of options. For example, on the motion "The Supreme Court should overturn the decision," the proposition team might argue for the overturn of any one of a number of decisions rendered by the court. A closed motion will normally dictate the subject matter for the debate, if not all of the specifics that could be part of the proposition team's case. For example, the motion "NATO should admit Russia as a member state" is a closed motion. The proposition team has some leeway to interpret the motion, insofar as they may suggest a particular plan for admitting Russia (sooner rather than later, phasing in membership, limiting influence, etc.). A relatively closed motion, on the other hand, will normally dictate a range or genre of subject matter for the proposition team's case.

There are other somewhat novel or experimental forms of motions.

There are motions that propose a general area of investigation, for example, "Africa" or "Olympic Games." Any reasonable idea generated from this kind of topic area could serve as a constructive interpretation of the motion and a foundation for debate. This form of motion design provides the proposition team with considerable interpretive liberty. The opposition might not be able to successfully anticipate either the issues for the debate or the direction of any suggested reform. (Will the proposition advocate more engagement with one or more African nations? Or will they suggest that nations withdraw support for national and sub-national groups engaging in human rights violations?) This motion form might be used in those circumstances in which a tournament director has determined that there is a decided bias for the opposition in the outcomes of debates on more specifically worded resolutions. The director might then use a focused but more ambiguous motion to provide an equal opportunity for the proposition side to participate in fair contests.

Another motion is the scenario. This motion offers an extended, detailed explanation of a crisis, condition, or bargaining position. Rather than a motion as a traditional single, simple, declarative sentence, the scenario may use one or several paragraphs to describe, through a series of chronological events, logical claims, or personal narratives, events that might constitute the subject for debate. Scenario construction necessarily limits substantive debating to the specifics designed by the tournament host. This may be appropriate as an academic exercise, a public event, or conference project, particularly for presentations to a specialized audience interested in the finely detailed descriptions of a case study. One example of a case study proposition is this one, used at a parliamentary tournament in the USA:

**Case Scenario:** A doctor has just learned that the patient she is treating will probably not live beyond the next day. The patient knows he is terminal, but thinks he has at least another few weeks to live and has hope that there is a slim chance to pull through. Family members are already near by. The doctor's dilemma is whether to reveal the truth about patient's anticipated time of death. The proposition team must support the statement "the physician must make a full and complete disclosure to the patient and his family."

This kind of case study or scenario for debate may be an interesting and relevant exercise for conference debates or other kinds of public events; however, its use in intervarsity tournament competition can be problematic. Longer topics can inadvertently advantage the opposition team by providing more grist for opposition arguments, while binding the proposition team to a relatively narrower area to defend. In the example above, the opposition team could persuasively contest the phrase "and his family," arguing that the doctor only has a responsibility to the patient, and that the patient (rather than the physician) should decide whether and how to inform the family.

The opening speaker of the debate is responsible for interpreting the motion for debate. The speaker typically defines key terms for the purpose of clarifying the motion and establishing an understanding of the controversy for debate. On the motion, "This House would establish a system of national health insurance in the USA," the speaker might define "system of national health insurance." There are many possible systems of national health insurance. Without a clear definition by the proposition team, how would the opposition know which system to consider? Is the proposition discussing an expansion of the Medicare system? A requirement that all employers pay for health insurance for workers? A new, federally administered national health program? Debate cannot proceed in a meaningful way until these questions are adequately answered.

There are, however, other methods to analyze a motion. Debaters should consider the following interpretive models. Examples follow each of the descriptions of interpretative models of several motions, with approximately the same amount of time devoted to the issues that one ought to use in a competitive debate. In addition to the arguments regarding the motion itself, the speaker should make sure to define any technical or difficult term in the motion and note that any issues not understood in the analysis of the proposition will be made clear "in the case proper." It is inevitable that additional clarifications of the motion throughout an opening proposition speech will assist an understanding of the proposition team's motion.

## A LITERAL MODEL OF INTERPRETATION

A literal interpretation is a conventional reading of a motion that presumes (1) a commonly held and exclusive understanding of the motion; (2) there is no metaphorical understanding of the motion; and (3) it is possible to understand the motion objectively, that is, the statement is independent of any interpretation or contextual understanding. (This is surely an ironic moment – a definition of literal meaning. Is there no literal meaning for literal meaning?)

In the example of the proposition, "This House would establish a system of national health insurance in the USA," a literal interpretation would presume a single available interpretation. A debater might introduce the interpretation in this way:

> "We are here to debate the motion, 'This House would establish a system of national health insurance in the USA.' It is evident that this resolution is discussing the ongoing controversy of a federal, single-payer system to provide universal health care coverage for all citizens and residents in the United States of America. That is the basis for today's debate."

## A PARAMETRIC MODEL

This method of interpretation presumes that literalism is problematic. Those debaters employing this interpretive method allege to account for the difficulties with literalism. They claim to appreciate that there is no singular and exclusive interpretation for a motion. They admit to a range or set of possible interpretations for any given motion. The range of interpretations is always in flux and somewhat arbitrary. There are no clear parameters on the set, although the interpreting team will admit to some parameters.

On the motion, "This House opposes the death penalty," a team using a parametric set or a model might acknowledge a number of reasonable interpretations:

- The proposition might call for an end to the administration of capital punishment, claiming that the death penalty, execution for special circumstances crimes and capital punishment are one and the same.
- The proposition might argue for the abolition of factory farms, arguing that modern farming techniques are certainly a death sentence for any animal unfortunate enough to be bred for slaughter.
- The proposition team could advance the idea that animal testing in research and development for the cosmetics industry, fatal to all tested animals, ought to be eliminated.
- The team interpreting the motion might abolish the estate tax, a federally imposed tax on the estate of a deceased person, often described as a "death penalty."

Likewise, on the motion "This House would establish a system of national health insurance in the USA" a proposition speaker might introduce the interpretation in the following way:

> "The motion before the House is to 'establish a system of national health insurance in the USA.' There are a number of reasonable national health insurance proposals that have been offered by government officials and public health experts. The most comprehensive and effective plan is the call for full expansion of the Medicare program, a position that we will endorse in today's debate."

## THE EXTENDED ANALOGY

In this case, the debater interpreting the motion argues that the motion may be drawn, by analogy, to correspond to a target statement. The latter statement is the proposition speaker's interpretation of the motion for debate. On the motion, "This House would fight the power," an opening speaker for the proposition might offer a case to stop or resist (fight) the bombing campaign in Afghanistan (the power). In interpreting by analogy, a proposition team should adhere to the semantic structure, grammar and syntax of the original statement when constructing the target interpretation.

- On the motion "This House would establish a system of national health insurance in the USA," a proposition speaker might draw the following analogy:

> "The motion before the House is to 'establish a system of national health insurance in the USA.' This motion represents the value of payments for the environmental or general health needs of citizens. Individuals are in the best position to determine the quality of their lives. As such, the motion is understood as a call for a guaranteed annual income for citizens and residents in theUSA."

## METAPHOR

Metaphors are the basis of much communication in everyday life as well as in parliamentary debates. Metaphors express a relation in which one thing stands for another ("people as plants," "life is a journey," "death is a journey"). In the interpretation of a motion, the opening speaker for the proposition would present a metaphoric understanding of the motion simply by having a case statement represent the language of the motion. The limited restrictions previously noted on extended analogy (consistency with number, semantic structure, etc.) are unlikely to apply.

- On the motion "Don't fear the reaper," a proposition speaker might argue for a policy of death education in schools. The speaker would say that to reject fear, we must institutionalize an educational policy. The relation with death comes from the speaker's connection of death and a reaper. A reaper is not an objectively accurate understanding of death. That fact is largely irrelevant to this sort of interpretation.
- On the motion "This House would establish a system of national health insurance in the USA" a proposition speaker might introduce the interpretation in the following way: "The motion is a metaphor for life's caring journey. Consequently, we will argue that society should better serve the needs of the elderly."

To be sure, there are problems with each interpretive method since it is possible to argue the merits of any of them. If one did not know this from the field of literary interpretation, surely he or she would understand it from the world of debate. Everything is up for grabs in debate. All ideas are subject to challenge. It is extraordinarily doubtful that literalism exists, and, if it does, it would seem to be of limited application. Is it the case, for example, that debaters share the knowledge base, worldview, identity and cultural history to have a singular and exclusive understanding of the terms of a motion? Literal understandings are more likely to be the ego projections of the judge or the opposing side in a debate. It is nothing other than one or more of those participants advancing their own knowledge base about a topic, subsequently reaching the conclusion that their understanding or interpretation of the motion is inevitably "intuitive," "conservative," or "better." (This suggests an insecurity that is better managed with years of intensive petting zoo therapy or "Up with People" counseling than participation in debating contests.)

Parametric interpretations are nothing other than samples of literalism – parametrics is literalism writ larger and softer (perhaps "flabbier" is the more accurate description). It is literalism + n, where the value of n is any non-zero number of interpretations. How any of this sets parameters in a reasonable, non-arbitrary manner has yet to be explained by its fans. The hallmark of the model is its capriciousness. Its advocates claim that it provides a predictable set of issues for debate. There is little way of knowing, however, in which direction the parameters are to be set or what they might potentially include or exclude. It is the three-card monte of interpretations, changing on the fly, scamming those earnestly playing along.

Extended analogies and metaphorical interpretations might provide too little focus for the debate. They seem to moot the point of having a topic for parliamentary debates. If the proposition only needs to substitute a target statement, any target statement, for the motion, and may do so by extended analogy or metaphor, then the topic itself is largely irrelevant. The proposition team will not need to adhere to any of the motion's language. They are free to abandon the motion and create their own debate resolution.

Proposition teams should take care to select the appropriate interpretive model in each debate. The language of the topic and the potential proposition case will strongly influence the opening speaker's choice of interpretation.

Opposition teams, particularly in the USA, are likely to argue that proposition teams have presented a case that is at odds with the motion for debate. This situation rarely occurs outside of the USA. In British debating, for example, opposition teams that challenge the proposition team's interpretation of the topic may be booed or otherwise heckled. On occasion, it is acceptable for debaters to disagree with the definition or interpretation of a motion, but it happens very infrequently. It also occurs only in circumstances in which the initial interpretation by the opening proposition speaker so violates principles of common sense that others in the debate must correct the interpretation in order to have a debate. Unless there is an egregious error by an opening proposition speaker, the other teams in the debate are expected to debate the motion as interpreted by the first proposition team. Deviations will likely receive a hostile reception from judges.

In those circumstances in which American parliamentary teams argue that the proposition team's case is at odds with the motion for debate, they are usually making a rather different claim. They are not actually suggesting that the proposition's case is inconsistent with the motion for debate. To the contrary, they are quite likely to ignore entirely the proposition team's interpretation of the motion for debate.

The opposition does not usually argue that the proposition team's interpretation is wrong or unreasonable, but that is not sufficiently right. The opposition team typically argues that there is another, and better, interpretation of the motion. They introduce the other interpretation and explain that it should be the basis for debate. The opposition might explain that their interpretation is more predictable, intuitive, or fair to all parties. The opposition team might offer one or more reasons why their version of the topic ought to serve as the interpretation of the motion for the debate. The opposition side concludes this **topicality** argument (an argument about the viability of the proposition case on the announced topic) by establishing that when the proposition team fails to offer a case that successfully matches the opposition interpretation of the topic, and the opposition interpretation is better than that of the proposition team, the proposition has not provided a legitimate interpretation of the topic and should lose the debate.

There are problems with this approach. The opposition merely offers a different interpretation of the motion. But there are always many possible interpretations of a given motion. The point of a fair debate is to permit the proposition team to select the more salient and defensible interpretations from among the potential ones. Opposition interpretation of the motion undermines this fundamental principle of equitable debating. Further, opposition interpretation of the motion is a way for the opposition team to duck the topic for debating. This is never a good way for either side to approach the debate. Just as the proposition team should not attempt to duck the subject matter of the motion, so too should the opposition team endeavor to confront the proposition team's case head-on.

One other problem with topicality arguments is the manner in which they seem to be at odds with lived experience about textual interpretation. The claims made for the argument include the following: (1) individuals share an understanding of the language, such that word use is common and universal; (2) the failure to abide with syntactic construction and grammar rules inhibits meaning; and (3) words are not understood contextually but have an objective meaning prior to their use. These points are routinely made or function as the subtext of topicality arguments without considering that these arguments represent controversial statements in the fields of philosophy of language, semantics, semiology, linguistics and communications. There is also an entire body of literature that repudiates the claims that language must be commonly and objectively understood and used according to fairly rigid grammatical principles in order to produce meaning. We call it poetry.

The proposition team answers a topicality argument according to the following guidelines:

- They may argue that the opposition team has failed to advance a theoretically sound position in the debate. The claim by the opposition that the debate ought to be about an "other" issue than that proposed by the proposition team seems fit here. Why should the opposition select the basis for debate? From where is the authority for an opposition interpretation of the motion? The opposition team does not have to defend the motion during the debate. The proposition has that duty. The proposition team has legitimate authority to define the motion because it has the burden of proof for it. The opposition team does not. The proposition may investigate the legitimacy of the theory supporting the opposition's topicality argument.

- The proposition team might argue against the construction of the topicality argument itself. In this way, the proposition speakers would consider the internal consistency of the argument, its relation to other opposition positions in the debate, the analytical or causal reasoning supporting the argument, or the examples proffered to support the argument. In other words, the proposition team would debate the issue in the same way they would consider any other argument in the debate.

- The proposition team's speakers might suggest reasons that their interpretation of the motion is consistent with the arguments offered by the opposition. These reasons would demonstrate that the interpretations are complementary, rather than contrary. It would show that the opposition position on the topic for debate is not a reason to reject the proposition interpretation.

- Finally, the proposition might establish some "affirmative" arguments (also known as "offensive" arguments, that is, an argument that establishes a winning position for its proponent. It does not mean an insulting or crude argument.). These arguments might include justifications for their particular interpretation of the motion. The proposition team would try to prove that to endorse the interpretation suggested by the opposition team would do violence or commit other serious harm.

For example, on the motion, "This House would have a new song for America," the proposition team might argue for significantly expanded affirmative action programs to redress race and gender inequality by business. The opposition could introduce a topicality argument, offering the claim that affirmative action is not a "new song for America," as affirmative action programs have been in place for many years. The proposition team might refute this statement, claiming that this opposition stance expresses the same rhetorical approach traditionally used to exclude women and people of color from business. In other words, they call for the suspension of discussion on the needs of socially marginalized people for a different or other agenda, the latter set by those privileged few (in this case, the opposition team and its differing interpretation of the motion.).

The de facto silencing of the advocates of dramatically expanded and substantially different affirmative action programs (the proposition team) is the tactic of those favoring business-as-usual approaches to race, gender and human relations. The opposition team, like those interested in further marginalizing socially alienated populations, always have another agenda to discuss, as they are endlessly bored with the plight of people unlike themselves. The proposition team might be able to argue that the topicality argument is a reflection of the very problem they are attempting to both reveal and ameliorate. According to the proposition team, the topicality argument is, therefore, not an effective reply to their opening speech. To the contrary, it produces marginalizing behavior that the proposition has proven ought to be disputed.

In addition, the opposition has an enormous conflict of interest when it interprets the debate motion. The opposition team opposes the motion in the debate and has every reason to provide a bankrupt or easily defeated interpretation. This tactic simply makes the debate easier for them. The debate then becomes a rigged game. The opposition side sets the agenda for the proposition and gets to argue against it. This situation would be similar to a state prosecutor autonomously setting the rules of procedure and evidence for a criminal trial and subsequently arguing the case. Of course, if the opposition speaker sets the agenda for the debate by interpreting the motion is her speech, the debate technically begins with the first opposition constructive speech. It is another rigged game. The proposition will have lost a constructive speech and must now prepare to debate against the first and second opposition constructive speakers.

If all this were not enough, the underlying assumption of much topicality argument is that the opposition side in the debate requires preparation time to effectively engage the proposition team's case. To the opposition, this requirement means they must have an idea about the direction or substance of the proposition case during the fifteen-minute preparation time period prior to the debate. Opposition teams seem to suggest that they are disenfranchised if the proposition presents a case they have not adequately anticipated during the preparation time period.

Preparation time is primarily for the proposition and it is not necessarily for the opposition team. The proposition team must make a convincing case for debate. This is a challenging enterprise. It is more difficult to build than to destroy. The proposition must provide consistent, unifying principles for its case. It is more likely than not that the proposition team will have to maintain several different arguments to maintain its logical proof of the case. The opposition team will not need to endorse unifying or terribly consistent positions to prevail. In fact, many opposition teams win debates because they are able to identify and support a single powerful argument against their debate foes.

The proposition team quite clearly and desperately requires preparation before the debate begins. The first speaker for the opposition, like the second speakers for the proposition and opposition, can make do without preparation time. If that is the case, there is no reason for advanced notice or predictability of the proposition team's interpretation of the motion. The opposition should be able to successfully debate in an extemporaneous manner. They should do so to facilitate meaningful debate on a single, focused topic. The topic is a guideline for debate. The point of proposition interpretation is not to provide the best or optimal interpretation of the motion for debate. Their burden is merely to provide one interpretation of the motion for debate.

Does this mean that there are no occasions for the opposition side to challenge the interpretation of the motion by the proposition team? Of course not. It is possible to argue that the proposition team has provided an illegitimate interpretation of the motion. Or, a particularly clever opposition speaker could argue that the proposition team has failed to uphold their interpretation of the topic as presented in the Prime Minister's constructive speech.

To accomplish this, the opposition should first identify the arguments in the opening speech that might constitute an interpretation of the motion for debate. There are always arguments in the opening proposition speech in support of the motion. Sometimes these arguments are highlighted or otherwise noted by the first proposition speaker. In many cases, the majority of the arguments involving interpretation of the motion are implicitly included in the substantive text of the opening speech. The fact that these arguments are not explicitly offered does not mean that they are not present in the speech. Instead of arguing merely a different or "other" interpretation of the motion, the opposition team should argue that the proposition team's case fails to meet the proposition's interpretation of the motion.

On the motion "This House would starve a cold and feed a fever," the proposition might introduce a case to increase the testimony of victims in criminal sentencing decisions in the USA. The opening speaker would argue that the criminal justice system should move from the sterility of formal due process protections exclusively for criminal defendants in order to embrace the concerns and passions of crime victims.

In this circumstance, however, imagine a case presentation that inadvertently supported due process: an opening speech in which the first proposition speaker endorsed the legitimacy of established constitutional protections. The opposition team might then legitimately argue that the first proposition speaker has every right to interpret the motion but once an interpretation is offered, the proposition team must show some loyalty to their argument for the motion. In this case, the proposition speaker has failed to offer a case consistent with the established interpretation of the motion, that is, an objection to due process coddling of criminal defendants. This combination of proposition arguments would be a strong reason for the opposition side to prevail on a topicality argument in the debate. The argument might be presented as follows:

"The proposition team has presented a case that is at odds with its interpretation of the motion. In the definition of the motion, the first proposition speaker explained his team's ambivalence, even hostility, to extant due process protections. This is their interpretation of the phrase "starve a cold" in the motion. To offer a proof for the motion, they must proffer a reduction in due process protections: they must starve the cold.

"But the proposition speaker supports constitutional due process protections later in her speech. This latter claim is at odds with their interpretation of the motion. It shows that the case does not reflect the motion. The proposition team must lose the debate, as they have presented a case that does not support the motion."

The point of all this argumentation about the definition and interpretation of the motion for debate is to establish a standard for the opening proposition team. The standard encourages the opening speaker to create a meaningful case that might be controversial and subject to dispute by each side. In other words, debate theory on the issue of the interpretation of the motion is designed to promote argument clash. There are three additional considerations to note: the matters of specific knowledge, truism and tautology.

**Specific knowledge** refers to a violation of the principles of fair or equitable debating. The popular conception of specific knowledge is that the proposition speakers possess information that is "specific" (that is, private). This information may form the basis of a proposition case. If it does so, it will undermine fair and meaningful debate. This argument against specific knowledge presumes that debates proceed best when based on shared information, that is, factual material, opinions and other data available in the public sphere or generally understood by informed university students and other parliamentary debate participants.

Specific knowledge claims are appeals to ignorance. They suggest that debaters should do little more than offer a least common denominator approach to a world of ideas, selecting out the challenging, intriguing, paradoxical, innovative, complex, and counterintuitive ones and excluding them from debates. It seems odd, indeed, that debaters might be penalized for knowledge or critical insight that goes beyond obvious, conventional wisdom. If debate is to accomplish anything, at least in a sophisticated way, it ought to both inform its participants and provide serious critical training. In other circumstances, we call this "education" and encourage its development.

Specific knowledge produces a race to the bottom. In other words, the student with the least information, the intellectual neophyte, may be better positioned for success in debate competitions. For that student, all the argument claims of the opposing side are examples of specific knowledge that ought to be challenged and excluded from debates. Specific knowledge functions to secure a win for the side that fails to answer the most arguments the fastest: "Brilliant opening speech, Prime Minister. I have never heard any such ideas before. Really. What a knowledge base! What an impressive command of the facts! Alas, it new to me. It is, therefore, not possible for me to debate. So, the matter of this debate is now settled. I win! Thanks, everyone, for attending. On to my next challenging round of debate!"

Specific knowledge turns the debate world on its head, providing a theoretical defense for anti-intellectualism. It suggests that debaters prepare for their event by "dumbing down" sophisticated ideas or creative perspectives. This bankrupt theory only puts a modern spin on the concession speech, attempting to turn surrender into a winning ploy. That anyone falls for this ploy reveals one of the great cons of contemporary debate.

The claim of specific knowledge is almost always suspect. It does not accurately describe the knowledge base of debate's participants. Debaters do not have "common understandings' of the issues introduced in debate topics. Students have very different personal knowledge, nationalities, cultural practices, identities, and histories. They concentrate their studies in different academic disciplines. (Is it specific knowledge for an economics student to exploit her knowledge against a religious studies student on an economics topic?) These differences actually serve as points of conflict and tension that ultimately produce debate. In addition, the information that students use in debates is not generated internally. Students read textbooks, newspapers, academic journals, novels, Websites, electronic newsletters, and magazines. They speak with faculty, friends and colleagues. They develop considerable life experience at work or during travel. The information they possess is externally generated. In other words, it is public information and should be considered in debates.

Many claims of specific knowledge are presented, paradoxically, in an attempt to censor public discourse that ought to be shared in parliamentary debates, including information regarding science and technology, decision theory, literature, new historicism, anthropology, art criticism, semiotics and postmodern geography. There is no logical reason to exclude complex and challenging ideas from contests involving sophisticated college students.

When confronted with the presentation of facts that seem to be specific knowledge, debaters should work with what they are given rather than react by simply crying "specific knowledge." Provided that the proposition team gives all of the relevant information to support a particular case, the opposition can still win the debate by referring to the information provided by the proposition team. If the proposition team withholds some information only to drop it on the opposition team in the next speech by saying "but what you do not know is…" the opposition can respond that this particular piece of evidence was not presented to them or something to this effect.

The truism, another example of a fairness violation in parliamentary debating, is equally suspect. The **truism** is an opposition argument explaining that the proposition team has offered an interpretation of the motion that is an objective TRUTH. As such, it cannot be debated. There are few propositions that can literally be considered truisms, and few ever appear in debate rounds. You will most likely not, for example, be asked to debate whether or not the earth revolves around the sun or whether two plus two equals four. Other propositions that are considered de facto truisms are propositions that are almost impossible to debate: "Child pornography is bad;" "Women should not be excluded from the workplace;" "The poor should not be forced to undergo involuntary sterilization."

In actual debate practice, the opposition's claim that the proposition's interpretation characterizes the proposition as a truism is unlikely to get them anywhere. The proposition team's interpretation of the motion is not objectively true. It is an argument that may be effectively refuted. Most opposition claims of truism are nothing other than hubris. The debater makes the claim that it is not possible to argue against the proposition team's case. The speaker is not arguing that she alone is incapable of arguing against the case. Rather, the debater is making the extraordinarily exaggerated claim that the case interpretation of the motion is unfair because no one could argue against it. Put another way, the debater seems to suggest that she has scanned infinite thought and reached the conclusion that no one could answer the proposition team's arguments.

In debates, you may have the occasion to debate proposition cases that seem to be truistic or otherwise unable to be debated. This does not mean that you should throw up your hands and roll over. Often these cases can be refuted by creative opposition strategies. For ideas, we suggest you learn more about the practice of criticism by reading Chapter Nine in this book. Remember that there are many ways to negate a case. One excellent strategy is to debate against the underlying assumptions of the case rather than the claims of the case itself.

Here is an example. On the topic "This House regrets the injustice," a proposition team argues that the Holocaust should be condemned. How should you, as an opposition team, debate this case that appears to be a truism? You actually have many possible lines of argument at your disposal. You might argue that the Holocaust shouldn't be removed from the category of genocide and condemned in an individual way. You could say that this creates a special status for the Holocaust, and that the Holocaust shouldn't necessarily have a special status, even in the confines of World War II (during which at least 75 million died), nor among other genocides in history in which tens of millions were killed. The danger here is the exclusion of other genocides in order to focus on the Holocaust. You could say that this exclusion risks causing us to ignore the genocides in our midst – we therefore do nothing about Rwanda or Bosnia-Herzegovina, or we don't do anything in circumstances in which aboriginal people are assimilated into cultures, lose their land, and simply die out in a passive rather than active way. We may actually generate victims by condemning the Holocaust or otherwise giving it a special status.

You could also argue that condemnation is an inappropriate and dangerous reaction to the Holocaust. You could say that it is the act of condemnation or isolation and exclusion of the Nazis, portraying the Nazis as non-human monsters or as symbols of evil, which makes us believe that it's appropriate to direct anger toward them. This portrayal means we fail to identify the similarities between Nazis and other people in positions of power today, risking the loss of our critical capacity to democratically engage people who commit evil acts.

Further, you could say that when we move to condemn the Holocaust, we bypass identification of our own moral culpability in violence. There are all kinds of privileges that allow people to commit violence. You can claim that by presuming to position yourself as a moral authority able to condemn people for their transgressions, you act as the Nazis did, condemning the Jews and Gypsies and other minority populations as sub-human and evil, allowing in turn their slaughter. The implication of this argument might be that you shouldn't externalize blame for the problem; instead you should look inward to your own moral culpability. If you think these arguments are long shots or irrelevant, you should think again. These are all serious arguments in the academy – for example, these arguments are made in Ward Churchill's book, *A Little Matter of Genocide*.

If you say there's no way to debate against this case, you effectively ignore learning all these other issues. Wouldn't you be better off if you were be able to say that you might be morally culpable in victimizing others and should investigate that, or that condemnation is inappropriate as is the search for vengeance? These are important arguments to air for debate, particularly the argument that the Holocaust shouldn't be the symbol for genocide. Many researchers and advocates argue that genocide may be perpetuated and, paradoxically, encouraged if we focus all our energies on the Holocaust. Arguing a truism means you lose the ability to learn about all these important issues. Ideally, the process of debate should force us to create and advance arguments against all positions. As this example shows, you do not need to argue directly against the claims of the proposition's case to refute it.

One other bit of advice: If the proposition team presents information that is objectively accurate, that is, a claim with which there can be no disagreement or debate, they will have ascended to divinity. Stop arguing with them and begin praying to them. In no circumstance should you argue with the divine or enlightened. (Punishment involves a smoting of some sort.)

**Tautology** is the final theoretical issue regarding the interpretation of any motion. A tautology, also known as circular logic, is an argument fallacy in which a speaker fails to engage ideas logically. The speaker merely repeats a claim again and again, typically confusing repetition of an idea with analysis. Do not do this. Instead, offer reasoning to support your interpretation. Tautology is a rare affliction. It is possible to debate or judge for years and never cross one of these creatures.

## Suggested Exercises

1. The debater selects a motion for interpretation. (There are more than 1,000 sample motions listed in Appendix 1.) She is given two minutes to imagine and outline an interpretation of the motion. She has one minute to make a verbal presentation of the motion. This exercise is repeated four or five times, with criticism from the audience regarding the following:

Is the interpretation convincing for a debate judge and why?
Has the speaker interpreted the motion to successfully restrict argument possibilities for the opposition?
What foundation is there for replies to opposition arguments about truism and specific knowledge?

In a 15 to 20 minute practice period, a speaker will be able to prepare interpretations for different kinds of motions. With a performance evaluation for five interpretations, the speaker is likely to make more interpretations and receive more criticism on motions interpretations than at a full invitational or intervarsity tournament.

2. Individual debaters are presented with a motion for debate. The debaters have five minutes to list as many reasonable and different cases for the motion as they can.

This exercise teaches debaters that language is subject to interpretation and recontextualization. The motion will not mean the same thing to all the assembled participants for a debate. In addition, the exercise will assist debaters in brainstorming a motion in order to select the best possible expression of opinion, the best case, for the motion.

# CHAPTER 3

# ARGUMENT THEORY FOR DEBATERS

## INTRODUCTION

Arguments are the most basic building blocks of debate. Understanding what makes arguments work distinguishes successful debaters from their less successful colleagues, and creates advantages for even the most experienced and precocious debaters. Arguments are like automobiles: If you understand how they work, you are likely to get more service out of them, understand what went wrong when they break down, and fix the problem before your next outing.

There is a considerable amount of literature dealing with argument theory and its minutiae. Most argument, speech, or communication texts include at least one chapter about argument theory. While this material goes into great detail about types of arguments and the most propitious conditions for their analysis and refutation, these theoretical elaborations are usually ponderous and mostly useless for the average debater. Debates proceed orally, at a relatively quick pace. Debaters do not have enough time to apply the detailed argument analysis techniques in the average debate and argumentation text. Most argument textbooks assume that students will be using their prescriptions to analyze texts rather than quickly developing oral arguments. Our goal in presenting the following analysis of argument theory is to make it useful for debaters, whose needs are different from those of academicians.

What matters most about argument theory to the average debater is simply this: What differentiates a bad argument from a good argument? This is, in many ways, an unanswerable question. There really is no such thing as a bad argument *per se*; rather, arguments must be judged on the basis of their relative effectiveness. To this end, we say that arguments can be more or less *persuasive*, a judgment always made in the complex contexts of audiences, purposes, and settings. Arguments that fail in some contexts may be very successful in others. If you were to argue in favor of trade restrictions to protect organized labor interests, you might fail to persuade the G-7. Does this mean your argument is bad? Not at all. It means that your argument has not succeeded.

Debaters must learn some basic concepts in argument theory so that they can make successful arguments and presentations.

## A BRIEF HISTORY OF ARGUMENT

Argument is distinct from debate. An argument is an attempt to influence someone else in some direction. Usually, this direction is a matter of belief, adherence, or action. Some arguments are about **facts**. These arguments deal with facts or definitions in controversy and attempt to get the listener to believe in certain facts. Other arguments are about **values**. These arguments try to persuade the listener to adhere to particular value systems; alternately, they may use given value systems to persuade the listener to accept certain states of affairs as consistent with their values. Finally, some arguments are about **policies**. These arguments attempt to influence the listener in matters of policy or courses of action. In real life as in debate, however, these distinctions are far from clear. For example, questions of policy always involve questions of fact and value, even if these associations are always made implicitly. Debate is not the same thing as argument. Debate is the infrastructure for the presentation of many and various arguments, all of which can and usually do serve distinct and disparate functions throughout the course of a debate. Of course, in debate as in life, not all arguments are created equally. That is, some are more successful than others. The immediately relevant question for debaters is how to make successful arguments and how to make these successful arguments work in debates.

Often, arguments are not successful because they are incomplete. It is important to remember that an argument is different from a simple *claim*. A claim is, most simply, an assertion that something is so:

"The death penalty is justified."
"Hyacinths are better than roses."
"Pitt the Elder was the greatest British prime minister."
"There is no such thing as reality television."
"The USA should eliminate its nuclear arsenal."
"Economic growth is more important than environmental protection."

Most propositions that you will debate will be simple claims about the world. They may take the form of propositions of fact, value, or policy, or of any combination of these. In everyday situations, many people mistake simple claims for their more sophisticated cousin, argument. This error leads to difficult and often unresolvable debates not unlike those had by children: "Is too." "Is not." "Is too." "Is not..." This method of argumentation is similar to the method of conflict resolution used by warring mountain goats, whereby both parties simply lower their heads and butt horns until someone falls off the cliff and dies.

An argument is more than a claim. While a claim asserts that something is so, an argument attempts to prove *why* that thing is so. Of course, as you might imagine, there are many schools of thought about how this proof is or should be achieved. Aristotle argued that proof was either created to suit an occasion or already extant and evident. He called these kinds of proofs, respectively, "artistic" and "non-artistic." Aristotle's great insight that persuasion is an art (rather than a science) is important for debaters of all stripes to remember. Debate is an art at least in this way: There is no one correct way to go about its practice and performance. Our proofs and arguments are artistic in that they

**53**

are creative enterprises that demand constant innovation. In debate, we rely on artistic proofs that we create to justify our arguments or tear down those of our opponents. To this end, we will discuss primarily how artistic proofs, or attempts at persuasion, are created and substantiated in the practice of argumentation.

Aristotle's theories of argument are still relevant to contemporary debaters. Of particular note are his concepts of *logos*, *ethos*, and *pathos*. For Aristotle, persuasion through *logos* attempts to show that a thing is so: It is primarily and classically understood as a logical proof. Proof through *ethos* attempts to demonstrate the credibility and good will of a speaker, since people have a tendency to believe people they trust or respect. Finally, proof through *pathos* tries to influence the feelings or emotions of an audience so that they sympathize with the issue or argument at hand.

After 24 centuries, good debaters still use these three types of persuasion to win debates and influence judges. Contrary to popular belief, the value and effectiveness of an argument should not be measured solely on its logical content, although logic is important. To be successful, debaters must have *ethos* – they must appear credible and confident. Debaters must also use *pathos* to persuade – they must appeal directly to the assumptions and emotions of their audience.

Debate is not a science. It has only a familial relationship to the practice of formal logic of the type used in classical mathematics or scientific proof. It is worthwhile to understand this relationship so that you can understand how persuasion works. The building block of formal logic is a form of reasoning known as a **syllogism**. A syllogism looks like this:

All dogs are mortal. (Major premise)
Roswell is a dog. (Minor premise)
Roswell is mortal. (Conclusion)

As you can see, the syllogism begins with a general premise, known as the major premise – in this case, the statement that "All dogs are mortal." It then proceeds to the minor, or second premise, usually an argument connecting to the specific case to be examined. In this case, the minor premise is "Roswell is a dog." Finally, the conclusion is reached: "Roswell is mortal."

In syllogistic reasoning, the assumptions, premises, and conclusions are all explicitly laid out for everyone to see. However, as Aristotle noticed, this method of proof is neither efficient nor effective in oral communication. Imagine how totally bored your audience would be if you spoke like a formal logician, defining all your terms and spelling out all your premises. They would no doubt be asleep long before you got to your conclusion. Syllogistic reasoning is also ill-suited for debate because debaters, like all public speakers, deal in *probabilities*, rather than *certainties* (as in the case of mathematics or science). Consider the following formal argument:

All dogs love to chase their own tails.
Roswell is a dog.
Roswell loves to chase her own tail.

Although this argument is structurally sound, its initial premise ("All dogs love to chase their own tails") is somewhat less certain than the initial premise of the previous argument ("All dogs are mortal."). The major premise is *up for debate*, because it retains an element of uncertainty, requiring persuasion to make others believe it. In fact, many dogs doubtless feel it beneath their dignity to entertain themselves or others with the pointless exercise of chasing their own tails.

The lesson here is that while formal syllogistic proof may work in math class, it is a poor fit for the uncertain realm of human (and animal – see above) affairs with which debaters deal every day. Even if you believe that mathematical and scientific concepts deal in irrefutable certainty or universal truths, it is difficult to extend the same status to statements about human affairs and relationships.

It is important to remember that proof in debate and argumentation is not like proof in mathematics or formal logic. Arguments that make logical sense can easily fail to be persuasive. By the same token, many arguments that are very persuasive may turn out to make little (if any) logical sense. In communication, we use a form of rhetorical proof known as an ***enthymeme***. Once again, this critical concept in argument theory originates with Aristotle. An enthymeme is a kind of rhetorical proof – the rhetorical version of a syllogism. Enthymemes deal with probabilities and uncertainties.

Enthymemes can also function as a kind of abbreviated, or truncated, syllogism – that is, an argument in which one or more premises are unstated. This technique allows alleviation of the boredom factor usually associated with formal logic. It also has other, more important benefits. Consider that every audience has internalized some arguments, usually cultural or social norms and expectations that vary based on a number of factors, including gender, ethnicity, class or social standing, political beliefs, and the like. Good speakers and debaters know their audiences. Even Aristotle emphasized the importance of knowing what kinds of assumptions and ideas your audience might hold. Because argumentation is fundamentally a process of *persuasion*, it is an activity that occurs between or among communicating individuals. All parties contribute to the process, not just the speaker.

So why leave premises (or even conclusions) unstated? This technique seems to run contrary to our ideas about good argumentation, but in fact is how everyday arguments function all the time. When you are trying to convince friends that you should dine together, you do not phrase your argument like this:

> All friends enjoy eating a meal together.
> We are friends.
> We enjoy eating a meal together.

or this:

> We should get a meal together.
> Dinner is a meal.
> We should get dinner together.

or even this:

> We are all hungry.
> When we are hungry, we should eat.
> We should eat.

You might simply say: "Hey, let's go get dinner," leaving unstated all the premises of such a claim. You do not need, given this audience, to elucidate all the parts of your argument. Your audience fills in the rest of the argument with you, perhaps thinking "Well … friends *do* enjoy eating together, and I *am* kind of hungry… yeah, let's go to dinner!" In fact, if you were to methodically lay out all the premises of your argument, you would probably not be invited along on the grounds that you were either clearly deranged or a colossal bore – neither of which is a desirable characteristic in a dining partner.

Debaters, however, rarely get to debate such uncontroversial topics (dinner) in front of such sympathetic audiences (friends). They need to craft persuasive arguments on difficult and often quite controversial topics in front of audiences or judges who may (often unbeknownst to them) be downright hostile to the position they are advancing. This task is much more difficult than trying to convince a group of hungry people to order a pizza.

What you need to know, then, is how to make rhetorical reasoning work for you in all kinds of situations. This task requires an understanding of the method of rhetorical reasoning: What is it that makes arguments work? What makes arguments effective? The British logician Stephen Toulmin made important contributions to argument theory that are useful for this line of inquiry. Toulmin found six components of arguments:

**Claim**: A statement that something is so.
**Data**: The backing for the claim.
**Warrant**: The link between the claim and the grounds.
**Backing**: Support for the warrant.
**Modality**: The degree of certainty employed in offering the argument.
**Rebuttal**: Exceptions to the initial claim.

This is an extremely formal model of argumentation. Few arguments, if any, display all of these components, particularly at first blush. Nevertheless, the Toulmin model provides us with useful tools for analyzing the components of arguments. Of these six characteristics of arguments, three are uniquely valuable for understanding basic argument theory. In this chapter, we will use primarily the concepts of *claims*, *warrants*, and *data*.

Simply speaking, all arguments have a *claim*, which is simply a statement that something is so. Arguments also have *warrants*, which are reasons why the claim is valid. Warrants are the "because" part of an argument. Finally, arguments have *data* – the evidence for the validity of the warrants. All three components are normally hallmarks of complete (and thus potentially more successful) arguments. A novice debater might simply offer claims to prove her point:

"The death penalty is justified."

A more sophisticated debater knows that her argument will be more persuasive with an accompanying warrant:

"The death penalty is justified because it deters crime."

Better yet is the technique of the advanced debater, who offers proof to cement the credibility and persuasive power of her argument:

"The death penalty is justified because it deters crime. Longitudinal studies conducted across the nation strongly point to this deterrent effect."

Referring back to the concept of the enthymeme, we can see how even this complete argument is itself incomplete:

| | |
|---|---|
| **Data:** | The death penalty has a deterrent effect. |
| **Warrants:** | 1. The death penalty deters crime. |
| | 2. (Policies that deter crime are justified.) |
| **Claim:** | The death penalty is justified. |

If this argument "works" (is persuasive), it will be in part because it plays on the audience's assumption that policies that deter crime are good. It may also be persuasive because the data is credible, or from a credible source. Of course, there are many other unstated assumptions of this particular argument. It assumes, for example, that the proposition has the moral authority to put people to death in the first place, an assumption called into question by many anti-death penalty advocates. This particular formulation of the argument, therefore, might not work with an audience whose assumptions are different from those the speaker assumed they would hold.

For successful debating, it is critical that you understand and elucidate the assumptions of the opposition. Many people argue by simply
rebutting claims with other claims. This is not a sophisticated or persuasive form of argumentation. Good debaters know that a claim is best
refuted by undermining its supporting *assumptions, warrants,* and *data.*

## ARGUMENT ANALYSIS

The Toulmin model is not just a vocabulary list for argument theorists. It
can also be a kind of checklist for aspiring debaters. In debate, we don't
just make arguments; we also *analyze* them. Argument analysis is a kind of
interrogation whereby we ask questions of arguments to determine their
viability as well as their potential weak points. Debaters need to learn to
think critically about arguments: There is little place for uncritical accept-
ance in debate, particularly if you want to have the best arguments or
rejoinders. When we encounter an argument, we should ask ourselves a
series of questions about it. Toulmin's model gives us a few pointers about
questions we can ask. For example, you might analyze a particular argument by answering the following questions about it:

- What's the claim being made? In other words, what is the thrust or
  gist of the argument? What is it that the speaker ultimately wants you
  to believe or agree with?
- Does the claim have a warrant? What reasons does the speaker give
  to support her claim?
- Is the warrant supported by data? What kind of data? What is the
  source of the data?

These questions for analysis are more or less purely informational,
because you need to know how an argument works in order to be able to
effectively criticize it. You should also ask more critical questions, such as:

- Are there exceptions that could be made to the stated claim? What are
  they? How do those exceptions affect the overall validity of the claim?
- Is the reasoning for the warrant sound? What kinds of assumptions
  are made in its reasoning?

• Is the data credible? Does it come from a credible source? What kinds of circumstances might the data not take into account?

In this section, you will learn how to analyze specific kinds of arguments with versions of these and other questions. It should be noted that there are as many types of arguments as there are debaters who do not want to have to memorize all the different types of arguments. We will discuss the strengths and potential pitfalls of a few basic types of reasoning.

One of the most common types of argument is the **argument from example**. When we reason with examples, we may proceed from a specific case to a general theory or conclusion. We may also use a general theory to predict how specific examples might play themselves out. The first kind of argument from example, where a speaker reasons from specific examples to a general hypothesis, is called *induction* in classical logic. By contrast, *deductive* reasoning begins with general theories and uses those theories to deduce the details of specific examples. The most relevant issue for debaters when thinking about reasoning by example is always simply this: What is the relationship between the specific cases and the general theories being presented?

Reasoning by example is a powerful way to prove a point, or make or negate a case. Proposition teams usually try to prove that there is a need for their proposed solution by providing examples of people or things that are harmed in the present system. They may show that their plan solves the problem by providing an example of a situation it would alleviate. Advertisers may sell a product using similar tactics. They may try to show that the average toilet bowl is filthy by showing the toilet bowl of the Jones family, thus creating a need. Then they may show that their product works by showing that same toilet, cleaned to a blinding white, presumably by means of their product. As a debater, you can use a variety of examples to prove your arguments. You might provide factual examples, drawn from research or personal experience. You might also use hypothetical examples to draw the listener into your story.

Many people use faulty forms of reasoning by example that an alert debater might catch and use to her advantage. Thus it is important to carefully analyze these arguments Ask yourself:

• Are there enough examples to prove the claim? Too often, debaters will reason simply from anecdotal evidence.
• Are there examples that might directly counter the given examples?
• Are the examples typical of the category the speaker wants to generalize about? It is important to have a representative sample if you wish to reason from example.

Finally, reasoning from example often falls prey to the logical fallacies known as the *fallacy of composition* and the *fallacy of division*. These are discussed in the next part of this chapter.

Another kind of reasoning is known as **reasoning from analogy**. When we argue from analogy, we are trying to show that what was true in one situation will be true in an analogous situation. An analogy is a comparison of people, places, things, events, or even abstract concepts. Debaters reason from analogy all the time. In making a case for non-violent resistance to a political policy, you might argue that since such resistance worked in the American civil rights movement, it could work in another case as well. Advertisers reason by analogy. In the case of the Jones's toilet, referenced above, the advertiser clearly wants viewers to draw an analogy between the Jones's toilet and their own toilet: "By God, if it worked for their toilet, it's *bound* to work in mine!" When analyzing analogical arguments, you should ask the following questions:

How strong is the analogy? Are there differences between the two situations, people, events, etc. that are being compared? What are those differences?

• What are the similarities between the two things being compared?
• Do the similarities outweigh the differences? Do the differences outweigh the similarities?
• Beware the fallacy of the false analogy. Keep your analogies precise

and sparing to maximize their effectiveness.

Debaters often try to establish causal relationships, either to prove their case or to negate the case of the other side. This technique is called **reasoning by cause**, and it can either be from cause to effect or from effect to cause. When you reason from cause to effect, you begin with a cause and attempt to show what its effects might be. You might argue, for example, that if propositions act to ban human cloning, the effect would be to drive that research underground into an unregulated black market. In debate, one of the most common forms of causal reasoning is the *disadvantage*, whereby the opposition argues that the proposition's proposed policy will cause negative consequences.

When reasoning by cause, you can also look at existing effects and try to determine their cause(s). Proposition teams use this tactic all the time when they make their case for change. If you were arguing for gun control, for example, you might start by showing how many deaths are inflicted by guns every day. You might then argue that these deaths are the result of (that is, they are *caused by*) the existing, permissive gun laws. This process would be an example of reasoning from effect to cause and is the same tactic doctors often use to make diagnoses: They will note that you have a cough and a fever, and will reason, based on these symptoms, that you have the flu. As you might imagine, though, reasoning by cause is a tricky business. A few questions to keep in mind when analyzing causal arguments:

Are there other causes that could have prompted the discussed effect?

What other effects does the cause produce? How do these weigh against the already specified causes?

Causal reasoning is also prone to many logical fallacies, such as the *post hoc* fallacy and the fallacy of *common cause*. It is worth noting here that there is another type of reasoning, closely related to causal reasoning, known as **argument by sign**. A sign, of course, is something that stands for something else. When you see a sign, you often assume that certain conditions are true based on your knowledge of what that sign usually represents. For example, when you see a "For Rent" sign on an apartment building, you might believe that you could rent an apartment in that building if you wanted to. Often we mistake signs for causes. It does not follow, for example, that the apartment is for rent *because* the sign is there. Correlation of events does not imply causality.

A final kind of argument is called **argument from authority**, or **reasoning from testimony**. Sometimes when we make arguments, we rely on the opinions or statements of others to help make our point. Most often, arguments from authority or testimony are found in the data component of an argument. Debaters routinely cite various studies or expert opinions to provide the proofs for their claims. The practice of evidence analysis and comparison is a critical part of successful debating, and the evaluation of arguments from authority or testimony is a good place to start in your quest to figure out what constitutes good evidence and what constitutes bad evidence. Here are some preliminary questions to ask of reasoning from authority:

• What are the qualifications of the person(s) cited as a source? Are they qualified to speak about the subject they are cited in?
• Is the source relatively more or less biased about the topic at hand?

Argument from authority is a good way to establish your credibility as a speaker. Audiences are more likely to believe speakers who appear to have credible, relevant facts and testimony to support their conclusions than those who appear to use mostly conjecture and hearsay.

## Suggested Exercises:

1. Find advertisements that represent each of the categories of reasoning listed above (from authority, from cause, from example, from analogy, from sign). Break down the argument made in each ad using the components of the Toulmin model explained in this section.

2. Examine the editorial page of your local newspaper. Take each edi-

torial and analyze the argument using the techniques listed above. What is the primary argument made by the author? What warrants does she use? What kind of data does she offer as support? Which of the major kinds of reasoning are used in the editorial?

# LOGICAL FALLACIES

In logic and the generalized study of reasoning, there are generally understood to be such things as *good reasoning* and *bad reasoning*. Typically, bad reasoning is characterized by falling into one or more of the classically compiled logical fallacies. A logical fallacy is simply a failure of logic. Arguments that are said to be fallacious have gaping holes or misleading leaps in their structure and reasoning. Debaters need to familiarize themselves with the logical fallacies: The ability to point out holes in your opponents' reasoning is a very powerful tool in debates. As we have learned, however, arguments are not necessarily intrinsically good or bad; rather, they should be evaluated in terms of their relative effectiveness. In fact, many arguments that are fallacious or otherwise fatally flawed are widely accepted. The argument type we call the *slippery slope*, for example, appears repeatedly in public policy speeches and analyses. Once you understand more about logical fallacies and learn to identify them, you may be surprised at how often they turn up in commonly accepted arguments.

APPEAL TO FORCE. This fallacy occurs when you tell someone that some kind of misfortune will happen to them if they don't agree with you, e.g., "If you don't believe that our utopia is ideal, then I guess we'll have to release the hounds."

APPEAL TO THE CROWD. Sometimes called the "bandwagon," or *"ad populum,"* this fallacy occurs when the arguer contends you will be left out of the crowd if you don't agree: "All of the cool kids smoke cigarettes these days."

APPEAL TO IGNORANCE. When an argument has not been disproven, it does not therefore follow that it is true. Yet the appeal to ignorance works a surprisingly large amount of the time, particularly in conspiracy theories and their ilk: "No one has yet proven that aliens have *not* landed on Earth; therefore, our theory about ongoing colonization should be taken seriously."

APPEAL TO EMOTIONS. This fallacy is what it sounds like. Speakers routinely try to play on the emotions of the crowd in lieu of making real arguments. "I know this national missile defense plan has its detractors, but won't someone *please* think of the children?"

APPEAL TO TRADITION. Often a substitute for actual argument, the appeal to tradition happens when a speaker tries to justify her arguments by reference to aggregated habits, e.g., "We should continue to discriminate against the poor because that's what we've always done."

APPEAL TO AUTHORITY. While it is often appropriate and even necessary to cite credible sources to prove a point, the appeal to authority becomes fallacious when it is a substitute for reasoning or when the cited authority's credibility is dubious.

AD HOMINEM. Sometimes, arguers will attack the person making the argument rather than the argument itself. This is an *ad hominem* (Latin for "to the man") attack, e.g., "I don't know how my opponent found the time to research this issue, since plainly he doesn't even have time to bathe."

BEGGING THE QUESTION. Begging the question occurs when the conclusion assumes what it tries to prove: "Of course he tried to fix the boxing match, since he was one of the people who stood to gain by fixing the boxing match."

RED HERRING. An old favorite, the red herring happens when the arguer diverts attention to another issue and draws a conclu-

ART, ARGUMENT AND ADVOCACY

sion based on that diversion. "The candidate has a weak stand on education. Just look at what she says about foreign policy."

**HASTY GENERALIZATION.** This fallacy occurs when a conclusion is drawn based on a non-representative sample, e.g., "Most Americans oppose the war. Just ask these three peace demonstrators."

**FALSE CAUSE, OR "POST HOC, ERGO PROPTER HOC."** This fallacy is just what it sounds like. In the English, at least. Sometimes, speakers will draw a faulty link between premises and a conclusion such that the link depends upon a causal connection that probably does not exist: "The sun rises every time I get out of bed. Therefore, by getting out of bed, I make the sun rise." It is important to remember that correlation does not imply causality, and neither does chronology imply causality.

**EQUIVOCATION.** In this fallacy, the meaning of a critical term is changed through the course of an argument. Lewis Carroll in *Alice's Adventures Through the Looking Glass:* "'You couldn't have it if you **did** want it,' the Queen said. 'The rule is jam tomorrow and jam yesterday - but never Jam today' 'It must come sometimes to Jam today,' Alice objected. 'No, it can't,' said the Queen. 'It's jam every *other* day: today isn't every *other* day, you know.'"

**SLIPPERY SLOPE.** One of the more popular logical fallacies, particularly in political circles, the slippery slope argument contends that an event will set off an uncontrollable chain reaction when there is no real reason to expect that reaction to occur. "If we start regulating carbon dioxide, the next thing you know the proposition team will be telling you what to eat for breakfast."

**WEAK ANALOGY.** While argument by analogy is a very strong, common form of argumentation, the weak analogy fallacy occurs when an argument's conclusion rests on a nonexistent similarity between two examples, e.g., "Well, if it worked in a college term paper, it'll work in American foreign policy."

**FALSE DICHOTOMY.** This fallacy occurs when the premise of an argument is a disjunctive statement that presents two alternatives as if they were mutually exclusive, e.g., "It's either free school lunches or nuclear war;" "Either you let me go to the concert or my life will be ruined."

**FALLACY OF COMPOSITION.** This fallacy happens when the conclusion of an argument depends on the erroneous transference of a characteristic from the parts to the whole: "Jake likes fish. He also likes chocolate. Therefore, he would like chocolate covered fish."

**FALLACY OF DIVISION.** The opposite of the fallacy of composition, the fallacy of division occurs when the conclusion of an argument depends on the faulty attribution of a characteristic from the whole to its parts: "The average American family has 2.3 children. The Jones family is an average American family. Therefore, the Jones family has 2.3 children."

**COMPLEX QUESTION.** Used in questioning periods, this fallacy occurs when a single question is really two or more questions: "Do you still cheat on your tests?;" "How long have you been smoking banana leaves?"

**SCARECROW.** Formerly called the "straw man" fallacy, this kind of argument is a diversionary tactic whereby an arguer exaggerates or mischaracterizes his or her opponent's position and then proceeds to represent this caricatured. This is a common tactic used in advertising campaigns: "Worried about your family getting critically ill? Better use our disinfectant." In some circles, this fallacy is known as the "fallacy of refutation," though nobody really uses this terminology anymore.

**SCAPEGOATING.** This fallacy is similar to the scarecrow fallacy.

The term "scapegoating" comes to us from the Judeo-Christian tradition. In the Old Testament book of Leviticus, Aaron confessed the sins of his people over a goat and sent the goat away, thereby absolving the sins of his community. In contemporary rhetorical theory, we say someone is scapegoating when he or she attributes a current situation to a group of people who may or may not be responsible for the problem. Politicians are notorious for scapegoating minority groups for broad social problems. In America, for example, illegal immigrants are often convenient scapegoats for budget or social services problems.

**NON SEQUITURS.** This is not so much a fallacy, *per se*, as a failure of reasoning. The Latin phrase *non sequitur* means "does not follow." Thus, reasoning that is non sequitur is composed of arguments that are irrelevant to the topic. As a debater, you should insist that your opponents' reasoning stick strictly to the topic(s) at hand.

**COMMON CAUSE.** Often, two things will occur together so regularly that you are tempted to assume that they are cause and effect. However, sometimes those two events are the cause of a third factor, which must be taken into consideration to make the reasoning complete. For example, noticing that there are many dead fish in a river and that the river's water is undrinkable, you might conclude that the dead fish caused the undrinkable water. However, in so doing you might miss that an industry's dumping into the water caused both pollutants.

## SUGGESTED EXERCISES:

1. Examine a popular magazine. Find advertisements that use one or more of the above logical fallacies. Explain how each advertisement uses faulty reasoning.

2. Each of the following arguments uses at least one logical fallacy. Identify why each argument is fallacious and explain how it

could be improved.

a) Every atom in my body is invisible. Therefore, I am invisible.

b) If you want to grow up to be like Wonder Woman, you'd better eat those carrots.

c) Friedrich Nietzsche's philosophy is bankrupt. Nietzsche was an immoral man who went mad from syphilis before he died.

d) Where did you hide the cookies you stole?

e) Pianist Ray Charles says Sinclair Paints are the best. So be sure to use Sinclair Paints when you redecorate your home.

f) Philosophers are highly intelligent individuals, because if they weren't highly intelligent, they wouldn't be philosophers.

g) Ronald Reagan met with space aliens in 1987, and that cannot be disproven.

h) Sodium and chlorine, the atomic components of salt, are deadly poisons. Therefore, salt is a deadly poison.

## PRACTICAL ARGUMENT THEORY

Now that you've learned a good bit about basic argument theory, you need to know more about how to use these concepts practically in debates. In this section, we will explore some ways you can do this. We have emphasized repeatedly in this chapter the idea that there is no such thing as a bad argument or a good argument *per se*. Remember that many arguments that are not structurally or logically sound are often very functional and persuasive. In communication, validity is not something that is given, but is a belief that is the product of successful persuasion. Advertisers know this and use this phenomenon to their advantage all the time.

Can you think of some examples of ad campaigns that are successful, yet make little (if any) logical sense? Consider how often advertisers use arguments that we would call logical fallacies. The appeal to the crowd and the appeal to emotions are very common advertising techniques. A car manufacturer, for example, might imply in their advertisement that their auto will make you more attractive to women. Does it therefore follow that their auto will, in fact, get you more dates? Of course not. Does the campaign work regardless? All too often. Audiences are very susceptible to appeals to emotions. This is one of the factors that makes these arguments so dangerous and often ethically suspect.

The appeal to the crowd is also a popular ad technique. A perfume manufacturer might use a bandwagon appeal to get you to buy their scent, perhaps by showing many attractive, cool young people with whom you might like to identify, all of whom happen to be wearing the perfume in question. Does it therefore follow that if you wear this cologne you will be attractive and cool? Certainly not. Does the campaign work regardless? Probably so. Audiences do not necessarily want to feel as if they do not fit in.

We can learn a lot about practical argumentation by studying advertisements. Consider that a typical advertisement is structured very much like a typical proposition case: i.e., an advertiser will establish a *need* or *harm* that exists in the present system; they will then propose a *solution* (the product being hawked, conveniently enough); then they will show that the product *solves* the problem. Because advertisers, like debaters, use enthymematic reasoning, they may leave out some of these components. Yet if you examine most ads, you will find that these components are almost universally inferred, if not directly present.

One of the advantages of learning argument theory is that this knowledge will help you become a more critical consumer of information and of products and their accompanying advertising claims. Another advantage, of course, is that it will help you become a better, more successful debater.

We have already learned about many types of arguments used in debates and in everyday reasoning. These arguments (by example, from authority, etc.) can be used in many different contexts by either side in a parliamentary debate. What we need is a way to take these formal categories of reasoning and make them functional for debaters. We suggest that in debate, there are really only two broad categories of arguments, separated by their strategic function: *offen-*

*sive* and *defensive* arguments. Offensive arguments are arguments *for your side*, or case, or position. When you argue offensively, you establish affirmative reasons for why your side should win the debate. When the opposition argues disadvantages to the proposition's case, they are arguing offensively. When the proposition argues link or impact turns (a type of argument discussed in the chapter on disadvantages) to these disadvantages, they are arguing offensively. When the opposition argues that adoption of their counterplan would be *net beneficial* over adoption of the proposition case, they are arguing offensively. When the proposition team argues advantages to adoption of their case, they are arguing offensively. Debates are won or lost based on the power and proliferation of offensive arguments. To win debates consistently, you must establish *why you win* early and often.

That said, debates are also won or lost based on defensive arguments. As you might imagine, a defensive argument is an argument that plays defense against the other team's arguments. Defensive arguments show why you should not lose the debate. When the opposition argues that there is no need for the proposition's proposed solution, they are arguing defensively. When the proposition argues link take-outs or impact take-outs (also discussed in the disadvantage chapter) to an opposition team's disadvantage, they are arguing defensively.

The distinctions between offensive and defensive arguments may seem hard to grasp. If you feel that way, you're not alone. In fact, the two kinds of arguments blur into each other quite a bit, but understanding the difference still serves an important functional purpose: *To win a debate, you must show <u>both</u> why you win <u>and</u> why the other team's arguments don't mean that you lose.* That is, you must argue both offensively and defensively to win a debate, particularly in the rebuttal speeches. This concept will be covered more extensively in the chapter on performance skills.

Another way to understand the concepts of argument offense and defense is to think of them as arguments of *advancement* and *refutation*. When you advance an argument, you are making a claim, hopefully (if you're doing it right) with an accompanying warrant and some data (if it is available). Remember: Arguments are not just claims. Arguments explain *why* something is so. So an argument of advancement is just what it sounds like: the opening salvo of a debate, whereby a claim and reasoning is advanced for discussion. But debates can't be composed just of arguments of advancement; if they were, they wouldn't be debates, but rather exchanges of unrelated ideas:

> **Speaker 1:** *Bananas are better than apples because they contain more potassium.*
>
> **Speaker 2:** *Circles are better than squares because their shape is more pleasing to the eye.*

What this "discussion" is missing is what in debate we call **clash**. Both speakers are advancing arguments, but their statements are unrelated to each other. Clash is one of the fundamental principles of good debate; in fact, it is fundamental to any debate. Unless arguments clash, there is no way to compare and adjudicate them. Debate deals with arguments that are in dispute.

To dispute an argument effectively, you must master the skill of **refutation**. Arguments of refutation serve as a rejoinder to arguments already in play. Refutation is necessary in debates because it promotes direct clash between arguments. You already know how to advance arguments; now, you need to learn how to refute arguments.

Just as questions have answers, arguments have answers called rejoinders and responses. There are many ways to answer an argument that has been advanced. Of course, some methods are better than others. The first, and unfortunately most common, way of refuting an argument is simply to provide a counterclaim:

> **Speaker 1:** *Bananas are better than oranges because they contain more potassium.*
>
> **Speaker 2:** *Speaker 1 says that bananas are better than oranges, but I disagree. Oranges are better than bananas.*

Speaker 2 has simply provided a claim to counter the claim of the first speaker. Who wins this debate? Clearly, Speaker 1 has the edge, since she is the only debater to have actually provided a warrant for her claim ("because they contain more potassium"). Good reasoning always trumps no reasoning at all.

A more advanced method of refutation is to provide a warrant for your counter-claim:

> **Speaker 1:** *Bananas are better than oranges because they contain more potassium.*
>
> **Speaker 2:** *Speaker 1 says that bananas are better than oranges, but I disagree. Oranges are better than bananas because they contain more vitamin C.*

What makes this rejoinder better than Speaker 2's previous attempt? Here, she is providing a warrant for her claim: "because they contain more vitamin C." Imagine that you are asked to adjudicate this debate. How will you decide who wins? You find that Speaker 1 has proven conclusively that bananas contain more potassium than oranges. You also find that Speaker 2 has proven that oranges contain more vitamin C than bananas. Neither debater really has the edge here, do they? Notice that while there is direct clash between the claim and the counterclaim, there is no direct clash between the warrants for each. Speaker 2 has not yet succeeded in completely refuting her opponent's argument.

Complete refutation is important to decisively win when arguments clash against each other in debate. In order to completely refute an argument, you must include what we call a "therefore" component. The "therefore" component of an argument of refutation is where you explain *why* your argument trumps the argument of your opponent. Observe:

> **Speaker 1:** *Bananas are better than oranges because they contain more potassium.*
>
> **Speaker 2:** *Speaker 1 says that bananas are better than oranges, but I disagree. Oranges are better than bananas because they contain more vitamin C. Therefore, you should prefer oranges because while many foods in an ordinary diet contain potassium, few contain an appreciable amount of vitamin C. It is more important to eat oranges whenever pos-*

*sible than it is to eat bananas.*

Speaker 2 wins. She has completed the process of refutation by including a "therefore" component in her rejoinder. Notice how this last part of her argument works. She compares her warrant to Speaker 1's warrant to show why her argument is better than that of her opponent. Almost all refutation can follow the basic four-step method demonstrated above. As you practice your refutation skills, consider starting with this model:

**STEP 1: "THEY SAY...."** It is important to reference the argument you are about to refute so that your audience and judges can easily follow your line of thought. Unlike the bananas/oranges example above, debates contain many different arguments. Unless you directly reference which of these arguments you are dealing with, you risk confusion on the part of your audience and judge, and confusion is seldom a good technique for winning debates. Good *flowing*, or note-taking skills, will help you track individual arguments and the progression of their refutation. We'll discuss how to take notes in the specialized form demanded by debates in the skills chapter.

One important thing to remember here is that when you refer to your opponent's argument, you should do so in shorthand. If you were to repeat all of your opponent's arguments, you wouldn't have any speech time to advance arguments of your own. So try and rephrase the argument you're about to refute in just three to seven words to maximize your speech time: "They say that reducing welfare benefits helps the economy, but...;" or "They say Batman is better than Superman, but..."

**STEP 2: "BUT I DISAGREE...."** In this part of your refutation, you state the gist of your counter-argument. This can be, in the case of the banana/orange controversy, simply the opposite of your opponent's claim. It can also be an attack on the warrant or data offered for your opponent's claim. The important thing is to state clearly and concisely the counter-argument you want the judge to endorse. You can elaborate on it later. For now, it is important to phrase your argument as concisely as possible. This tactic helps your judge, audience, and opponents to remember it and get it on their *flows*, or notes. Word economy is a very important skill for successful debaters. We will discuss this aspect of debate more in the chapter on skills.

**STEP 3: "BECAUSE ...."** Having advanced your counter-argument, you need to proceed to offer a warrant. Arguments of refutation need to be complete, just like arguments of advancement. Your warrant can be independent support for your counter-claim, as in the case above. It can also be a reasoned criticism of the opposition's argument.

**STEP 4: "THEREFORE...."** Finally, you need to draw a conclusion that compares your refutation to your opponent's argument and shows why yours effectively defeats theirs. This conclusion is usually done by means of comparison, either of warrants or data or both. You need to develop a variety of strategies for argument comparison and evaluation, as this is a critical skill for success in competitive debate. What you need to accomplish here is to show that your argument is better than their argument because....

> **It's better reasoned**. Perhaps their argument makes some kind of error in logic or reasoning, of the kind discussed earlier in this chapter.

> **It's better evidenced**. Maybe your argument makes use of more or better data. Perhaps your sources are better qualified than theirs, or your evidence is more recent than theirs.

> **It's empirical**. When we say that an argument is *empirically proven*, we mean that it is demonstrated by past examples. Perhaps your argument relies on empirics, while theirs relies on conjecture or speculation.

> **It takes theirs into account**. Sometimes your argument may take theirs into account and go a step further: "Even if they're right

about the recreational benefits of crossbows, they're still too dangerous for elementary school physical education classes."

**It has a greater expressed significance.** You can state that your argument has more significance than their argument because (for example) it matters more to any given individual or applies more to a larger number of individuals.

**It's consistent with experience.** Perhaps your argument is consistent with experience over time, a in different place, or in different circumstances. This technique is particularly effective with audiences: "Hey, this is something we can all relate to, right?"

These are only some examples of techniques you can use for argument comparison. In this book and through your debate education, you will find others.

### SUGGESTED EXERCISES:

1. Play a game of "I disagree." Generate a series of claims of various types (fact, value, policy). Then refute each claim using the four-step method. Try this exercise with a partner. Have one person generate claims while the other person refutes them. After ten repetitions, switch roles.
2. Analyze the following excerpted arguments using the tools you have acquired.
   - What is the main claim each author is advancing? What warrants do they offer to support their claims? What data do they advance to back up these warrants?
   - What kinds of reasoning does the author use to advance their claim?
   - Construct two different refutations of the argument. Choose either the author's main claim or one or more of their subclaims or warrants.

a) "The United States of America should end its trade embargo against Cuba. The embargo violates the International Covenant andofarguably, the 1994 General Agreement on Tariffs and Trade (GATT), ). The embargo is a policy of starvation that offends the moral sensibility of the world. In other situations, the USA claims to be working against starvation and international isolation. Why, then, does it persist in its trade embargo toward the people of Cuba? Alfredo Duran of the Cuban Committee for Democracy, has said that 'the embargo hasn't worked and everyone knows it. The starvation in Cuba is what the embargo has created.'"

b) Education is vital for any civilized society. If citizens are not adequately and properly educated, they cannot be expected to participate meaningfully in important decisions that affect their lives. Education also provides long-term economic benefits, both to individuals and to their society at large. This does not mean that education should be mandatory. In democratic societies, citizens should not be forced to attend school if they choose not to do so. We do not require our citizens to quit smoking, even though that behavior would be beneficial. Likewise, we do not require our citizens to work at a job, although they clearly suffer if they do not do so. Education should be treated in the same way. If we are truly a society committed to ensuring choice for our citizens, we should end mandatory school attendance.

3. Using the four-step refutation model, refute each of the following simple claims:

   - The government should increase regulation of the mass media.
   - The USA should lift its sanctions against the nation of Iraq.
   - Sunbathing causes cancer.
   - Drug testing violates individual privacy.
   - Environmental protection is more important than economic

growth.
- Nations should open their borders to immigration.
- Military spending is detrimental to society.
- You don't need a weatherman to know which way the wind blows.
- The debt of the third world should be forgiven.
- Silence means consent.
- Science is more dangerous than religion.
- NATO intervention in Kosovo was misguided.

# CHAPTER 4:

# CASE

# CONSTRUCTION

In the American and British debate formats, strategic planning and construction of the proposition case is essential for success. In the American format, it appears that the proposition team has some decided advantages because it has the first and last speeches in the debate. Through interpretation of the motion, this team determines, to some extent, the subject matter for the debate. The proposition team establishes the decision making framework for the debate.

There are fewer advantages for proposition teams in the British format. The first proposition team presents a case to open debate on the motion. The second proposition team offers a case, which is understood to be an extension of the original proposition position. In this way, the proposition teams enjoy the same advantages of the first proposition team in the American format; namely, they initiate debate on the motion and design the debate's framework.

Despite these obvious format advantages, there are substantial advantages for the opposition as well. The opposition may well be in a superior position in parliamentary debates. All things may not be equal.

In the American parliamentary format, the opposition has a time advantage during the debate. The opening speaker for the proposition has seven minutes for her speech. During this time, the speaker must offer an entertaining introduction; define the motion; establish a decision making framework; present a logical, organized case for the motion; and summarize the speech in a convincing conclusion. These duties mean that the first proposition speaker realistically has approximately five or five and one-half minutes to make a proof for the motion.

After the initial proposition presentation, the time advantage for the balance of the debate shifts to the opposition team. The first proposition delivers her speech, with an effective five-minute argument for the motion. The first speaker for the opposition has eight minutes to respond to the speech. The opening opposition speaker is able to argue efficiently, concentrating her arguments to precisely the weakest elements of the case.

The second speaker for the proposition, also known as the Member of Government, also has an eight-minute speech. This timing might help right the imbalance of the first two constructive speeches, except for the following opposition stand on the floor. At the conclusion of the second proposition speech, the opposition has two consecutive speeches with a total of twelve minutes of speaking time (an eight-minute second opposition constructive speech followed immediately by a four-minute opposition rebuttal speech). These consecutive speeches, occupying as they do a considerable amount of time in the debate, are known as the **opposition block**.

The opposition team has more than enough time to manage the argumentation from the second proposition speaker. And with a twelve-minute block of time, they can create a considerable amount of havoc for the final proposition speaker, who has but five minutes to answer their arguments. In sum, the time advantage clearly favors the opposition team during the debate. This imbalance, with other factors, has traditionally led to a small but significant opposition bias in parliamentary debating in the USA. This bias may also occur in parliamentary debating with the American format outside the USA.

The British format gives the opposition a different advantage. The first proposition team and second proposition team each introduce a case in the debate. The opening proposition team makes the original interpretation of the motion. The second proposition team extends the interpretation of the motion and advances the issues in the debate. In each of these cases, however, the opposition has the final word in arguing the case. The second speaker for each of the first and second opposition teams effectively closes argument on the proposition case. In the latter case, the second speaker for the second opposition team has the final word in the debate.

This position is a significant advantage for the opposition. It is easier to tear down than to build a case. Opposition arguments might only need to target a single dysfunctional element of a case for a decisive victory in a debate. The proposition team must usually defend every element of a logical proof in order to prove its side of the motion. With the last word on a case or in a debate, the opposition is in a powerful position in debates. Because of some important format advantages for the opposition, the proposition team must take great care in the selection, organization and execution of its case.

## PREPARATION TIME PRIOR TO AND DURING THE DEBATE

Technically, there is one preparation time period in parliamentary debating – the period between the announcement of the motion and the opening presentation by the first proposition speaker. There are other opportunities to prepare during the debate and those will be investigated as well.

Typically, debaters receive 15 minutes to prepare for debates after the revelation of a motion for debating. Usually this will be the full amount of preparation time available to the debaters. Sometimes, though, debaters will have little or no knowledge of the motion itself nor the academic discipline, subject field or public policy arena related to the topic. In these cases, the participants muddle through as best they can, hoping to make a connection to the language of the proposition.

In the majority of circumstances, the debaters are sufficiently familiar with the motion and related information to begin preparation in earnest. How should they prepare? There is no one, uniform guide to debate preparation. The language of the motion and the manner in which the motion connects to the knowledge base or academic interests of the proposition team will influence preparation plans. There are, however, some general recommendations for preparation time:

- Teams should complete individual work and teamwork during preparation time.
- Debate preparation should be comprehensive.

Proper preparation time management involves individual work and teamwork. Although it may be evident that preparation time should provide opportunities for a proposition team to organize the opening case and for the first speaker for the proposition to outline her speech's major lines of argument, it is less evident how a team may accomplish these goals efficiently.

To be sure, some very experienced debaters, working with a regular debate partner, have established a collaborative relationship in which they seem to have a symbiotic connection. Preparation time brainstorming and organizational matters appear to be effortless. It is possible to hope for this sort of cooperative interaction with a debate partner, which brings us to the rest of the debating universe. You need more than hope. You need an arrangement, an accommodation, with another person to efficiently share the responsibilities of designing your case and constructing your argument during preparation time.

Team collaboration should not trump individual analysis of the motion or case during preparation time. If there is a common error debaters consistently make, it is sharing time for the full duration of preparation time. This error limits preparation time (more on debate mathematics in a moment). It might produce the most dreaded consequence of shared labor with your debate partner: groupthink. Also known as tunnel vision, groupthink frequently occurs when the two parties on a debate team share an agenda set by one of the parties. There is insufficient critical analysis of the issue, with no outside vision and no one to mirror or function as the opposing side. This error inevitably narrows the task of generating ideas during preparation time (you produce fewer arguments) and fails to consider critical logic gaps in your arguments (you limit your ability to successfully anticipate arguments). Debaters with tunnel vision are more prone to the production of unseen errors in case design – unseen, at least, until the opposing side gets a chance to listen to the first proposition speaker.

What should the proposition team do during preparation time? Our recommendation is for the members of the proposition team to work separately (individually) for a minute or so, carefully analyzing the motion prior to a team discussion on case design for the forthcoming debate. The speakers then collaborate for a minute or two, sharing ideas on interpretation of the motion and a successful case. At this point, the debaters work individually. The first speaker for the proposition should immediately begin preparation of the opening speech, generating lines of argument and organizing them for a coherent and entertaining address. At the same time, the second speaker for the proposition should begin preparation of her speech.

How should the second proposition speaker prepare her stand on the floor? Is preparation possible without a fair hearing of the first opposition speech? Of course, the proposition team's second speaker should anticipate the opposing side's likely strategy for the debate and prepare her arguments accordingly. This speaker should begin to analyze the forthcoming debate from opposition's perspective. This step accomplishes the following: (1) Preparation for the second speech. The second speaker in the debate has little free time to craft an organized and clever speech once the proceedings are underway. It is, quite obviously, better to begin preparation in a less stressful environment. (2) Argument anticipation. The second speaker can identify potential flaws or inconsistencies in the opening speaker's argument using argument anticipation techniques described above. This step is not due to any self-destructive urge on the second speaker's part but rather an acknowledgement that she must adopt an *oppositional stance*. Instead of collaborating with her partner, she will be in a strong position to critically investigate the logic of her partner's case and have an opportunity to expose problems with the case at the only time available for their simple and convenient correction, namely, the period of time before the debate begins. Also, anticipating the opposition's arguments allows the second speaker to advise her partner about potential changes or additions to the first proposition speech.

After the individual preparation, the speakers need to join together and review ideas for several minutes. Sharing information at this point is particularly valuable, as the opportunity for some quiet time and private deliberation on the motion has doubtlessly spurred creativity, so there are plenty of new ideas on the table. The debaters use the final few minutes of preparation time to complete the case outline or second speaker's replies to opposition points. The second speaker may have also found one or more clever ways to amplify or extend the arguments in the opening speech.

Debaters are advised to have and use an inexpensive digital timer for preparation time management. Although many debaters develop an effective "internal clock, " a valuable skill, to be sure, for the proper organization of a speech with rigidly set time limits, it is easier to look at the face of a timepiece or listen to its infernal beeping. It is too easy for debaters to become distracted during preparation time. A digital clock keeps debaters on task.

A sample 15-minute preparation period might look like the one below:

| | |
|---|---|
| Individual assessment of the motion | 1 minute |
| Shared discussion of the motion | 3 minutes |
| Individual preparation of speeches | 5 minutes |
| Shared discussion of speech preparation | 3 minutes |
| Final speech preparation | 3 minutes |

Debate teams should experiment with different times to accomplish these tasks. They may be adjusted for different partners, motions or other circumstances.

There are ancillary benefits to this preparation model. It provides more than 15 minutes of actual preparation time, with some time devoted exclusively to the second speaker's preparation. In our model, only six minutes of the 15-minute preparation period involve shared time. The remaining nine minutes involve individual work, meaning that the team has essentially doubled its preparation time for nine minutes of the period, bringing total preparation time to 24 minutes for the team. Of equal importance is that a significant percentage of the nine individual minutes allocated to the second speaker involve anticipating arguments and preparing for her speech. The second speaker may have as many preparation minutes prior to the debate as her speaking time during the debate.

When preparing for debate, you should carefully consider the balance of issues on a motion. You ought to anticipate several of the main lines of argument from the opposing side. Preparation time should include preparing speech introductions and conclusions, interpreting the motion, and framing the debate and the elements of the case proper. Time should be devoted to speech structure and humor. In other words, preparation ought to be comprehensive. Notes on many of these matters, as well as preliminary information to support the factual material of a case, should be prepared in advance of the tournament competition. Debaters might then refer to different kinds of information (that is, information on the public policy matter, debate practice, rejoinders to conventionally introduced arguments, as well as notes on initiating humor and responding to heckles). Organizing some previously briefed debate materials means that debaters will not have to "reinvent the wheel" before each debate. Notes might offer tactical reminders for sound practice or serve to jog your memory on the facts of a particular case or opposition argument.

In an ideal model, members of a debate team would brainstorm their ideas and prepare speeches independently. Preparation would both increase the number of serious issues and provide depth of reasoning and evidence to each of the elements of proof. In this model, teams would have 30 minutes of genuine preparation time, double the amount of officially declared time for preparation, which provides a significant advantage over teams that are less efficient in their preparation period. Debaters should use the ideal as a standard, attempting to increase their preparation to 30 minutes. This is ideal, of course, but it is not readily achieved. Debaters need time to inform partners of ideas, a task rarely accomplished in nanoseconds. Debaters might not succeed in expanding preparation to a full 30 minutes, but they might get a lot closer than the conventional approach of shared time for 15 minutes.

# THE CONSTRUCTION OF THE PROPOSITION CASE

Debates can be complex. The motions normally relate to fairly sophisticated philosophical, economic, social, political and cultural matters. Debaters introduce as many as a dozen major lines of argument in each debate, with accompanying examples. There are, in addition, a number of less significant challenges presented in a round of debate, as well as back and forth during points of information (and, in the American format, points of personal privilege or points of order). For more on parliamentary points, please refer to the chapter by that name at the end of this book. There is some discussion of the appropriate guidelines for framing and deciding a debate; this is the meta-debate discussion (i.e., "the debate about the debate"). Simple and elegant case design is a profound way to address the potential chaotic presentation of many disparate issues on a subject.

A conventional proposition case is based on a direct and appealing narrative form – introduction, body and conclusion. It is a bit more difficult to achieve in practice than in theory. The opening speaker for the proposition should include the following:

• A speech introduction.
• An interpretation of the motion.
• A framework for the debate.
• A case proper that supports the motion.
• A speech conclusion.

## INTRODUCTION TO THE SPEECH

It is appropriate to use a speech introduction to establish your credibility with the judge and audience, create favorable expectations regarding your performance and offer a powerful introduction to the subject matter of the case. Many academic parliamentary debaters, however, make a quite limited effort and provide rather trite introductions in the opening proposition speech. All too often, the introduction is a perfunctory exercise, a quick round of "thanks" to the Speaker of the House, opposing side, colleague, and audience. At that point the proposition speaker might suggest that there is "a lot of work to do" and, thus, it is time to "jump into the case." This is not an interesting speech introduction, let alone one that can stand to be constantly repeated from debate to debate, tournament to tournament, region to region.

It is well past time for parliamentary debaters to revise the introduction, providing meaningful presentations prior to a round of thanks. For example, on the motion, "This House would right the wrongs," a proposition team might argue for institutional legal checks on the presentation of eyewitness testimony. Although eyewitness testimony holds particular persuasive power over the decisions of jurors and, therefore, the outcome of criminal trials, it is notoriously unreliable. Thousands of individuals are wrongly convicted each year due to the prosecution's presentation of eyewitness accounts of crimes.

A first proposition speaker might offer the following introduction for the case:

> "There is no greater wrong, no greater injustice, no greater deprivation of liberty than the wrongful conviction of an innocent person. When considering the circumstances leading to a wrongful conviction, one is likely to imagine gross prosecutorial error or misconduct. But the fact is that the leading cause of wrongful conviction is the testimony that jurors hear from eyewitnesses.
>
> Ladies and gentlemen, the proposition team has an opportunity to address a disgraceful problem that victimizes thousands of people annually. We do so with our support of the motion, 'This House would right the wrongs.' Thank you, Mister/Madame Speaker."

You could begin with a quick thank you to the Speaker of the House, a polite reply to her recognition of your speech. It would then be appropriate to thank others at the conclusion of the preamble of your speech.

"Thank you, Madame/Mister Speaker. There is no greater wrong, no greater injustice, no greater deprivation of liberty than the wrongful conviction of an innocent person. When considering the circumstances leading to a wrongful conviction, one is likely to imagine gross prosecutorial error or misconduct. But the fact is that the leading cause of wrongful conviction is the testimony that jurors hear from eyewitnesses.

Ladies and gentlemen, the proposition team has an opportunity to address a disgraceful problem that victimizes thousands of people annually. We do so with our support of the motion, 'This House would right the wrongs.' Thank you to participants and the assembled audience."

The introduction should be brief. It should not replace the substantive information in case proper. It should provide striking information to get the attention of the judge and audience, without undermining the rhetorical power of the speech. An effective introduction provides a preview of the case without giving away the more salient issues in the opening 15 to 30 seconds. If the speech introduction offers too much information, the opposing side will immediately begin preparing the refutation for their speeches, allowing the opposition more time for preparation during the debate. In a typical debate ideas unfold throughout the proposition team's opening speech, delaying the opposition's preparation of effective refutation strategies.

All speakers in a debate should have a speech introduction. It is evident that the opening speakers for the proposition and opposition should establish themselves in the debate before engaging an audience. Debaters may want to court favor with an audience through the use of humor in a speech introduction. There is nothing quite as powerful as meeting the expectations of the assembled audience that they will be entertained during the round of debate.

Subsequent speakers in the debate should present introductions that will recall their debate partner's speech. Too often, later speakers introduce their presentations as a *reaction* to an opposing side's preceding speech. This technique subtly shifts the debate's focus to your opponent's issues. The ideas that you want to present in the debate might be lost along the way. It is better to establish your foundation for argument – the main lines of proof for your side or the issues neglected by an opponent – *before* issuing a reactionary presentation. (Save that fiery negation for the Guild Hall, talk radio, pulpit, or Masonic Lodge.)

## INTERPRETATION OF THE MOTION

The first speaker for the proposition team interprets the motion to give meaning to it for the purpose of focused and informed debate. Without this attention to detail in the opening speech, it is likely that the debate motion would have a different meaning for different teams in the debate. Language is abstract. Words' meanings are not fixed and change with the context of their use. (For more on this subject, consult a dictionary. A dictionary is a history of the use of words and includes numerous understandings of individual terms over space and time.)

There are many potential interpretations of any given motion. Some of the possibilities are reasonable and might serve as a foundation for a powerful case on the motion. Other potential interpretations are incoherent for debate, maniacal, or genocidal. For example, on the motion, "This House would significantly reduce free speech," there are a number of possibilities for the proposition.

• Reasonable interpretations:

**Campaign finance reform:** The proposition might argue for restrictions on campaign advertising in the interest of "fair" elections.

**Group libel law:** The proposition team would call for the extension of libel laws for individuals to groups. This extension would restrict false and malicious speech targeting racial, ethnic, religious and other groups.

**Broadcast regulation:** The proposition might advocate that the government should restrict entertainment and other programming to increase public service announcements and programming.

• Incoherent interpretation:

> **Eliminate opposition speeches:** The proposition could demand a restriction on free speech by eliminating the opposition speeches to its case in the debate.

• Maniacal interpretation

> **Muzzle all dogs:** The proposition argues that dogs channel demonic messages and, subsequently, their speech must be curtailed. The opening speaker for the proposition cites, as reference material for the case, the disturbing facts of the Son of Sam murders, as well as books on the White House by former First Ladies Barbara Bush and Hilary Rodham Clinton, purporting to comment on presidential life from a dog's point-of-view.

• Genocidal interpretation

> **Eliminate political liberals:** Political liberals support free speech. The proposition team might argue for an executive order or other governmental decree authorizing the detention or summary execution of political liberals with a history of free speech.

The proposition team is responsible for selecting a meaningful interpretation for debate. There are several options here for the proposition team but many are unsavory or fail to focus the discussion in a coherent fashion. The proposition side of the motion is self-interested about the interpretation of the motion, to be sure, but they are biased in the interest of effective argumentation. They will not able to sustain a case without sophisticated lines of argument offering a proof for the motion.

The opposition team has no such interest. The opposing side is not concerned, in the same manner as the proposition team, about the successful interpretation of the motion. If the motion is dysfunctional, it is a simple matter for the side opposing the motion to win the debate. This is a primary reason that the interpretation of the motion ought to remain, with few, if any, reservations, within the exclusive control of the proposition side. Additional possibilities and limitations on the interpretation of motions are listed in the chapter on topic interpretation (Chapter 2).

## FRAMING THE DEBATE

Debaters compete to win debates. *Framing* a debate, a technique of argument contextualization, is a tool to increase the probability of proposition victories. With framing, the opening speaker for the proposition team creates a context for the appreciation and resolution of argumentation. Framing is done for three primary reasons:

- It is a gatekeeper matter.
- It anticipates argument comparison for the rebuttal and latter speeches of the debate.
- It establishes a context for the judge's decision making.

Gatekeeper ideas can be powerful tools in contest debates. A *gatekeeper* argument is one that determines if other arguments are permitted to enter the debate. In this way, the gatekeeper argument allows some ideas in (presumably, ideas favorable to your side of the motion) and keeps other arguments out (the challenges from your opponents). For example, the interpretation of a motion operates as a gatekeeper issue. The proposition team's interpretation, if sustained, eliminates other, competing interpretations of the motion in a debate. This technique compels the opposition to debate the issues initiated by the proposition team. On the motion, "This House would restrict the authority of the World Trade Organization in one or more areas," a proposition team could interpret the motion to discuss new restrictions on WTO authority to improve international environmental regulations. This interpretation opens the gate for a discussion of free trade and environmentalism and at the same time, closes the gate on debate on labor law, telecommunications, and other issues that might conceivably be part of a general discussion on WTO regulatory power.

The opening speaker for the proposition team should be able to frame or contextualize the debate to limit the possibilities for argument from the opposing side. The first speaker accomplishes this task by stating the point of the controversy for the proposition side of the motion and subtly setting a refutation argument agenda for the opposition. In other words, the opening speaker claims to establish a proof for the motion in a particular way and suggests to the judge the argument options available to the opposing side to dispute the claims of the proposition's case. For example, on the motion, "This House would limit military intervention against terrorists," the proposition might make a case to stop British and American bombing campaigns in Afghanistan. The opening speaker for the proposition side of the motion might argue that his team will prove that the bombing campaign has three serious negative consequences: (1) It creates a false sense of security about anti-terrorist policies, making it less likely that governments will initiate comprehensive anti-terrorist policies in a timely manner; (2) It produces regional instability and threatens to destabilize Pakistan, a nuclear nation; and (3) It has led to a humanitarian crisis in Afghanistan, as the bombing campaign has disrupted the shipment of food and other relief supplies. The proposition speaker might add the following to "frame" the issue as a gatekeeper device: "Each of these claims is an independent proof of the our interpretation of the motion for debate. If we are able to prove any of these issues, we will have successfully accomplished the goal of demonstrating a proof for the motion. The opposition team must refute each of these claims to disprove the case in the debate." This rhetoric restricts argumentation to any of these three issues in the debate. It attempts to narrow the options for the opposing side, by insisting that the opposition team defeat all of the proposition team's arguments to have a chance of success.

Framing anticipates the comparison of issues at the latter stages of the contest. Ideas are introduced in the debate with a particular goal in mind: the effective relative comparison of the arguments' merits at the conclusion of a round of debate. The outcome of a debate necessarily involves the relative positioning of teams. In the American and other two-team formats, debates are zero-sum contests and one team is designated a winner and the other team the loser. In British and other formats with more than two teams in a single round of debate, the outstanding team is ranked first, with lesser teams in the debate receiving correspondingly lower rankings. Because teams are evaluated on their relative achievement (that is, a higher ranking or a win is awarded based on a comparison to the performances of the other competitors), it is simply not enough to have an opinion in a debate. You must have the best possible expression of an opinion *and* your opinion must trump the opinions of the other participants in the contest. Achievement in debates, therefore, requires comparing the stances of each of the competing teams.

Debaters should anticipate their final stands on the floor and plan accordingly. It is not enough to know how to begin a debate. We know, for example, that any and all ideas are subject to disagreement and disputation. We know that it is inevitable that debaters will present opposing viewpoints on the subject matter of a motion. For us, this does not fully describe debate. Debate does not concern itself exclusively with disputing facts or informed opinion. Clash on factual issues is a necessary, but not sufficient condition for debate. The art of debate is about the effective resolution of facts and opinions already in dispute.

Debaters should frame issues for comparison at the conclusion of debates. As experienced competitors know, what matters is not how debates begin but how they end. Judges are persuaded by the final stands on the floor, the manner of resolution of contested issues. Framing ideas by anticipating the "end game," introducing arguments in a debate to move both you and your opponent to an inevitable conclusion favoring your side of the motion, is a valued skill of the experienced competitor.

Framing might also be used to influence the judge's decision making. In some parliamentary formats and leagues, most notably in some regions within the USA, debaters present formal decision-making **criteria** to assist the judge. This is hardly done as a favor to judges. The reason they give assistance to judges is to set the decision-making agenda for the judge, another way to tilt the debate toward one's side for the motion.

Debaters are fond of presenting an exclusive decision-making criterion to a judge for a debate. (Although it is typically a single evaluative instrument, the overwhelming majority of debaters refer to the issue by the plural, as "criteria." This is somewhat confusing for inexperienced debaters, who are always waiting for the other shoe to drop. When will the proposition team present a second or third decision making tool? The use of the term "criteria" in this context is admittedly vexing for the last three standing Latin scholars in the USA as well.) The criterion may be a statement of a valued principle: "The issues of the debate should be considered through the lens of Rawls' conception of justice." "Privacy interests of the individual are of utmost importance. They are essential to the protection of other political and social rights. As such, this debate must involve an exclusive assessment of issues from the position of privacy interests."

The decision-making criterion may involve general guidelines for a judge's consideration of the debate's arguments. Debaters often call for judges to decide debates on "the preponderance of the evidence" or "a cost-benefit calculus." These proof standards mirror decision making in civil trials or regulatory agencies.

Decision-making criteria educate inexperienced judges about their responsibilities as judges. They encourage judges to evaluate the debate on the issues raised by debaters, rather than on personal prejudices about the motion. They may also subtly support the logic of a proposition team's case. If the proposition team has a case that suggests that the government of a country could take a small action that would produce a large benefit, it is, quite obviously, in the interest of that team to argue that a judge should evaluate the debate based on the overall policy advantages (that is, a cost-benefit calculation of some sort). If a proposition team, on the other hand, has a case that relies on factual material generally thought to be beyond serious dispute, it is in the interest of the team to employ a decision making criterion on "the preponderance of the evidence," as it is unlikely that the opposing side will be able to disprove the factual foundation of the case.

The problem for proposition teams using this framing strategy is the exclusive use of a single criterion for decision making. Decision making is complex. Many factors are involved in reaching a conclusive decision. Even a relatively modest decision, for example, ordering food in a restaurant, involves a series of important decisions. A person ordering a meal in a restaurant would not use price alone as a basis for making a decision. ("The quality and taste of the food do not matter, just bring me the cheapest item.") Nor would a diner base a decision exclusively on a food's taste, presentation, nutritional content or another factor. It is the combination of these decision-making elements that lead to an action.

Debate decisions are even more complex. The issues of a debate may involve sophisticated discussions of comprehensive public policy reform. They might involve multiple actors and stakeholders. They might operate in national and international contexts. A single, exclusive criterion probably does a disservice to the kind of decision that is required to evaluate a debate.

Additionally, the proposition team would like to achieve victory in a debate on any issue that might ultimately support its side of the motion. It probably does not matter to the proposition side if they win the debate on an issue they have initiated or on a matter that was introduced in the debate by the side opposing the motion. An exclusive criterion (that is, a request that the judge should consider only those arguments that support one perspective on the motion, for example, "liberty interests") might too narrowly limit the proposition team in a debate, reducing their potential for success by taking off the table issues on which they could win.

## CONSTRUCTING THE CASE PROPER

A case is a set of arguments that supports a logical proof for a motion. The **case proper** refers to the substantive matter of the debate directly providing support for the motion, rather than any preamble to the case or meta-discussion appropriately framing the material substance of the debate.

The majority of parliamentary cases, in all debating formats, could generally be described as policy cases. A **policy case** endorses a specific public policy reform. The opening speaker for the proposition does this in a two-stage process, a logical construction that both identifies a problem and proposes a solution to the problem. In other words, the proposition team offers a case that attempts to correct a serious economic, social or political problem.

With this case form, the proposition team constructs a comparison between the status quo and a hypothetical future. The opening speaker for the proposition identifies core problems of the status quo. The **status quo** is said to be a description of extant policies and institutional structures. (It is important for debaters to recognize that there is no "status quo." It is a fiction. Policy is not unchanging, unyielding or static. Institutions can and do change their policies. New administrative regulations are adopted and rescinded on a regular basis. Political changes [e.g., new presidents, prime ministers and cabinet or military leaders] will necessarily lead to policy reforms, even in those circumstances in which the core governmental institutions do not change.)

The proposition establishes a comparison between dysfunctional institutions and a **hypothetical future**, i.e., a plan of action producing a better world. In the expression of the difference between the world in which we actually live and the world in which we ought to reside, the proposition team is able to identify benefits associated with its advocated position in the debate.

The speaker has certain obligations in order to prove the legitimacy of the case. The speaker must first identify a **problem**. Debaters are aware of many of the world's problems, social crises, and other calamities. But what are the constituent elements of a problem? You'll need to know these to offer a proof that an intractable problem does indeed exist. There are two. A condition is said to be a problem if it is (1) **ongoing** with (2) **serious negative repercussions.**

Debate terminology for these conditions includes the concept of **inherency**, which involves an examination of the ongoing nature of problems. If an issue is no longer a contemporary economic, social or political matter, it is not a problem. Few people today are worried about the potential of forced conscription to participate in the Crusades. (We are likely to worry about those few people made nervous about that possibility.) But many individuals are concerned with increasing cycles of violence and intolerance in the Middle East. Considering the ongoing nature of the matter, the former is not a problem but the latter most definitely is.

Negative repercussions are often identified as matters of **signifi-**

cance. The significance of an issue reveals its qualitative and quantitative dimension. For example, how seriously does the issue profoundly affect the life of an individual and how many individuals are troubled by this matter? The more an issue bothers a person and the more lives are touched by that matter, the greater the problem.

In a debate, you should include an explanation of the ongoing nature of a problem and the degree of its significance. It is not necessary to include formal debate jargon while undertaking these tasks in a speech, but it is important that you (and by extension, your audience) understand the elements of a problem. This knowledge is the only way to ensure that you will have a comprehensive and logical presentation of a proof. In addition, the logic of the construction provides some basic structure to a speech. It assists the speaker to organize her comments for easy understanding by a judge or audience.

After establishing the foundation of a problem, the speaker proposes a **solution**. The argument involving the solution to a problem is known as **solvency**. Once again, it is not necessary to use debate jargon in an actual debate to discuss arguments involving solutions. Jargon and technical speech are frequently an inelegant form of communication and can also confuse an audience unused to the terminology. It is, however, helpful to be familiar with technical debate speech, if only to understand an opponent who might use such language.

The solution to a problem should be well defined and technically feasible. (We know that in your private affairs, you prefer magic, ouija boards, tarot, palmistry and other "psychic arts" to accomplish your tasks. Debate judges tend to be skeptical of these solutions.) A comprehensive solution to a problem should include a plan of action and sufficient argumentation and information to sustain the claim that the plan adequately fixes the problem.

The **plan** is the formal expression of a solution to a problem. It should be brief but sufficient to provide a meaningful solution to the identified problem. The plan is generally a summary of model legislation, agency or executive action, a sample court decree, etc., that would successfully address the problem.

A plan might answer the following questions regarding agency, scope of regulatory authority and implementation:

- Who will do it?
- What are they required to do?
- How will they accomplish their goals?

Answers to these questions will satisfactorily address the issues regarding a solution to a problem, at least for the purposes of initiating debate on the matter. The proposition team should identify one or more of the parties responsible for an action, describe the scope of their authority, and discuss the manner of policy implementation. As for the latter issue, the proposition team ought to demonstrate that like policies, perhaps identical ones, have been previously adopted in other jurisdictions or in the same political jurisdiction on a different occasion in the past.

On the motion: "This House would legalize one or more recreational drugs," a proposition team might argue for the decriminalization of marijuana in the USA. They could identify the responsible parties for decriminalization (federal and state governments), examine the scope of their authority (rescinding all legislation criminalizing possession of marijuana and substituting a system of civil fines for public possession of the drug or behavior under the influence of the drug and make available drug rehabilitation programs for those with more than one civil violation), and discuss successful policy implementation (previous decriminalization efforts and one state, Alaska, has legislation that might serve as a successful model for the plan).

There may be ancillary advantages to a plan of action. The opening proposition speaker may discuss the scope of a problem, its proposed solution and additional benefits. For example, a proposition team might argue for a single-payer system of national health insurance in the USA. The reason for the proposal might be to offer a proof for the motion that "This House would bring them in." A proposition team might construe this motion to be a reference to those individuals currently without health insurance or underinsured. The case may be based on principles of equality but might have the additional benefit of spurring health and medical research, as more stakeholders in the public health care system makes it easier for investors to commit funds to health research and development, because the addition of tens of millions of new health and medical consumers is likely to add to the pay-offs of future research and development.

In addition to the policy case, there are other case models used in parliamentary debates. Some debaters use what might be described as a **fact case**. This case offers a proof for a so-called proposition of fact, a case that is difficult to prove and, if successfully proven, impossible to dispute. (This is the nature of "facts." The problem with facts is that they are "incontrovertible." They are, by definition, not subject to disputation and are therefore anathema to debate.) The other problem is the prohibition on the use of published material during a parliamentary debate. Facts cannot be verified in the course of a parliamentary debate. This situation creates a condition in which the judge, too often, is called on to insert her judgment for that of arguing debaters, deciding the outcome of the debate on the "facts she knew" before listening to the speeches. This judgment vitiates the point of debating. It is better for the authors of motions and proposition teams to avoid the fact motion or case entirely.

Debaters may also present a **value case** on a value motion. This matter has been discussed in some detail in the chapter on topics and their interpretation. The value case provides a proof for the motion in support for a particular value. On the motion, "Give me liberty or give me death," the first speaker for the proposition team would identify reasons and evidence to support the value of liberty, in direct contrast with the value of life.

There are some problems with most value motions and cases that purport to support those motions. Each value claim, liberty, for example, is packed with multiple meanings, some of them contradictory. (We suppose this compression of meanings makes sense for issues that have been debated for thousands of years.) It is difficult to discuss these issues in the abstract because of the differing understandings that accompany the use of value terms. In addition, each value claim incorporates the elements of other value claims. Life includes a liberty interest, as death typically interferes with the appreciation of civil and political liberties. Liberty incorporates life interests, because one is more likely to face arbitrary death in conditions of tyranny and slavery. It is nearly impossible to identify the exclusive "core" of a value claim for the purpose of focused debate. In other words, each side of a debate on the matter of liberty versus life ultimately seems to endorse both liberty and life interests. Of course, many values do not necessarily trade off with each other. It is possible to advocate two or more values in support of an idea (for a thought experiment, identify at least two values that are used to support any public policy). Many artificially constructed value motions, intending to produce a clash of values, merely confound participants who spend an entire debate trying to identify the Archimedian disputation point to begin serious debating.

Although it is now disfavored in parliamentary debate communities, the **time-space case** is important to note. This case attempts to analyze the basis of decision making by "moving" the debate to another time or place. It involves role playing for the debaters. In the shift of the debate through imagined time or space, typically a move to the past, debaters revisit historically influential decisions. On the motion, "This House would ban the bomb," a proposition speaker might make the following time-space introduction:

"It is 1945. The USA and Japan are locked in brutal struggles throughout the Pacific. This debate will examine the final stages of the war and the proposition will argue that the USA should not use atomic bombs on Japanese cities. The judge will evaluate the debate from the perspective of the decision-maker at the time, President Harry Truman. The proposition, as noted, will argue against the use of the atomic bombs. The opposing side should take the role of Truman's military and political advisers who favored the use of these devices. No material information revealed after August 1945 should be permitted in the debate."

The primary challenge associated with time-space case is that it is impossible to discern which knowledge comes from any single historical period and which arguments and ideas might spill over to another time. Quite often, it is extraordinarily difficult for debaters to fulfill their roles in a meaningful way. Of course, moving the debate to another time or place reduces the knowledge base of debaters, who inevitably know more about the world they live in than about any potential parallel world that might be discussed.

It may, in fact, be better to have a more contemporaneous discussion. In this example, the speaker calls for the excision of facts after 1945. Wouldn't debates be improved with more, rather than less, information? The atomic bombings of Hiroshima and Nagasaki are controversial events today but there is new evidence to bolster the case for either side of a motion on the justification of the attack. The debate can be fully engaged in the current period, with additional information after 1945 used to support fresh views on the event.

The time-space case has lost much of its former popularity. It is no longer a staple of debate teams and you might compete for years and never personally experience the traditional form of case. There is, however, a time-space element that persists in parliamentary debating. It pertains to the definition of "this House" in debates.

In many debates, the interpretation of the phrase "This House" is uncontroversial. The "House" is the debating chamber. The participants in the debate try to persuade the House to vote for or against a motion on the floor. In tournament competition, there is usually a designated voting representative for the House, namely a single judge or a panel of judges. In practical terms, the person or persons judging the debate, formally deliberating on the motion, are the House.

A number of debaters define "This House" to mean something other than the debating chamber and its deliberative membership. In these cases, the first proposition speaker moves the debate from its location to another place (occasionally, but infrequently, another time). The proposition speaker might define the House as the "United Nations," "European Union," "International Criminal Court," "Government of Costa Rica," "Saddam Hussein" or any other decision maker. The speaker expects that the debate will proceed in the context of a decision by that selected actor. For example, if the House is defined as the "U.S. Federal Government," the debate will only consider the motion from the perspective of the jurisdictional authority of the USA. Although not popularly known as a time-space case, this approach functions in precisely the same way as the traditional time-space model.

## Suggested Exercise:

Debaters should take a motion and construct a model opening speech for the proposition side of the motion, including introduction, interpretation of the motion, framing, case proper, and conclusion. This exercise should be repeated using any of the sample topics from the selection in the back of this book.

## The Speech Conclusion

Like the introduction, debaters should deliver a powerful final comment in support of its side of the motion. A concluding remark of no more than 10 or 15 seconds ought to summarize the relative positions of the teams in the debate, identify a consistent and powerful theme associated with the presentation of the case, or remind the judge and audience of the serious and salient matters under consideration. This technique will leave the judge with a final persuasive appeal for the case, rather than a perfunctory or pro forma conclusion, namely "I beg to propose/oppose." Don't beg. It is unseemly.

# CHAPTER 5:

# ARGUING
# AGAINST THE
# PROPOSITION CASE

## BASIC OPPOSITION TO THE CASE

The opposition team is able to challenge the proposition case with both direct and indirect refutation. We discuss indirect refutation in the chapters on disadvantages, counterplans, and critiques. This chapter discusses how to engage in direct oppositional refutation. Direct refutation involves specific challenges to the arguments in the opening proposition speech. The opposition arguments that specifically address the major lines of proof of the first proposition speaker are called **case arguments** or **"on-case" arguments**. They fundamentally challenge the original case position.

There are, however, a number of issues in a debate that might be relevant to the discussion but do not have a corollary in the proposition team's opening remarks. After all, the proposition team tries to put on its best face in the opening speech. The proposition case includes the outstanding arguments for a proof of the motion and little else. The proposition team does not present information that might do harm to its position. There are, inevitably, many issues excluded, or even self-censored, by the proposition team. The opposing side may wish to introduce one or more of these otherwise excluded ideas into the debate. In addition, the opposition might choose to present major arguments – disadvantages, counterplans, and critiques – that are premised on the proposition case but move well beyond the case text. These ideas are often known as **"off-case" arguments**, because they are not found within the text of the proposition team's case arguments.

The opposition team ought to counter the substantive material of the proposition team's case. It is not necessary to disagree with each of the major elements of proof of a case. Strategic agreement, a sound tactic for the opposition, is a method of argument by which the opposing side concedes one or more of the proposition side's arguments in order to advance their own interests in the debate.

Agreement might focus the debate on more salient matters. For example, a speaker might agree to relatively modest claims that serve as a distraction for them and the judge. If a case supports restrictions on immigration, the proposition side might argue that closing national borders could (1) improve security against terrorists who would potentially use weapons of mass destruction and (2) save some administrative costs for government processing of immigrants. The advantages of this case might fairly be described as a battleship pulling a dinghy. The former advantage could affect the lives of tens of thousands or millions of people. The latter one is modest and might save some money, which politicians would surely waste on improving their salary structure. It is perhaps a better approach for the opposition team to cut off the proposition team's dinghy, simply ignoring the relatively modest advantage of unspectacular savings of government administrative expenditures in order to concentrate their rhetorical resources on the more significant issues related to terrorism and weapons of mass destruction.

An argument concession might permit the opposition side to present another and more compelling idea in the debate. Disadvantages are an apt example. Many disadvantages presume that a plan of action is successfully implemented but that it has grave and (at least for the proposition team) unseen consequences. For example, a proposition team might support the adoption of mandatory helmet laws for motorcyclists. The opposition might concede the proposition team's argument that the law could be successfully enforced (i.e., after the adoption of a mandatory helmet law, the overwhelming majority of motorcyclists would wear helmets). The opposition team might concede that more motorcyclists would wear helmets so that they could subsequently make a rejoinder that new research on motorcycle helmet laws demonstrates that mandatory use increases injury and death because helmeted riders develop a false sense of security and take more risks.

Debaters will inevitably disagree with some elements of the proposition team's case. If the opposition team confronts a policy case (the majority of parliamentary debate cases), it may want to challenge any of the case elements describing the extant problem and the proposed solution. These include the issues of inherency, significance, and solvency, concepts describing the nature of the problem and its solution.

To challenge the proposition team's inherency argument, that is, the proof that a problem is ongoing, the opposition team will want to offer an explanation for the failure to implement the proposition team's proposal. The risks of policy failure associated with the plan might be one reason that well-intentioned individuals have yet to act in accordance with the proposition team's suggested reform. The opposition might also argue that more study is required before one should attempt policy action.

Of course, the opposition might also identify other causes of the problem. The suggestion of another reason for the problem, an alternate causality, undermines the claim that a particular institutional flaw is responsible for the problem. For example, the proposition team might claim there is an ongoing crime problem and propose a guaranteed annual income to alleviate the cause of crime – that is, poverty. If the opposition is able to identify other major causes of crime (family violence, intercultural prejudices, drug abuse and sociopathologies), then they will be able to demonstrate that the problem is unrelated to the cause identified by the proposition team. The purpose of this line of argument is to show that the problem is not amenable to reform by the plan.

The opposition team may choose to refute the significance or harms of the case. This text includes some additional tactics for arguing impact assessments and issues of significance in the chapter on debate skills. Basically, there are three primary strategies for refuting claims of significance:

- The opposition team may attempt to minimize an argument.
- The opposition team may turn or capture an argument.
- The opposition team may choose to answer an argument.

Arguments have different expressions of qualitative and quantitative significance. Some issues matter a great deal to an individual. In other words, they have qualitative dimension. For example, the wrongful incarceration of a person is a grave matter. The loss of a job due to race discrimination is a compelling violation of individual liberty. As serious as these conditions may be for any single person, however, the arbitrary loss of liberty for a single individual may not be a sufficient reason to reform the entire criminal justice system. Some expressions of significance have qualitative authority but do not have quantitative dimension. They are serious matters, indeed, but relatively inconsequential to comprehensive reform of a public policy field.

Other expressions of significance might apply to a large number of people but have relatively little consequence. A modest increase in the price of a postage stamp or additional waiting time for public transportation may affect the lives of tens of millions of individuals, but the degree of disruption in people's lives is so modest that it could not be said to describe a serious problem. A debater might minimize a significant argument, i.e., an argument describing a harm or benefit, by identifying the way it fails to prove that it has both qualitative and quantitative scope.

It is possible to compare the qualitative and quantitative measure of an argument with the qualitative and quantitative measure of another argument. Debaters should evaluate the commensurable outcomes of their lines of argument. If, for example, a proposition team suggests a public policy reform that would save 1,000 lives and the opposition team is able to demonstrate that the same policy will cost 10,000 lives, it is quite obvious that the opposition team should contrast the advantage of the policy and disadvantage of the policy in like or commensurable terms: number of lives saved.) Debaters may also evaluate incommensurable ideas. Please see the section in Chapter 10 on impact assessment for a comprehensive description of debating incommensurable values and policies.

In addition to minimization, the opposition team may turn or capture an opponent's argument. An argumentative **turn** is a technique in which a debater takes an argument from a team arguing one side of a motion and makes the claim that the argument is better suited to support the opposing side (their side) of the motion. This is a highly effective argument strategy because it does not necessarily resist or refute the material substance of an opponent's argument. In its most effective form, this tactic "spins" the opposing side's issue. When you turn an opponent's argument, you take one of their arguments and proceed to use it for your own purposes, usually by showing that it better supports your side of the motion.

There are two types of turns: link turns and impact turns. A **link turn** is a claim that a causal connection (or "link") for an argument better supports the opposing side of the topic. For example, a proposition team might argue for a motion to increase the war on drugs, with the expressed purpose to reduce criminal drug use. The opposing side might respond that the war on drugs paradoxically increases criminal drug use, as it forces drug users, particularly novice users, to associate with criminal drug dealers to purchase recreational drugs. These new associations would increase the possibility of new and inexperienced users being recruited as drug sellers or couriers. It also initiates drug users to a world of lawbreakers who might lead them into other criminal activity. In this case, the opposition team agrees with the proposition team's premise. Both teams are interested in reducing criminal drug use. The fundamental difference in the teams' position is that the opposition team makes the claim that the war on drugs is responsible for increasing criminal drug use. The increase in the war on drugs, therefore, is likely to concomitantly increase criminal drug use, rather than reduce it. The opposition team, by agreeing with the proposition case, has successfully identified an error in causal reasoning and is able to turn the argument to theiradvantage.

An **impact turn** is an argument that reverses the claims associated with an argument's impact or outcome. For example, a proposition team might argue about the risks associated with nuclear proliferation. They might suggest that proliferation is destabilizing and leads to the possibility of nuclear conflict. The opposition team might reply that proliferation is actually a valued public policy rather than a reason for fear. The opposition speaker would claim that the history of effective nuclear deterrence among major nuclear powers for the 50 years of the Cold War, despite considerable antagonism and high-stakes international conflicts, proves that nuclear proliferation increases stability and reduces the potential for nuclear conflict. In addition, the team might argue that nuclear proliferation would also deter the use of chemical, biological, and conventional weapons, making conflict dramatically less likely with new nuclear regimes. In this case, the opposition team is able to reverse the standing of the issue of significance in the debate. That which was "bad" is now determined to be "good." There is additional information on link turns and impact turns in Chapter 7 on disadvantages.

In the event that your opponent introduces a relevant argument that has a substantial degree of significance and cannot be turned, it is then necessary to answer the argument. Many effective debate arguments are supported by examples. The most effective counter is to directly refute the examples initiated by your opponent.

Examples may be nullified with counterexamples. These counters should match the original example in scope. In other words, the opposition team has a duty to provide appropriate counterexamples that consider the scale of the proposition team's examples and try to either (1) directly match or exceed the significance of the original example in the same area of inquiry (e.g., the opposition could use an example of a favorable military intervention to counter a claim of an unfavorable military adventure) or (2) make analogies to counterexamples in other fields (e.g., the opposition might argue about regulatory excess in environmental policies to counter a proposition team advocating new regulations in consumer product safety).

There are additional challenges to examples: They ought to be *representative* or *typical* of the analytical claims made by the proposition team. They should express significance. They ought to reveal that problems can be resolved and are not intractable. There should be sufficient examples to prove the core elements of a motion. It is also possible for the opposition team to counter the solvency claims of the proposition. Will the proposed solution resolve the problem? Alternate causality arguments could effectively undermine a proposition team's claim that they have proposed the correct solution to a discrete problem. The opposition team might carefully examine the elements of the plan. Have they identified the appropriate agent, with the necessary legal jurisdiction and resources, to successfully administer the proposed reform? Does the agent have sufficient legal authority, expressed in the mandates of action provisions of the plan, to carry out its mission? Are there difficulties that might occur during program implementation? Are there sufficient constituent groups to sustain the program in the long term? Would any social groups opposing the plan or any other party engage in a backlash against new policy initiatives? These questions might produce a significant number of objections to the technical implementation and ultimate success of a policy proposal.

On a cautionary note, the opposition team should exercise considerable care when introducing inherency and solvency arguments into the debate. The proposition team's inherency argument explains that there is an ongoing problem. That team argues that no agent is effectively moving to adopt the suggested plan. Too frequently, the opposition replies to this position in a reactionary manner, indicating that there is some movement in the direction of the proposition policy, that government or private interests endorse or otherwise adopt elements of the proposition plan. Rather than helping the opposition cause, these arguments are likely to undermine it.

The best position for the opposition is to argue that the proposition case is "bad." By that, we mean that the proposition makes a case that is an expression of a "good." It is not an effective counter to say that the case may not be good enough. If the proposition team lowers their original expectations (that is, they are not "good enough") but they are still superior to the opposition team, who would logically prevail in a debate? The proposition team. The opposition team should show that the proposition is counterproductive, dangerous or demonic. On the occasions that the opposition team defends a position that suggests movement in the direction of the proposition position in the debate, they are unable to credibly argue that movement in the direction of the proposition team's advocated position is a bad idea.

In addition, strong opposition arguments, such as the disadvantage, may rely on the successful implementation of the proposition team's plan. The better arguments for the opposition presume that the plan comes into fruition but is a bad idea. If the opposition team argues (usually, with solvency arguments) that the plan is not fully implemented, it may limit the introduction of arguments that presume that the plan is both implemented and counterproductive. Debaters should be careful to introduce inherency and solvency arguments that do not contradict the substantive material of other powerful and effective opposition strategies.

## SUGGESTED EXERCISE:

In Appendix 4, you will find a transcript of the opening speeches for the proposition and the opposition sides of the motion: "This House should return the goods." Debaters should work as individuals or in small groups on the full text of a speech or a speech section, analyzing it for (1) the five elements of a narrative construction of a proposition case, including introduction, interpretation, framing, case proper, and conclusion; (2) effective opposition argumentation, identifying argument typologies; (3) speech structure and argument organization; and (4) argument clash.

## STRUCTURING OPPOSITION ARGUMENTS TO THE CASE

Just as it is important to make good arguments against the proposition team's case, it is also important to structure your opposition arguments appropriately to maximize their effectiveness. Appropriate structure is particularly important for the arguments made in the constructive speech of the first opposition speaker, because these arguments frame the rest of the debate on the proposition team's case. There are at least two faulty and mutually exclusive strategies employed by the first opposition speaker:

**THE UNDIFFERENTIATED MASS.** Sometimes the lead opposition speaker will advance her arguments against the proposition team's case consecutively and without structure. This kind of presentation may be pleasing from an oratorical perspective, but its lack of structure can be ultimately crippling to the opposition team and annoying to the judge. ("This plan is a bad idea, and it's not inherent, and it has little significance, and here's an example of why it wouldn't solve the problem, and the plan makes no sense, and...")

THE HYPER-STRUCTURE. Sometimes the lead opposition speaker will advance her arguments using too much structure, rather than not enough. This presentation strategy is, in effect, the opposite of the undifferentiated mass strategy. It meets the organizational needs of the judge and the other team and then goes too far, cluttering the debate with needless detail, much to the annoyance of all the participants. ("Off of their first observation, in their A subpoint, on their small two point, sub 'b...')

Each of these strategies has specific disadvantages and advantages. Neither strategy is optimal. Instead, the first opposition speaker should seek to differentiate and explain her arguments using a simple structure to facilitate flowing, refutation, and consolidation in the later parts of the debate.

The problem for the first opposition speaker is how to respond to specific components of the proposition team's case without devoting too much confusing time and energy referencing the specific (and often highly detailed) structure of that case. Let's consider an example to see how this might work in practice. Perhaps the proposition team has presented a case that contends that the USA should get rid of its nuclear weapons arsenal. The basic outline of the case might look something like the example that follows. We do not here go into the full articulation of the arguments that might be made by a first proposition speaker defending disarmament; rather, we want to show a potential outline for refutation.

Observation I: There is a pressing need for the nuclear disarmament by the USA.
    A. Accidents are likely and dangerous
        1. False alarms. Empirically, nuclear powers' early warning systems receive false alarms that could cause an automatic launch of nuclear weapons. This has almost happened many times in the past, and reliable sources assure us that it is only a matter of time before an accidental nuclear war breaks out for real. (Examples follow.)
        2. This situation is particularly true in Russia, where deteriorating command and control systems, as well as an underfunded military and reliance on hair-trigger alert status mean

that accidental launches could happen at any time.

3. Even one accidental detonation would kill tens of thousands of people – every additional warhead detonation would of course add to this death toll. There is a serious risk that an accidental nuclear war might break out, killing millions.

B. Proliferation

1. By refusing to commit to nuclear disarmament, the USA is essentially in the process of spitting in the eye of the international nonproliferation regime, as codified in the Non Proliferation Treaty (NPT). In that treaty, the USA and other nuclear powers agreed to a goal of disarmament; they just have not yet put that goal into practice.

2. This policy poisons the well of non proliferation. The USA's hypocrisy on this issue communicates the message that what the NPT is *really* about is dividing the world into two classes: the nuclear "haves" and "have nots." This state of affairs is perceived as colonialistic, unfair, and unacceptable by the majority of the world. Thus the NPT, the linchpin of the global nonproliferation regime, has largely been rendered obsolete by the obstinance of the USA.

3. Proliferation is risky business. As more states acquire nuclear weapons, their use becomes more likely. Because nuclear deterrence is largely a fictive construct with no empirical evidence, it is really only a matter of time before all kinds of conflicts begin to escalate to the nuclear level, killing millions.

The Plan: The USA should formally commit to nuclear disarmament, pursued in an expedient manner, while assuring that all relevant safety and security steps are made in the interim. This policy will be pursued in consultation with all relevant actors.

III. Solvency

A. Antiproliferation credibility. The plan will bolster the nonproliferation regime, assuring that international nuclear proliferation can be effectively checked.

B. Norms. The plan will establish an international norm that clearly communicates that nuclear weapons are not an acceptable currency or lever in politics and thus will not be tolerated. C. Other nations will follow. The international community has repeatedly communicated that if the USA were to pursue meaningful nuclear disarmament, others would follow its lead. D. Moral imperative. It is in all nations' best interests to work towards nuclear disarmament. The weapons themselves are so immensely destructive, both physically and psychologically, that we must commit to rid the world of them. The plan is a giant step in this direction.

The first opposition speaker and her partner should generate arguments against this case as it is being presented. As arguments against the case are generated, they should be flowed in the column next to the part of the first proposition speaker's case to which they correspond. As a general rule, the first opposition speaker should use only the *most general structure* of the proposition team's case to signpost her arguments. All debaters must *signpost* their arguments in the refutation and extension process. By this we mean that you should provide a signpost for the judge that clearly states which argument or group of arguments you are refuting or extending. Signposting fulfills the "they say" step of the four-step refutation process discussed in Chapter 3. Many first opposition speakers will carry this signposting process too far, resulting in the "hyper-structure" problem discussed above. Let's say that you wanted to make some arguments against the "accidental launch" claims of the proposition case above. You would phrase your arguments in this way:

"I'll begin by answering their first observation, which is their statement of harms. They give two specific scenarios, which I will answer in order. On their accidental launch scenario – scenario A, I have a few answers:

"First, the false-alarm risk is low. This is empirically proven by decades of nuclear possession by many countries. There has never been a single accidental nuclear launch, much less an all-out nuclear exchange, which is what their impact claims assume. This scenario is nothing but reckless fear-mongering on the part of the proposition team.

"Second, safety is high. We have hotlines, diplomacy, constructive engagement, and other weapons mitigation procedures *because* of the risk of accidental launch. The accidental launch possibility is *why* we have all of the existing safety procedures.

Third, a turn: This scenario encourages the nonproliferation regime and additional safety procedures. The possibility of an accidental launch encourages other countries to think twice about weapons buildups. By disarming, the proposition case makes it seem that the threat is ending, paradoxically increasing the risk of accidental launch by decreasing overall vigilance."

This is excellent technique for structuring and presenting the initial opposition arguments against the proposition case. Notice that the opposition speaker numbers her arguments consecutively, rather than trying to signpost them off of specific components of the presentation of Scenario 1. Also notice that the speaker *tags*, or assigns a concise label to, her arguments before relating the substance of the argument: "First, the false-alarm risk is low;" "Second, safety is high." This is a good debate habit because it enables the judge to get a concise summary of each argument onto her flow. The average judge will only get the first three words of each argument onto her flow, so it is incumbent upon debaters to make sure that those first three words are the most important.

Notice also that the speaker answers the first scenario as a whole, without attempting to refute all of its constituent parts. This is good technique. You can easily refute a specific scenario, or a whole contention, without directly referencing each of its constituent parts. You should try to *group* arguments, whenever possible, to simplify the record of arguments as exemplified by their presence on the flow of the debate. *Grouping* arguments is just what it sounds like — a tactic that answers a few similar arguments as a group, rather than individually. In the example above, the speaker has grouped together all the arguments in the first scenario to answer them more effectively. Yet she has still answered the scenario effectively.

This speaker, after making the above arguments, should continue on to answer the second scenario and the solvency contention. She should group each of those sections rather than answering the substructure of the case specifically. This does not mean that the speaker should not *answer* the specific components of a proposition case contention. You can easily answer specific proposition arguments using the grouping method. Consider the following potential answers to the proposition team's solvency contention:

> "First, norm establishment won't solve the problem. This has been proven again and again with international treaties – the Chemical Weapons Convention has been ratified, but countries still pursue chemical weapons. Likewise, the United Nations Declaration of Human Rights establishes norms, and those aren't followed, either. There's no reason to believe the plan would induce others to disarm.
>
> "Second, nuclear weapons deter conflict. This means that after the plan, more wars will occur as deterrence evaporates. Also, this means that existing nuclear weapons states won't have an incentive to get rid of their nuclear weapons because they believe in deterrence.
>
> "Third, the antiproliferation regime is doomed anyway. The plan can't revitalize the nonproliferation regime because it relies on outdated supply-side controls that have never worked. Countries like India, Pakistan, and Israel haven't acquired nuclear weapons because the USA has failed to get rid of its nuclear weapons."

These arguments answer parts of the proposition team's solvency contention specifically, but without using confusing signposting to refer to overly specific parts of the proposition team's case. The speaker does *not* say:

> "They say in their B subpoint of their solvency that the plan will encourage other countries to give up nuclear weapons and that this will create some kind of norm, but…"

The speaker here has not yet made an argument, despite having spoken for about ten seconds. This preface to an argument commits several common errors. First, obviously, it is too long. Second, it gives too much credit to the proposition team's argument by repeating it at length. Third, the speaker is trying to respond to each sub-point of solvency individually rather than responding to the observation as a whole. Finally, the speaker damages her own credibility by failing to state her argument clearly and concisely at the beginning. The speaker could improve her presentation a bit by saying something like the following:

> "They say that their plan will create a norm against nuclear weapons, but this won't work because…"

This is still a sub-par framing of a response. The speaker is still beginning her argument by reiterating the proposition team's argument rather than by declaratively making one of her own:

> "First, norm establishment won't solve the problem. This has been proven again and again with international treaties…"

You should practice this technique of phrasing your arguments offensively and concisely rather than defensively and in a verbose manner.

A few final notes about opposition arguments against the proposition team's case. First, while you should definitely make arguments about the plan (e.g., its inadequacy, its poor wording, its foolish and naïve assumptions about the world), you should make those arguments where they will impact the substantive claims of the case. For example, if the plan has no possibility or provisions for enforcement, it is unlikely to solve the designated problem. Make this argument on the solvency contention. Do not confuse the matter by signposting your argument on the plan. Perhaps the plan does not account for alternate causalities discussed in the harms contentions. Make this argument on the relevant harms contentions, rather than on the plan. This technique points to a more general rule about placing opposition arguments – *make your arguments against the part of the case that they impact the most.*

Second, you should always design your opposition strategies with an eye toward crystallization in the opposition's final stand (or stands, depending on the format for debate) on the floor. This means you should try to ensure that your arguments are relatively consistent with each other and appropriately diversified. Do not put all of your oppositional eggs in one basket in the first opposition speech. Make several different kinds of arguments, both on the case and off the case, to ensure that you will have a broad spectrum of arguments to decide among when your subsequent speeches come around.

# CHAPTER 6:

# EVIDENCE AND

# RESEARCH

## BASIC RESEARCH ISSUES

Research on the debate's subject matter improves the quality of debating. More importantly for debate's practitioners, informed argument may produce more debate success. It will provide an edge in debates: The informed have a greater range of issues on which to draw. Additional information also assists debaters in providing more analytical depth on any given issue. Good debates require extensive preparation. It is a terrible experience for audiences and judges to listen to speakers try to debate a subject about which they are not knowledgeable. You should not even think of debating if you are not committed to reading and researching current issues.

Research supports argument anticipation, which is the single most important skill for consistently outstanding debate performances. If a debater is able to make strategic moves in anticipation of the ideas and tactics of an opponent, she is more likely to triumph on those issues and in the debate. Subject knowledge puts debaters in a position to anticipate and evaluate the merits of issues.

Research for effective parliamentary debating includes issue preparation – a knowledge base of current events and notes from previous debates. A number of issues constitute core value or policy claims that are regularly repeated in parliamentary debates. Value claims – such as life, liberty, equality, justice, privacy, and aesthetics – form the foundation of many debate motions. Research on these matters would greatly assist preparation for debates.

But what does it mean to research "liberty"? This issue has been investigated for thousands of years. There are millions of pages of texts on the subject. Liberty interests are relevant to discussions of virtually every public policy issue. Liberty is hardly a static notion: There are new understandings of liberty and its application to personal or political behaviors, reflecting the dynamism of the value. There are hundreds of thousands of Web pages exploring its elements. How is it possible for debaters to carefully investigate this issue? (It would take much longer to research the issue of liberty to prepare for a debate than the available years of one's lifetime. It's the Tristram Shandy paradox, to be sure.)

It is important to consider the use of research in preparation for a parliamentary debate. Research on a single subject will support argument on a single issue or small argument set. It will rarely serve as the foundation for even a full speech because parliamentary debate speeches do not frequently and exclusively discuss a single line of argument. It is in your interest to present multiple, independent arguments, any one of which will offer a winning position. Breadth of argumentation increases the likelihood that at least one winning position will obtain at the conclusion of the debate. The reality is that you are unlikely to devote more than two or three minutes to a major line of argument. Debaters, therefore, do not need to master an academic discipline to have a sufficient knowledge edge. You need only that information that will produce an advantage relative to the information possessed by your opponent.

In addition, there are a limited number of applications for your knowledge in a debate. On an issue like liberty, you will need to have sufficient information to discuss differing ideas about liberty. You should be able to compare the value of liberty interests to other value claims (e.g., why liberty interests ought to trump equality or privacy rights). You will want to describe examples of liberty interests and the impacts associated with liberty gains and losses. Your information should be sufficient to anticipate and counter the rejoinders of those from the opposing side.

Debaters should read at least one newspaper every day. There is no substitute for the diversity of information available in a daily newspaper. Because of the nature of parliamentary debate, debaters must have at their disposal a variety of information on a wide array of topics. If you read the newspaper every day, you will at least be up to date on current events and topics of general importance. When you read the newspaper, read it with an eye towards debate. Try to identify articles that might contain the information necessary to make good cases for future debates. Take notes. We suggest that you keep a notebook where you store notes from articles and publications that you read so that you will be able to access this information when you are writing cases or putting together information to oppose the cases argued by other teams.

Different debate motions frequently raise similar public policy issues. Immigration reform, peacekeeping forces, tax reform, gun control, educational reform, affirmative action, terrorism, drug legalization, and other popular topics are often debated on more than one motion or as a subset of a motion each year. A database file of topics and issues, that is, an institutional history of debate practice, will direct research and preparation for competitors. Some of this information is already collected in parliamentary argument texts, sourcebooks and Websites. Debaters can examine texts on current events, including newspapers, Websites and electronic journals, academic and other periodicals, and government documents. You might review multiple periodicals in libraries rather than rely on personal subscriptions (unless you invested in Microsoft early and often). It is possible to subscribe online to wire service digests and newspapers worldwide. As the majority of debate topics are drawn from current events, these sources of information are valued sites. They are particularly important sources of information immediately prior to invitational and inter-varsity tournament competition.

Debate squads can coordinate research. Burden sharing among a number of debaters, each researching a value claim, can increase the production of information without a concomitant increase in work for any single debater. You should compile notes for each researched topic, building up the base of research over time. We suggest that each squad, or group of colleagues on a debate team, divide up responsibilities for examining different periodicals and publications throughout the year for maximum efficiency in obtaining information. Come up with a list of uniquely useful weekly, monthly, or quarterly publications and assign everyone on the squad to one or more of these resources. That person should be responsible for reading their assignments and reporting to the rest of the group on the interesting content they found. This way, a team can maximize the information accessible to all debaters.

## ETHICS AND EVIDENCE

Parliamentary debate is unique among debating formats in that it accepts the voice of the debater as an authority on the subject being debated. Other formats, in which debaters read quoted evidence from outside sources, often diminish or devalue the expertise of the debaters themselves on the subjects for debate. This feature of parliamentary debate places a tremendous responsibility on the debater, who thereby shoulders the ethical responsibility to represent her sources and information fairly and honestly. At times, some unsavory elements in the parliamentary debate community have disregarded or ignored this responsibility and invented facts, figures, and case studies to bolster their arguments in debates. These tactics are to be deplored. *It is not acceptable to make up information in debates*. This is not ethical behavior. It is also not polite – your opponents deserve your respect and the opportunity to engage in a fair debate.

Falsification of evidence so breaches the mutually agreed upon standards for the event that individuals who violate these standards ought to be excluded from competitive debate leagues and clubs in the same way that individuals who plagiarize are excluded from academic circles. Consider that you ought to treat others as you yourself would want to be treated. When you enter a debate, you expect that your opponents will behave in an ethical and respectful manner. They will expect the same of you. We urge you to act accordingly.

On occasion, you may encounter a debater who, you believe, has her facts wrong. What should you do in this situation? We advise you not to assume that the opposition is deliberately distorting the truth in order to trick you. They may have made a simple factual error. They may also be simply uninformed in comparison to your superior knowledge on the issue. We encourage you to give your opponents the benefit of the doubt, just as you would want in this situation. You may be wrong about the facts. Many people are convinced that they know "the facts," but are later proven to be gravely mistaken (e.g., the critics of Galileo, flat earth theorists, phrenologists, particle physicists – all people allegedly operating under the high evidentiary standards of physical science).

## PREPARING CASES

In addition to general preparation, it is wise to prepare proposition and opposition argument positions through the development of case ideas and opposition argumentation. Case development includes the following steps:

- Identifying a public policy issue framed in problem-solution language. For example, there is an emerging AIDS crisis in Southeast Asia. The crisis is magnified by needle sharing among intravenous drug users and the failure of sex partners to use condoms. A needle exchange program, with distribution of clean hypodermic needles and bleach, as well as an educational program for condom use, would dramatically reduce the incidence of AIDS.
- Doing advanced research on the issue. The debater will conduct sufficient research to have a knowledge advantage relative to the informed opinion of opponents.
- Anticipating arguments. The debater will imagine the possible counters by the opposing side in the debate and prepare effective replies.
- Practicing. A debate team will engage in one or more debates with the information on the AIDS crisis. The proposition team will attempt to apply the case idea in full or as an example on more than one motion.

This model of case construction, which follows a logical pattern, provides many direct and ancillary benefits for participants and is a routine matter for experienced debaters. One thing that debaters develop over years of debate participation is a reservoir of knowledge about motions and issues. Experienced practitioners are likely to rely on that information during formal preparation time immediately prior to debates as well as during the actual contest. For this reason, it is inaccurate to say that parliamentary debaters are exclusively engaged in extemporaneous argument. In fact, many argument positions are "scripted" ideas: The issues have been discussed in previous debates. Experienced debaters often replay the speeches of a debating career, exploiting lesser-trained or experienced participants who are yet to create their institutional memory of debate practice.

The model successfully replicates the stages of argument analysis on a case, from initial brainstorming to generate an interpretation of the motion, to establishing a foundation of analytical reasoning and examples, to execution in speeches. This sample practice set slowly traces the techniques on display in tournament competition each round. This patient method of instruction, carefully detailing the basics of case construction for novice and advanced debaters, is a valuable instructional tool. It reveals that research, from the personal information of participants, public policy literature, current events information, and notes from previous tournaments, may assist debaters' educational and competitive success.

We strongly recommend that debaters and their extended squads build a library of pre-prepared cases for use in tournament debates. This exercise fulfills two major purposes: It prepares debaters, through practice, to construct a variety of cases; in addition, it ensures that debaters will not be caught wholly unawares and unprepared at tournaments when they are called on to debate on the side of the proposition. Using the guidelines for case construction, debaters should generate a series of prepared cases on a variety of topics they are likely to encounter in their competitive debate season. Your pre-prepared case should contain the following components:

• A detailed outline for the first proposition speaker's speech, including an introduction, statement of harms, a plan, a statement of solvency and advantages, and a conclusion.

- A list of potential opposition arguments and appropriate proposition rejoinders to these arguments.
- A list of humorous, issue-specific items that can be used to enliven the debate and persuasively convey critical arguments.

Keep these pre-prepared cases in a notebook for reference before your debates. They will help you use your preparation time more productively and efficiently. For more on how to use preparation time, reference the section in the next chapter.

Make sure that your pre-prepared cases span a broad range of potential topic areas to maximize their potential applications. During the course of a debate season, you may have to debate issues of environmental policy, constitutional reform, trade policy, labor relations, military intervention, public health issues, and drug policy. You should develop at least one pre-prepared case for each of these topic areas. You should also develop pre-prepared cases that deal with issues of your particular interest.

Opposition research includes disadvantage, counterplan, and critique preparation. (Comprehensive information on the theory and practice of these opposition arguments is contained in subsequent chapters of this text.) Opposition teams should prepare arguments on issues that recur in debates, including research on popular cases, such as gun control, immigration reform, the application of United Nations peacekeeping forces, and tradeoffs between the economy and the environment.

The opposition should anticipate and research conventional arguments that are frequently (and sometimes subconsciously or unconsciously) used by proposition teams. For example, a substantial number of proposition teams in the USA routinely include arguments indicating that they ought to defend a framework for the debate by which the decision is given to the team best upholding utilitarian principles. Utilitarianism is often described by the first proposition speaker as a model for debates in which the judge should ultimately rule for or against debate teams based on principles of "net benefits," "cost-benefit analysis," or "greater advantages." In these cases, there is almost never a defense of the core elements of utilitarianism, nor does it seem to be the case that the proposition team has carefully considered the implications of strict utilitarianism (although the Nazis figured it out early on). This is precisely the kind of argument that the opposition might identify, research, and prepare to answer prior to tournament competition. Other matters include core value claims (life, liberty, equality, justice, privacy, order, aesthetics, etc.) and opponents' cases.

## FINDING EVIDENCE

We have already said that you should read a wide variety of magazines, books, and newspapers in order to be a well-researched debater. Of course, reading is only one part of the equation – you must also work to comprehend and appropriately process the information contained in the books and periodicals you read. Reading for debate is similar to other reading you may do for classes you are taking or have taken in the past. Since you should expect to read many sources and articles for preparation in parliamentary debate, you will have to develop good skimming and reading comprehension techniques to maximize your efficiency.

Journalists and other authors often (but alas, not always) craft their writing to make it interesting to their audience. Their care does not always result in articles that are immediately useful to researching debaters, who must poke through many articles on the same subject in order to construct a good case or a solid opposition argument. The best advice we can give you for critical debate reading and research is this: Don't collect facts more or less at random, hoping that they will prove useful at some future point. Every time you collect data, collect it for a specific purpose.

Since successful debaters must read a wide variety of publications, they must develop techniques for skimming the sources they evaluate, gleaning the relevant facts and circumstances as they read. Learn to use keyword identification as you read: Try to identify causal relation-ships established by authors, conclusions about policy recommenda-tions, and statements of quantitative and qualitative significance.

When reading longer articles or books, read the introduction and conclusion of the piece to determine if it will be useful to you. Books, in particular, should be skimmed: Read the table of contents or other chapter list, and use the index to identify facts and sections of particular utility to your research project.

## USING EVIDENCE

In parliamentary debate, debaters are not permitted to read directly from researched materials to prove their various points. This rule does not mean, however, that parliamentary debaters should not make informed and well-evidenced arguments. Complete arguments include evidence that substantiates the claims and warrants of the speaker. In the previous chapter on argument theory, you learned that there are many kinds of evidence that debaters can use to prove their points. In many parliamentary debates, as in most public policy discussions, the primary form of evidence is the *example*. Good parliamentary debaters have at their disposal a variety of anecdotes and examples. In the previous chapters on case construction and negation, you have seen how examples should be deployed to set up or knock down a case for the proposition. Examples must be accumulated through a process of research and careful note-taking and memorization. The goal of research in parliamentary debate is to build a substantial knowledge basis from which you can draw to support extemporaneous speeches on a wide variety of topics.

You might, during the course of preparing arguments for various subjects, accumulate quotations of support from various experts in the field. We caution you against trying to reproduce these quotations in parliamentary debates because there's no ability to verify the quotation. Additionally, because there is no accompanying text, this practice is really nothing more than name-dropping. The substance of the idea ought to "speak for itself," so quotation from others is largely unnecessary. This practice also undermines the credibility of the speaker, as the speaker is no longer an authority on the issue but functions as a mouthpiece. Finally, quotation of others can serve an intellectually limiting function, as your agenda is then set by someone who is not inside the debate. Instead, you need to be more flexible to the needs of arguments as they develop in the debate to promote clash.

Consider bringing a selection of texts to a debate tournament to aid in your preparation. Statistical reference texts and other almanacs are a great resource, as they will give you relevant and useful information on a wide variety of topics. You must bring a dictionary to every debate tournament: It will prove invaluable in the enterprise of defining words and interpreting motions during preparation time.

One kind of evidence is specialized or technical information. This information is not technical in a way that excludes people from the debate; rather, it is technical in a way that assists understanding of a specialized issue. For example, when discussing the Comprehensive Test Ban Treaty, you ought to possess information about recent international discussions of the issue, the Non Proliferation Treaty (NPT), and the Low Level Test Ban Treaty. An uninformed discussion about the merits of a nuclear test ban treaty will not suffice. Debaters must have a sense of history and contemporary debates to be able to fully and appropriately engage an issue. Details are important.

Finally, we encourage debaters to continue to identify news stories during the course of the tournament. All too often, debate tournaments seem to occur in a news blackout. However, it can be very persuasive to refer an audience or opposing team to a story in that morning's newspaper as support for your argument.

All evidence falls under the categories of data and warrant, as discussed in Chapter 3 on argument theory. A review of that chapter will suggest several typically underutilized kinds of evidence, including analogical reasoning and empirical reasoning. Your research will help you make better, more successful arguments. If you use research appropriately in conjunction with other debate skills, such as argument anticipation and refutation, you will experience more success in your debate performances.

# CHAPTER 7A

# OPPOSITION
# STRATEGY
# – DISADVANTAGES

## INTRODUCTION TO DISADVANTAGES

As we learned in Chapter 4, proposition teams design their cases largely on a problem-solution model. They identify a problem, thereby showing that there is a *need* for the plan. They then present a solution, or plan, to deal with those needs. Finally, they demonstrate that their proposal will be an adequate solution to the problems that require redress. Usually, proposition teams employ a cost-benefit approach to show that their plan is a good idea. They argue that their plan has more benefits than costs, or that its benefits *outweigh* the potential or actual accrued costs.

In debate, we talk a lot about *weighing issues*. What does this phrase mean? In Chapter 3, we talked extensively about comparing and analyzing arguments. We use the metaphor of weighing to visually demonstrate how arguments are compared. Debaters and judges are constantly in a position of trying to decide which arguments are more important than other arguments, either in terms of significance, probability, soundness of data or reasoning, or some combination of all these factors. We *weigh* these arguments against each other in a comparative analysis to determine which are the most important. One argument is said to *outweigh* another if it is more significant according to the established, agreed-upon criteria (which in turn are, of course, always up for debate).

The proposition team, then, tries to ensure that the benefits of their plan outweigh its potential costs. One important strategy the opposition team can take to counter this approach is to show that, in fact, the costs of their approach outweigh the benefits. We have already learned some basic techniques for refuting the proposition case. We've seen how to frame and debate attacks on significance and solvency. A solvency turn is one example of an opposition argument that tries to show that the proposition team's plan accrues more costs than benefits. Another such argument is the *disadvantage*.

A disadvantage argues that adoption of the plan will cause something bad to happen. In formal debates, opposition teams argue disadvantages when they want to show that adoption of the government's plan will lead to far greater undesirable consequences than desirable consequences. Disadvantages are causal arguments, often composed of several cause-effect relationships, leading to an ultimate impact. Disadvantages are also, typically, known as *off-case arguments*. Far from being irrelevant to the case, an off-case argument does not directly refute the foundational arguments of the case proper, i.e., the first proposition constructive arguments. "Off-case" generally refers to the opposition's forms of indirect refutation by the opposition, e.g., topicality arguments, counterplans, disadvantages, and critiques.

We have already learned what an *impact* is. Case advantages have impacts. Perhaps the proposition team claims that their plan will save lives, improve the economy, preserve constitutional or human rights, or attain any number of other benefits. Disadvantages also have impacts. Opposition teams may argue that adoption of the plan may end lives, hurt the economy, decimate constitutional or human rights, or cause any number of other harms. Disadvantages are an oppositional version of advantages.

Opposition teams may, in theory, argue any number of different disadvantages in a given debate. The purpose of these arguments is relatively unified: to prove, at the end of the debate, that it would be undesirable to adopt the proposition team's case.

## BASIC ANATOMY OF THE DISADVANTAGE

Disadvantages are causal arguments that have the same basic structure. Opposition teams arguing a disadvantage try to prove that the plan causes something bad to happen. It is important to note that disadvantages, like most debate arguments, can be generic or specific. Of course, we will need to have many kinds of disadvantages prepared in advance. But you will always have to make these general disadvantages apply *specifically* to the proposition team's case. In this section, we will see how disadvantages work. First, we'll look at some examples to see what disadvantages look like and how they may be argued. Then, we'll offer some vocabulary to use in discussions about disadvantages.

### EXAMPLE #1: ALLIANCE CREDIBILITY

PROPOSITION PLAN: "The USA should withdraw from the USA-Japan Mutual Defense Treaty."

OPPOSITION DISADVANTAGE: "Withdrawing from the US-Japan Mutual Defense Treaty would be a disadvantageous and dangerous policy. If the USA says it will no longer commit to defend its longtime ally Japan, that otherwise peaceful nation will have no choice but to arm itself to prepare for its defense. This will no doubt massively destabilize the fragile peaces all over Asia and heighten the risk of war. Furthermore, such a withdrawal will threaten the credibility of all other USA treaty obligations, as that country will no longer seem to be a trustworthy ally. Other alliances will begin to crumble, and many nations will feel insecure as the shelter of the USA's nuclear umbrella is removed. This will mean that weapons will be put on a hair-trigger alert, increasing the risk of accidental conflict."

COMMENTARY: Here the opposition presents the disadvantage as a causal chain, explaining each step as she reasons her way through the argument. The gist of the alliance credibility disadvantage is that once a nation begins to break treaties, it loses its credibility as an international ally in other areas. The credibility gap is said to *spill over* into other areas, causing bad things to happen. In this case, the opposition team is trying to show that if the USA develops a reputation as an alliance-breaker, then wars will ensue. Do you think the speaker persuasively makes the case for the disadvantage? How could the speaker make her case in a more persuasive manner?

## EXAMPLE #2: BUSINESS CONFIDENCE

PROPOSITION PLAN: The government should increase taxes on corporate profits to facilitate the redistribution of wealth.

OPPOSITION DISADVANTAGE: "The proposition plan will cause a near-total collapse in business confidence, destroying the economy as a result. The economy is teetering on the edge of collapse right now for a variety of reasons. Although ultimately it will probably pull through, the proposition plan will doubtless reverse this state of affairs and send the economy into a tailspin. Corporate profits are low enough as it is, and we depend on the strength of corporations to pull us out of the current recession. If the proposition plan passes, corporations will not only lose money in the short term, but they will lose confidence in the government for the long term. This loss of confidence will cause some businesses to go bankrupt and others to flee the country in search of greener pastures. The net result will be the collapse of the economy. Millions will be out of work and hungry. Inflation will soar as money is 'redistributed' into the economy. Too bad there won't be anything for the poor to buy after the proposition plan succeeds in closing down all our industries and shops. So, when they collapse the economy, they won't even be able to solve their own advantage."

COMMENTARY: In this example, the opposition is using a three-tiered strategy to relate their disadvantage to the plan action. Notice how the opposition speaker makes three distinct arguments about why the plan will be bad for business:

- Businesses will go bankrupt because they will lose money.
- Other businesses will leave the country because they are losing money here.
- Redistribution of wealth will cause inflation, devaluing currency.

This is a sophisticated strategy for arguing a disadvantage. You should try to relate your disadvantage to the plan in as many ways as possible to make it more convincing to the judge. Also, note how the speaker argues that if the economy collapses, the plan will be unable to fulfill its goals. In essence, the speaker proves that if she wins the disadvantage, the *case will be turned* because it will cause the opposite of what it tries to accomplish. Does the speaker make a persuasive case for the disadvantage? How does her disadvantage compare to the disadvantage in Example 1? Is it more or less persuasive? Why?

## EXAMPLE #3: PROTECTIONISM

**PROPOSITION PLAN:** The European Union should ban the import of food products made with genetically modified organisms (GMOs).

**OPPOSITION DISADVANTAGE:** "The proposition plan is a protectionist policy that will cause a massive trade war and most likely be struck down by the World Trade Organization (WTO). The whole reason we have an international trade regulation regime is to prevent plans like this one. If the European Union begins to institute these unilateral, non-negotiable trade barriers, other nations will respond in kind. This action will result in a trade war as tariffs and taxes spiral out of control. Whole sectors of the economy could be devastated as other nations target European businesses for retaliation. In these tense times, a trade war could easily turn into a shooting war. Meanwhile, the WTO will surely strike down the proposition team's mandates, leaving them with zero solvency and a whole lot of conflict. Better to stay with the present system, imperfect though it is."

COMMENTARY: The opposition speaker takes great pains to walk the judge through all the steps involved in her disadvantage. There are at least four different internal causal relations involved in this disadvantage:

- Other nations will respond in kind with their own trade barriers.
- These actions will result in a trade war.
- Whole sectors of the economy will be devastated.
- A trade war could become a shooting war.

The more you describe the causal chain of the disadvantage, the more likely the judge is to find it credible. The speaker also argues that the result of the disadvantage will be that the plan is struck down by the WTO. This is a useful argument for the opposition. *Notice how this works*: Even if they are not able to win that the proposition plan causes a trade war, the opposition team can still win the debate on this argument because they can prove that the plan will never be implemented; that it will be rendered void by the WTO. Finally, the speaker sets up her rebuttal strategy in the last sentence: "Better to stay with the present system, imperfect though it is." This is good technique. It is useful to tell the judge early and often why the disadvantage is a reason to vote for the opposition. Does the speaker satisfactorily explain the causal relations in her disadvantage? How could she improve the presentation of these relationships?

## EXAMPLE #4: COURT CREDIBILITY

PROPOSITION PLAN: The U.S. Supreme Court should overturn Roe v. Wade. The Congress should pass legislation mandating a right to abortion based on equal opportunity.

OPPOSITION DISADVANTAGE: "The proposition plan is terribly disadvantageous. It will destroy the already fragile credibility of the Supreme Court, eliminating the Court's ability to serve as a necessary check on the unconstitutional excesses of the legislative and executive branches. When the Court overturns Roe v. Wade, it will be in essence admitting that it was wrong for decades about a popular decision.

People will have no reason to trust them about future decisions because the Court will be seen as fickle. When Congress passes legislation, this overturn will add insult to injury. Essentially Congress will be saying that the Court is totally useless. Unfortunately for the proposition team, this deathblow to the Court's credibility will have lasting and devastating consequences. The Supreme Court is vital to maintaining our system of checks and balances. If they aren't credible, no one will enforce their decisions. The net effect of the proposition plan will be unchecked tyranny of the legislative and executive branches. Might as well use the Constitution to light a cigarette – it won't be good for much else."

COMMENTARY: One of the strong suits of this disadvantage, as presented, is its strong wording. The speaker uses words like "fickle," "deathblow," and "devastating." In debate, we call this *power wording* – the idea being that one should use striking words with a lot of force whenever possible, as such phrasing helps cement your ideas in the mind of your judge. Notice also that the speaker advances the claim that the "net effect" of the plan will be "unchecked tyranny." This is a setup for the rebuttal calculus, when she will have to prove that her disadvantage outweighs the case impact. The court credibility disadvantage is particularly useful for *agent counterplans*, which are discussed in the next chapter. How is this disadvantage different from the previous examples? How does the speaker's use of humor at the end of her presentation affect the overall persuasiveness of the disadvantage?

## EXAMPLE #5: SYMBOLIC ACTION

PROPOSITION PLAN: The United Nations should pass a resolution stating its support for fair trade instead of free trade.

OPPOSITION DISADVANTAGE: "The proposition team's plan is a purely symbolic action that will only forestall and co-opt real, lasting, meaningful social change. It is disadvantageous. Right now, a variety of social movements are mobilizing to promote fair trade and protest against the corporatist practices of agencies like the World Trade Organization. The plan's action serves as a Band-Aid solution, i.e., it is a superficial solution to a deep and abiding wound. Activist movements are on the verge of reaching critical mass to effect lasting change in the area of fair trade policies. Meanwhile, the proposition team's plan acts to take the wind out of their sails, quiescing new social movements just as they're about to achieve some of their goals. The question is this: Is it better to have social change from above or from below? The proposition team's plan dictates change from above, and so must fail because it doesn't wait for the all-important consciousness-raising period. Plus, it serves as a purely symbolic action, neutering potentially revolutionary social movements that, left to themselves, would solve the case harms and so much more. The plan is therefore, on balance, not beneficial."

COMMENTARY: The symbolic action disadvantage serves a wide range of interests against a wide range of cases. The gist of this argument is that the proposition team's case is basically a purely symbolic, fundamentally toothless action. This is bad because such incremental, cosmetic reform directly de-mobilizes social reform movements that would otherwise work to solve the problem in question. When you argue a disadvantage like this, you should emphasize that if they were left to their own devices, the social movements in question would solve the problem. Notice how this speaker creates a sense of urgency about the status of the movements. She says that the fair trade movements are "on the *verge* of reaching *critical mass*," thereby communicating to the judge that now is the key time for these movements. The implication is that if the plan were implemented at this unique junction in history, it would have particularly bad consequences. Do you find the presentation of this disadvantage to be persuasive? Why or why not? How does it differ substantively and structurally from the presentations of the previous disadvantages?

Now that we've seen a few examples of disadvantages in action, let's learn some general vocabulary to use when talking about them. Note that these vocabulary words are mostly *not* for use in debate rounds. Judges and audiences, in general, will not have a working knowledge of formal debate vocabulary of any kind. Use of excessive debate jargon in your speeches will sound silly and almost certainly lose and confuse the judge. That said, it is also the case that debate, like all other disciplines or activities, has its own jargon and slang.

There are only a few key terms to keep in mind when thinking about disadvantages. The first is the concept of a *link*. In formal debates, a link is the relationship of one's argument to the opponent's position in the debate and the internal chain of reasoning in a complex argument. More specifically, links are how disadvantages apply to a proposition team's case. In the examples above, the *links* to the proposition team's case occur first in the disadvantage. In example #4 above (the court credibility disadvantage), the initial disadvantage link is that an overturn of Roe v. Wade would hurt court credibility.

Disadvantages also have *internal links*. These are just more links in the chain of causal reasoning that is a disadvantage. The claim that trade barriers will escalate into a full trade war is one internal link that is used above. Sometimes disadvantages will have many internal links; at other times, they will only have a few. One challenge a proposition debater faces is identifying and responding to the internal links in disadvantages. Diagram or flowchart a few disadvantages, at least initially, until you develop a better understanding of how they work. To make disadvantages more persuasive to your judge and audience, keep the number of internal links to a minimum. Judges and audiences tend to get bored, annoyed, and skeptical of long and tenuous chains of reasoning.

Internal links lead, ultimately, to the *impact* of a disadvantage. In Chapter 5, we introduced the concept of an impact. The impact to an argument is similar to the "therefore" step used in the four-step refutation process: It is the ultimate result of your preceding reasoning. Impacts used above include "tyranny," a "shooting war," and, in the case of the symbolic action argument, "sweeping fair trade reforms."

## SUGGESTED EXERCISES:

1.  Identify the link arguments used by each of the above disadvantages. How does each argument relate to the specific plan offered as an example?
2.  Identify the impact arguments used by each of the above disadvantages. Be specific. Which disadvantages, if triggered, might implicate the proposition team's ability to solve their designated harms? How?
3.  Identify the internal links used by each of the above disadvantages. Using a simple flowchart or other diagram, explain what steps each disadvantage must go through in order to reach its impact.

## ADVANCED DISADVANTAGE ANATOMY

Disadvantages must have a link and an impact. This is the nature of a disadvantage argument. The opposition wants to show that the plan will cause some bad thing to happen. In order to do so, it needs to show that this bad thing is not happening now. This is true in everyday argument:

Parent: If you make that face for too long, it'll freeze that way.
Child: Too late. It's already frozen that way.

Consider the example of the court credibility disadvantage detailed above. The opposition team is arguing that the plan will hurt the credibility of the Supreme Court, which would be bad. What if the proposition team responded by saying that the credibility of the Supreme Court was *already* terrible, especially given the controversial *Bush v. Gore* decision made in 2000? Why would this be a good argument for the proposition team to make?

Think about it: If the proposition team can win that court credibility is already low, then they have a pretty good shot at disproving the disadvantage. They can show that *their plan* cannot make the problem any worse, and so the disadvantage is not a reason to vote for the opposition team. This kind of argument is called a *uniqueness* argument in formal debates.

Uniqueness is the part of a disadvantage that proves that the proposition plan and only the proposition plan could trigger the impacts. Affirmative advantages can also have a burden of uniqueness: If their harm is being solved now, then there is no unique need for the plan.

So when we say that disadvantages must be *unique*, we are saying that the opposition team must prove that the causal chain of events will not be provoked in the status quo (present system). By extension, the opposition team must show that the plan will uniquely provoke the disadvantageous reaction outlined in the disadvantage argument itself. Opposition teams generally advance uniqueness arguments in their first presentation of the disadvantage. What kinds of uniqueness arguments are made in the disadvantage examples 1-5 listed above?

• **Business Confidence:** The speaker makes a uniqueness argument when she says this: "The economy is teetering on the edge of collapse right now for a variety of reasons. Although ultimately it will probably pull through, the proposition plan will doubtless reverse this state of affairs and send the economy into a tailspin." This reasoning is a uniqueness argument because the speaker is trying to demonstrate that the economy will be fine now, but that the implementation of the plan will upset that balance.

• **Symbolic Action:** The speaker is trying to establish that movements are mobilizing now: "Right now, a variety of social movements are mobilizing to promote fair trade and protest against the corporatist practices of agencies like the World Trade Organization." This statement is a uniqueness argument for the disadvantage because it tries to show that everything is fine now.

The concept of uniqueness can be one of the most confusing for beginning debaters. Remember that the opposition wants to prove that the present system is fine now, and that the proposition plan will upset this balance.

Other useful concepts in arguing disadvantages include the con-

ART, ARGUMENT AND ADVOCACY

cepts of *brink, time frame,* and *threshold.* When we say a disadvantage is on the brink, we mean that it is an immediate possibility. It is on the edge of occurring. An opposition debater wants to claim that the proposition plan is enough to push the chain leading up to the impact over the brink. An example of a *brink* argument can be found in the symbolic action disadvantage presented above: "Activist movements are on the verge of reaching critical mass to be able to effect lasting change in the area of fair trade policies." Some key words here, used to indicate that a brink is near, are "verge" and "critical mass."

The *time frame* is the amount of time it takes for a particular condition to occur, usually (in the case of a disadvantage) its impact. It is usually said that disadvantages with a quick time frame – i.e., whose impacts will happen quickly rather than over the long term – are more persuasive. This is not, however, always true. We will examine the issue of time frame more completely in the section on impact analysis and comparison.

Finally, disadvantages often have a *threshold.* A *threshold* is the degree of change necessary to precipitate a particular outcome. In debates about disadvantages, a threshold is usually the degree of change of an affirmative plan from current policy that will trigger undesirable consequences. All links, internal links, and impacts have thresholds, i.e., they have a trigger point which, when passed, will kick in the next level of the causal chain. To remember this term, think of the threshold of a doorway. You can approach a door all you want, but once you have passed through the threshold, you have unmistakably walked through the doorway. Some phenomena have higher or lower thresholds than others. For example, it may take a lot of doing to you to take out the trash, but very little effort to get you to eat a delicious gourmet meal. Trash removal, then, has a high threshold. Gourmet meal consumption, however, has a low threshold.

All of these words may seem complicated, but in fact they are fairly commonsensical and can be easily remembered and applied once you figure out what makes a disadvantage work. In order to win debates on disadvantages, you'll need to come up with a reliable stable of arguments to deploy on demand. The examples provided in this chapter are a good start, but you'll need a wider variety in order to succeed. How can you come up with good ideas for disadvantages? The best place is to begin with the proposition team's case. Why isn't the plan being done now? Odds are that if the plan is, in fact, a good idea, then someone or something pretty important is keeping it from being done. Some examples might be:

- **Vested interests.** Sometimes powerful political forces conspire to keep certain items off the policy agenda because they stand to lose influence or money. Fossil fuel industries, for example, lobby furiously against legislation to tax carbon emissions. These vested interests are grounds for a disadvantage: Ask yourself what would happen if these industries were hurt financially or if they felt betrayed by government action that ran contrary to their perceived interests.
- **Financial shortages.** Some policies aren't being done now because there isn't enough money to do them, or they are too expensive. Perhaps money is tight and implementing the new policy would result in a tradeoff with another, more desirable, program.

The idea here is to figure out who or what stands to lose if the plan is adopted.

## SUGGESTED EXERCISE:

Below are a few examples of proposition cases. Generate a disadvantage argument for each plan. Try to make your link arguments and impact arguments as specific as possible.

- The government should ban all possession of handguns.
- The United Nations should make all decisions with a vote of the General Assembly, rather than using the Security Council.
- The European Union should abandon use of the euro and return to national currencies.
- The USA should recognize Taiwan as an independent state.

## ANSWERING DISADVANTAGES

A proposition debater has to learn how to answer disadvantages in a comprehensive and persuasive manner. This task can sometimes be a difficult enterprise, as it is hard to predict what disadvantages the opposition team will argue. Many proposition debaters have great difficulty answering disadvantages in a constructive way. Often, they will simply make one response or ignore the disadvantage altogether, no doubt using the strategy of "ignore it and it'll go away" that works so well for children. Below is constructive, step-by-step advice to proposition teams about how to debate disadvantages.

### STEP 1: ANALYZE THE DISADVANTAGE.

This is the most important part of the process. If you misread the disadvantage, you could fail to answer it properly. You might even answer it entirely backwards, and lose the debate. (Don't laugh! It happens to everyone sooner or later.) To analyze the disadvantage, you must answer the following questions:

- What's the link? What is it about your plan, specifically, that supposedly triggers the disadvantage?
- What are the internal links? The opposition team is alleging that your plan causes something, which causes something else, which causes something bad to happen. Figure out what those internal links are. They are often the weakest part of any disadvantage.
- What's the impact? What is the bottom-line bad thing that the opposition team says will happen?
- How does the impact compare to the impacts of your case advantages? Is it bigger or smaller? Will it happen sooner or later? Is it a one-time event or a systemic problem?

## STEP 2: GENERATE ANSWERS TO THE DISADVANTAGE.

Once you've identified the critical components of the disadvantage, you need to generate answers to it. The best place to do this is on your *flow* (your notes for the debate) or even on a separate piece of paper. Even if you are not planning to number your arguments in your speech, consider numbering them on the page so you can easily check for duplication and relevance. We suggest generating more answers than you will eventually make in your speech and then paring the list down to the best two or three arguments. A few things to keep in mind:

ANSWERING LINKS. You almost always need to answer the link when debating a disadvantage. Generally speaking, disadvantages come in two kinds: those whose link to the plan is virtually certain, and those whose link is tenuous. When you assess that the link is very strong, don't waste valuable speech time attacking it. Instead, focus your energies on other parts of the disadvantage. When you think the link argument is tenuous and easily dislodged, concentrate your fire at that level of the disadvantage rather than scattering your answers around.

Link arguments come in two varieties: simple (defensive) "no link" arguments and offensive "link turn" arguments. When you argue that there is no link to the disadvantage, you are saying that its relationship to the plan is nonexistent or negligible at best. Phrase your argument in a simple, declarative fashion:

> "On the business confidence disadvantage. There is no link to the plan, because we don't take enough money from corporations to cause a loss in confidence."

Remember that it is the *opposition's responsibility to establish the link to the plan*. As a proposition speaker, you should emphasize this allocation of burdens to the judge.

You can also make offensive "link turn" arguments. A *turn*, also known as a "turnaround," or, historically, as "turning the tables," is an argument that reverses the position of an opponent. Link turns are arguments that attempt to reverse a link established by the other team. For example, if the opposition team argued a disadvantage that said the plan hurt economic growth, the proposition team might argue a *link turn* by saying that their plan actually helped economic growth.

Remember the distinction we drew in the argument chapter between offensive and defensive arguments? Link turns are offensive, since they seek to turn the disadvantage into an advantage for the proposition team. Think about it: What if, by proving that your plan helped the economy, you could argue that saving the economy was actually an *advantage* for your plan rather than a disadvantage? Link turns are powerful arguments.

**ANSWERING UNIQUENESS.** Most disadvantages are vulnerable at the level of uniqueness. That is, there are many things that could potentially trigger the impact without the aid or succor of the plan. You need to think of what those things are and say them, like so:

> "They say our plan will collapse the economy, but we disagree. If record unemployment, low consumer confidence, and a burgeoning recession haven't collapsed the economy, then our small, fiscally responsible policy will certainly not accomplish this."

Proposition team uniqueness arguments generally come in two kinds: historical and predictive. Historical uniqueness arguments show that there are present or historical conditions that should have triggered the disadvantage. The economy example given just above is a historical uniqueness argument. It has the added advantage of showing that the internal link to the disadvantage is *empirically denied*.

When you make a predictive uniqueness answer, you are saying that some thing will happen in the future that will cause the disadvantage. In the case of the protectionism disadvantage above, you might show that the EU will adopt other regulations in the future that will be equally, if not more controversial. This argument proves that the disadvantage is not a reason to reject the plan, since its consequences will happen with or without the plan.

**DEBATING IMPACTS.** It is **vital** that you debate the impact to disadvantages you hear in debates. Even if, in your judgment, the impact is inconsequential or negligible, you still need to say so in your speech:

> "They say that the plan will increase bureaucracy, but we think that's a small price to pay for lifting millions out of poverty."

Notice how it is *not enough* merely to say that the impact is small. From a galactic perspective, the Earth is pretty small. You must always say that the impact is small compared to something else, in your case, the impacts to your case advantages.

Just as with links, there are two basic ways to argue against impacts. You can argue defensively, saying that the impact is not really bad, or that other things will remediate it (for example, coming adjustments in fiscal policy might stop any adverse economic impact). You can also argue offensively, *turning* the impact just as you might turn the link. An *impact turn* is an argument that tries to reverse an established impact. Using the economy example, a proposition team might argue that economic growth is devastating to the environment, thereby *turning* the impact of the disadvantage.

**HAVING OFFENSIVE ARGUMENTS.** It is important to try and have at least one offensive argument against every opposition disadvantage. BUT (and this is VERY important), **you should never argue link turns and impact turns against the same disadvantage.** This unfortunate occurrence is called a *double turn*. In answering a disadvantage, a double turn takes place when a team argues a *link turn* ("We solve that problem") AND an *impact turn* ("That problem is actually a benefit") on the same disadvantage. When this happens, the proposition team is saying that they stop a good thing from happening; in essence, running a new disadvantage against their own case. Even if you do not choose to continue arguing your turn in the rebuttals, it is usually a good idea to have turn arguments in your constructive speeches: Turns make it more difficult for opposition teams to conclusively win disadvantages.

**BRAINSTORMING ANSWERS.** It is difficult to answer disadvantages on the fly, in debates with very little preparation time, but you can do a lot of planning before the debate begins.

- Make a list of common disadvantages for any topic. Use the examples in this book as a starting point for such a list.
- Make a list of disadvantages that apply specifically to your prepared cases. Ask yourself: What disadvantages would I run if I were the opposition?

Then, generate a few generic answers for each of the disadvantages on your list. Take stock of your pre-prepared cases and figure out what disadvantages they potentially link to so that you can be ready for pre-pared opposition teams.

The most important thing to remember when debating disadvan-tages is to *use your case* to answer them. As we discussed in the chapter on case construction, your proposition case should be structured in such a way as to preemptively address the major opposition arguments. You can do more than this initial effort, though. You should use your case to make link turn and uniqueness arguments. In a debate where the proposition team has advocated providing comprehensive national health insurance, the opposition has argued that this plan would hurt the economy. What is the proposition's response?

"They say that our plan will hurt the economy, but this couldn't be further from the truth. The existing lack of comprehensive nation-al health insurance is already hurting the economy and will contin-ue to do so. This is true for a couple of reasons: When people don't have health insurance, they are likely to see a doctor only when they need acute care. Because these people don't have insurance, taxpayers end up footing gigantic bills. Preventative medicine is much cheaper in the long run than the painful lack of a system we have now. Also, with a single-payer system, the government will be paying out less in Medicaid/Medicare benefits than it is now. In the long run, we will massively help the economy."

The proposition speaker is using her case to turn back the disadvantage. Notice how she makes a coordinated attack on the disadvantage. She begins by making a uniqueness argument: "The existing lack of comprehensive national health insurance is already hurting the economy and will continue to do so." This argument is designed to show that the harm to the economy is both *ongoing* and *inevitable*. Its ensuing explanations are also link turns to the disadvantage. The speaker makes three distinct link arguments: acute care, preventative medicine, and Medicare/Medicaid payouts.

You should also use your case to address the impacts to the disadvantage. We will discuss this more in the section on impact assessment. Remember to explicitly compare (hopefully, for your sake, in your favor) the relative weights and merits of the case impacts vs. the disadvantage impacts.

## Step 4: Make your answers

A final question is this: When you answer disadvantages (and we hope that you will, indeed, answer them rather than merely looking confused at the prospect), how should you phrase your answers? There are at least two schools of thought on this issue, and how you debate should always vary based on your audience, judge preferences, and the habits and norms of the community in which you are competing. You may find you want to make a few arguments but don't know how to present them. Don't panic. You have at least two options:

COMBINING. You can combine your arguments into a cohesive whole, in essence offering a short speech in response to the disadvantage. The above response defending national health insurance is one example of this technique.

SEPARATING. You can also offer your arguments individually, phrasing them as discrete entities. For this technique to succeed, we suggest you number your arguments or use some kind of transitional language to ensure that everyone involved is able to follow you. This technique is discussed in greater detail below.

If you are debating in the USA, either technique is certainly acceptable, although the majority of parliamentary debaters these days seem to separate out their arguments for more direct clash and easier note taking. If you are debating outside of the USA, you may find that your judges prefer that you combine your arguments into a more cohesive whole. There are certainly exceptions to this generalization. Many international debaters and international judges prefer the rigorous, specific refutation enabled by separating out individual arguments.

This concept of separating out your arguments may seem a bit confusing at first, but really it's quite simple. When you generate answers to a disadvantage, you'll end up with a few discrete and potentially unrelated answers. Remember the "symbolic action" argument from a few pages back? You might come up with three different answers and, in lieu of "speechifying" them, decide to offer them up as a multi-pronged attack on the disadvantage. You would then end up saying something like this:

"On the symbolic action disadvantage. We have three answers.

1) It doesn't apply to the plan. Our proposal is certainly not a Band-Aid solution. A United Nations push to pressure for fair trade would constitute major progress in the fight for environmental and labor protections.

2) Movements are doomed now . Fair trade movements are struggling now. Just look at the present protests. Sure, they're big, but they don't achieve any consensus for change. In the present system, movements will surely fail to enact lasting change.

3) The plan saves the fair trade movement. Our plan puts wind into the sails of the movements by sending a critical signal of support from the United Nations. The resolution of support is a win for movements, giving them a success at a critical time when they must have something to rally around. They will also be able to use the resolution to build larger, more diverse coalitions."

The proposition speaker has taken three discrete arguments and offered them separately, yet as a concerted attack. The first argument is a "no link" attack. The second is a "uniqueness" argument. The speaker concludes with a "link turn." Notice that she has not felt compelled to use debate jargon to talk about her arguments. Avoiding jargon makes her arguments better and more effective.

These arguments are phrased and structured in a very precise manner. Each individual argument begins with a "tag line," a summary of the argument that is to follow, also called the *claim*. The warrant and the data follow in the subsequent part of each argument. Why are the arguments structured this way? There are several reasons. First, when you offer a quick summary of your argument, you help the judge and audience to follow your reasoning because they know what to expect. Second, having quick and simple tags for individual arguments facilitates effective note taking (more on this in the skills chapter). Finally, if you phrase your arguments in this way, you will find them easier to continue through to the rebuttals. You will be able to say to the judge:

> "As to the symbolic action disadvantage. The team from State State still hasn't addressed our argument that this disadvantage plainly does not apply to the plan, which is a large-scale action..."

This way, with only a few words, you and the judge are instantly on the same page. Pity the team from State State (Go State!). Their debaters are obviously not taking good notes. If they were, they might have clashed directly with your argument rather than ignored it.

Why would you separate your arguments out with numbers or other explicit transitional language? Aside from the reasons given above, many involved in debate feel that this added bit of structure promotes direct clash by facilitating comprehensive refutation of individual arguments. Many debaters, however, have a tendency to get carried away at the "microlevel" of the debate and miss the big picture. It is important to balance attention to individual arguments with attention to the bigger concerns, such as: Why, exactly are you (choose one) a) winning the debate; b) losing the debate; c) wearing that hideous tie?

NOTE: The strategies described above are generally used for answering all kinds of off-case arguments. With disadvantages, counterplans, critiques, and topicality arguments, you will always have the option of combining your arguments or separating them out.

## Suggested Exercise:

Using the five example disadvantages listed in the first section (alliance credibility, protectionism, symbolic action, court credibility, business confidence), generate four answers for each. Assume you are defending the sample case offered in each example. Write out your answers for each disadvantage in both the separated and combined formats given above.

# CHAPTER 8

# OPPOSITION
# STRATEGY
# – COUNTERPLANS

## INTRODUCTION TO COUNTERPLANNING

Traditionally, the proposition team is the advocate of change in a formal debate, while the opposition denies the necessity for change by defending the *status quo*. This model is based on legal argumentation, whereby the prosecution argues for change in the defendant's status (i.e., from free to incarcerated) while the defense argues for no change (i.e., the defendant should remain free).

The ability to defend the *status quo* carries certain advantages for the opposition. The opposition is said to have *presumption*, so that it becomes incumbent on the proposition team to shoulder the burden of proof. The proposition team has the responsibility to prove their case is better than maintaining the present system. Many opposition teams find the present system easy to defend, as it is relatively stable and predictable.

By no means is the opposition's strategic arsenal limited to defense of the present system. The status quo is only one way to delegitimize the need for, or viability of, the proposition team's case. Another, very powerful, option is the *counterplan*. A counterplan is a proposal offered by the opposition that provides a reason to reject the proposition team's plan or proposal.

In everyday discussion and argument, we argue counterplans all the time without even realizing it. If you are discussing dinner plans with your friends, you do not feel bound to defend the status quo if you disagree, do you? If you did, the discussion would look something like this:

> Friend: Gee, I'm hungry. Let's go get hamburgers.
> You: No, let's just not eat.

Unless you and your friend are on a hunger strike, your statement is likely to be a foolish and unpopular suggestion. Instead, you might counter with a plan of your own:

> Friend: Gee, I'm hungry. Let's go get hamburgers.
> You: Let's get Chinese food instead.

You have just proposed a counterplan. Not only that, by using the word "instead," you have argued that your counterplan is a reason to reject the original plan. We make "instead" decisions between plans and counterplans on a daily basis. For example, every morning we have to decide whether we are going to go to work or stay in bed. Clearly, if we stay in bed we cannot go to work. Those two options are competitive. That is, they compete for the same resources and time. A counterplan is an "instead" argument for the opposition.

Counterplans are everywhere in practical decision making. How do counterplans work in debate? Consider again what the basic role of the opposition team is in any formal debate. Broadly speaking, opposition teams win debates by showing that the proposition team's proposal or position is a bad idea. So what a counterplan needs to do in a debate is show that the judge should not endorse the proposition team's plan; *instead*, the judge should endorse the opposition team's counterplan. How is this accomplished?

First things first: A counterplan, just like a plan, should have a *text* that lays out what exactly the opposition team is advocating as a response to the proposition team's proposal. If the proposition team proposes a particular course of policy action, the opposition counterplan should do the same. If the proposition team proposes a particular stance on values or facts, the opposition's counterproposal should do the same. For maximum effectiveness, it is important that the counterplan (or counterproposal, or counterposition) mirror the proposition team's proposal. It is important to have a text so that the proposition team has a fair chance to debate what exactly it is that the opposition is proposing. This requirement is reciprocal to the opposition's (eminently fair) demand that the proposition team spell out what exactly it is that they are proposing.

Once the counterplan text is written, the opposition needs to figure out why the counterplan is an "instead" option. In formal debate, we call this *competition*. We say that a counterplan is *competitive* with a plan when it *forces a choice* between the two proposals. **A counterplan must compete with the proposition team's plan if it is to have a chance of winning the debate for the opposition team.** This is easily illustrated by extending the above example:

Friend: Gee, I'm hungry. Let's go get hamburgers.
You: Let's get Chinese food instead.
Friend: Well, why don't we get hamburgers *and* Chinese food?
You: Oh. Okay.

Here we see that the "Chinese food" option hasn't proven to be a reason to reject "hamburgers." Your counterplan has failed to provide a reason to reject your friend's case. What you need to do is to substantiate your claim of *instead*, which is the claim of counterplan competition. How do you show that a counterplan forces a choice between the plan and the counterplan?

After you present the text of your counterproposal, you must show how your counterplan competes with the plan. In formal debate, we demonstrate counterplan competition using the concept of *net benefits*. That is, in order for the counterplan to be a reason to reject the plan, it must be on balance the best option for action or advocacy. Counterplans compete with plans because they are *net beneficial*. In the ongoing dispute about what to eat, you need to convince your friend that Chinese food is the net beneficial lunch option. There are a few ways you can accomplish this. To establish that the counterplan is net beneficial in this example, you'll have to show that Chinese food is superior to hamburgers – at least in this specific case. There are two basic kinds of arguments you can make to establish net benefits for your counterplan in any situation.

First, you can argue that the plan is a bad idea, i.e., you can find disadvantages to, critiques of, or solvency problems with the proposition team's plan. In this case, you could:

a)  Show that eating hamburgers is bad for one's diet (calories, fat, cholesterol, etc...). This argument would be a disadvantage to the plan in that it claims the plan causes some bad effects.

b)  Show that eating hamburgers would not alleviate your hunger. This argument would be a solvency answer to the plan because it shows that the plan will not solve the stated harm (hunger).

c)  Show that the assumption that hamburgers are an acceptable food is fundamentally flawed. You could argue (from the perspective, perhaps, of an ethical vegetarian) that consuming meat is always wrong, and that therefore the plan should not be endorsed because of the values it rests on.

Second, you can argue that the counterplan is a good idea. That is, you can find advantages to the counterplan that the proposition team's plan does not accrue. In this case, you could:

a)  Show that Chinese food tends to contain more vegetables, allowing you to get more vitamins and servings of healthy greens.

b)  Show that Chinese food is generally low in fat and cholesterol, making it a healthy cuisine.

All of these arguments serve more or less the same function: They establish that the counterplan is a better option than the plan; it has more net benefits. The result of net benefits argumentation should always be that the counterplan ends up being a reason to reject the plan.

Because counterplans must be net beneficial, they function in precisely the same way as a disadvantage. When we argue disadvantages, we are saying that adoption of the plan will cause some bad result. When you say a counterplan is competitive, what you are really saying to the judge is: "Don't vote for the plan, because if you do you will forego this superior policy option." When we argue counterplans, we are saying that adoption of the plan will cause some bad result. In this case, that bad result is the loss of the superior option of the counterplan.

At one time, it was believed that to compete, counterplans had to be *mutually exclusive* with the proposition team's plan. Mutual exclusivity, simply put, is the idea that the plan and the counterplan literally cannot coexist with each other. There are perishingly few circumstances in which you can argue that your counterplan is *mutually exclusive* with the plan:

> Friend: Gee, I'm hungry. Let's go get hamburgers.
> You: Let's get Chinese food instead.
> Friend: Well, why don't we get hamburgers *and* Chinese food?
> You: We don't have enough money to get both.

By arguing that both options cannot be done at the same time, you establish that they are mutually exclusive with each other. But you still haven't proven that your option is superior. Mutual exclusivity is not a good method for proving counterplan competition. Even if your counterplan is mutually exclusive, it must still be net beneficial.

Another way of thinking about counterplans is as an *opportunity cost* of the plan. An opportunity cost is the sacrifice made when selecting one policy over another. Think of it this way: when you choose a particular course of action, you always forego other opportunities. This happens in everyday life as well as in public policy decisions. If you choose to drive to the movie theatre, you have implicitly rejected the other available means of transportation (bus, dogsled, bicycle, skateboard, rickshaw, etc.). Your choice has *cost* you those other *opportuni-*

*ties*. Every decision has opportunity costs. There are always other things you could do with the time and energy you invest in a particular course of action.

Government officials deal with the implications of opportunity costs all the time. It is the responsibility of public policy makers to evaluate the costs and benefits of policies they implement. Sometimes they have to make tight decisions based on available resources – for example, if there is only a finite amount of resources available to solve a given problem, legislators may have to choose between several options because there is simply not enough money to fund everything. Other decisions are forced because of political pressures, yet have lasting opportunity costs. One such commitment was the decision in Europe to use North Atlantic Treaty Organization (NATO) instead of European defense forces to intervene in Kosovo. The decision to use NATO had many opportunity costs: Europe lost the benefits associated with European military integration as well as the opportunity to use the European Defense force as a legitimate institution. Further, NATO intervention guaranteed the continued involvement of the USA in European affairs, a move that has been criticized by many.

In the end, whether or not you agree that the decision to use NATO was correct, there is no denying that it had palpable opportunity costs. In formal debate, those opportunity costs of a potential policy decision are the stuff counterplans are made of. As an opposition debater, your job is to find the most viable opportunity cost of the proposition team's case and defend it as well as you can. Try to convince the judge or audience that their policy is ultimately undesirable because it necessitates forsaking another, more beneficial, course of action.

As you can imagine, counterplans are a powerful strategic option for the opposition. As a debater, you might quite justifiably be nervous about debating against counterplans. What is to stop the opposition team from simply counterplanning with something that is much, much bigger than your case? Consider this frightening possibility: You begin the debate advocating that a commission should be established to investigate the return of pilfered relics. You think you're doing pretty well, and are pleased with your small case, until the opposition counterplans with a proposal to give massive food aid to starving refugees in Africa. On balance, their counterplan probably solves a bigger problem than your case and saves more lives. What do you do?

First, don't panic. This counterplan does not compete with your proposal. The two policies are *cooperative* rather than competitive, i.e., they do not resist each other and instead can (and probably should) work in concert with each other. As in the example of the Chinese food and hamburgers, you can (and probably should) do both policy options. Remember that it is the burden of the counterplan to provide a reason to reject the proposition team's plan. A counterplan must be *counter* to the plan. If the policies can cooperate; if they do not compete, then the counterplan is *not a reason to vote against the proposition.*

The proposition team needs to test the competition of the counterplan so that they can clearly communicate to the judge their argument that the counterplan does not compete. In formal debate, we call this kind of argument a *permutation.* In its simplest sense, to *permute* means to combine. When we permute the plan and the counterplan, we experimentally combine them to test how competitive the counterplan is.

> Just as a counterplan tests whether the plan provides a compelling reason to change the present system, so the permutation tests whether the counterplan provides a compelling reason to reject the plan.

The ability to argue permutations is the first line of proposition team defense against opposition team counterplans.

When you defend the proposition, you should always attempt to permute the opposition counterplan. The permutation argument needs to be advanced at the first opportunity your team has to respond to the counterplan. Permutations do not need to be complicated; in fact, they are most effective when they are simply phrased. In the example above, where your team has argued for relic return and the opposition has argued for food aid, you can simply phrase your permutation argument as follows:

> "Their counterplan is simply not competitive with our plan. It does not *counter* our case. In other words, it is another public policy. It might prove that the opposition team has opinions, but it does not

mean that their opinions undermine the case as presented. We can demonstrate this with the following permutation: it would be possible and net beneficial to do *both* the plan and the counterplan. You can give back relics *and* give food aid. Thus, the counterplan does not provide a reason to reject the plan."

Notice that this argument does more than just advance a permutation. It also provides a theoretical justification for the permutation, and in doing so attempts to teach the judge a little something about counterplan competition. Theoretical justification is an important component of the argument. Remember that many or most of your judges and audiences will be extremely unfamiliar with the formal debate terms we use here. There is, ultimately, no need to use the word "permutation" to talk about this critical proposition team argument. However, the vocabulary is useful shorthand for the more developed discussions about counterplan theory and practice that follow later in this chapter.

## COUNTERPLAN TOPICALITY

Before we move on to discuss types of counterplans, we should offer a few thoughts on counterplan topicality. Some people believe that counterplans have to be nontopical. They argue that to effectively challenge the topic, the opposition team can only defend nontopical action. We believe that this philosophy is fundamentally bankrupt. The *plan* is the focus of the debate. As long as the counterplan is counter to the plan, it is a legitimate subject for discussion. In a debate, the plan becomes the embodiment of the resolution – it is a living interpretation of the topic. Once the plan is the interpretation of the topic, any policy that's not the plan is *automatically not the topic*. Consider: You would never say that a disadvantage about the topic is illegitimate because it is about the topic; yet, folks say this kind of thing all the time about counterplans. Let us emphasize again: The *plan is the focus of the debate*. It is said that topical counterplans are unfair because they force the proposition team to debate against the topic. This is untrue. Once the case for the topic has been made using the plan and its advantages, anything that counters that case, topical or not, is intrinsically counter to the topic.

## SUGGESTED EXERCISES:

1.  Pretend that you are defending a proposition case that has the United Nations pay reparations for its inaction in Rwanda. Prepare and deliver a permutation argument for each of the following counterplans:
    - Counterplan: The USA should pay its back dues to the United Nations.
    - Counterplan: The Organization of African Unity should develop an autonomous self-defense force to deter future conflicts.
    - Counterplan: The European Union should adopt a policy to intervene in future African conflicts.

2.  Below, find a list of different actions. For each action, think of at least three opportunity costs you would forsake if you were to take that action.
    - Intervene, as the government, to stop a strike by workers in the airline industry.
    - Criminally penalize chemical industries for water pollution.
    - Restrict the transfer of copyrighted music on the Internet.
    - Support World Trade Organization authority to arbitrate trade disputes.

## TYPES OF COUNTERPLANS

Just as there are many types of proposition team cases, there are many different types of counterplans that you can learn to use strategically and effectively. Counterplans fall into two basic categories: those that are *generic* and those that are *specific* to the plan you are debating. A *generic* counterplan is one that can be argued in a wide variety of debates against many different types of proposition cases. A *specific* counterplan is targeted directly at the case or plan you are debating against. This distinction, while important, may be a bit misleading in this way: Generic counterplans must *always* be tailored to the specific proposition plan. Without a strong element of case-specific competition, they will usually fail to persuade your judge because they will not *clash* directly with the proposition team's case.

To say that there are many different proposition cases is a gross understatement. In the third appendix to this book alone, you will find more than a thousand potential topics for debate. For each of these topics, there are at least dozens of potential different topical cases – even if you were to use the strictest interpretation of each topic. As a parliamentary debater, you will have to be prepared to debate an enormous variety of specific cases and plans. To be consistently successful on the opposition, then, you will need some generic strategies that can apply to *types* of plans. Generic counterplans are indispensable for this endeavor. We will discuss several generic counterplans and explain how they can be used against a variety of cases.

## AGENT COUNTERPLANS

One thing that almost all plans have in common is that they all have an *agent of action*. That is, every proposal has an *actor* who must carry out the proposition team's recommendation. In the USA, the agent of action is usually the U.S. Federal Government. Sometimes, proposition teams will specify their agent even further and argue that a specific *branch* (legislative, judicial, executive) or *division* (i.e., the Environmental Protection Agency, Bureau of Indian Affairs, Department of Justice, etc...) of the federal government should implement their proposal. In Europe, it is common for proposition teams to say that their proposal should be enacted by a national government, or perhaps by the European Union or the United Nations. This specification in the plan is curious, given that it is rarely mandated by the resolution for debate. Some teams justify their move to specify an agent of action by defining "This House..." as whatever agent they wish to discuss, but there is good reason to be critical of this practice, as we have shown in the chapter on propositional interpretation. In any case, no matter the justification, most propositional teams do specify (and are *expected* to specify) the agent of action for their plan.

This specification gives the opposition more than adequate grounds to what is called an **agent counterplan**. An agent counterplan is a counterplan that argues that *the plan the proposition team implements through one agent of change should instead be implemented through another agent of change.* So, for example, if a proposition team argues that the USA should provide free malaria medication for children in Central America, you might propose a counterplan to enact the basic mandates of the plan through a different agent:

Counterplan: The World Health Agency should provide free malaria medication for children in Central America.

At first glance, it appears that this counterplan does not compete with the proposition team's plan. After all, it is possible to act both through the World Health Organization and through the U.S. government. But would such cooperative action be net beneficial?

To resolve this question, you'll have to think back to the comparison between hamburgers and Chinese food we laid out in the previous section. Remember that there are two basic kinds of net benefits arguments you can make in debates: You can argue that the plan is bad and you can argue that the counterplan is good. In this case, since the difference between the plan and the counterplan is the agent of implementation, you'll want to stick to net benefits arguments having to do with the respective agents. So you'll need to generate a few arguments *attacking their agent of action.* You might phrase your attack like this:

"There are a few reasons that the USA is a bad actor for this policy. First, the USA has a history of using these kinds of humanitarian campaigns as cover for military or other bad and dangerous interventions. Just look at how they use food aid as an excuse to deploy troops and stage covert operations. Second, the USA has a specifically bad record when it comes to malaria prevention. After the dangerous pesticide DDT was banned in that country, they proceeded to export and promote it for malaria control worldwide. Surely we don't want to risk these kinds of consequences."

After you argue that their agent of action is bad, you'll need to *defend your agent of action.* You need to show that your proposed alternative agent will do a good job of addressing the harms specified by the proposition team. You might phrase your defense like this:

> "The World Health Organization would be at least as good as the USA for the distribution of malaria medication and treatment. The WHO has extensive experience in organizing and carrying out broad international health campaigns. They also have extensive international support and can draw on a wider range of international resources and volunteers. The USA is comparatively limited in these regards."

When defending this kind of counterplan or any other kind of counterplan, you need to advance both of these kinds of arguments. To win that your counterplan competes with the proposition team's plan, you must argue *both* that the plan is bad *and* that your counterplan is good. Once you have made these arguments for your counterplan's competition, it is appropriate to offer some kind of summation that explains to the judge why the counterplan is a reason to vote for the opposition team. This summation might look something like this:

> "The bottom line is that the USA is a bad actor for this course of action. Our counterplan will better solve the problems of malaria in Central America, while avoiding all of the terrible costs historically associated with the USA's actions. Thus, when weighing your options in this round, you should prefer our counterplan and endorse the oppositional stance."

This summation should be made early and often throughout the opposition speeches in the debate round in order to *set up* the final *decision calculus,* or final reason to vote, that you present in your last opposition rebuttal.

When planning what kinds of arguments to make to defend your counterplan, always anticipate what your response will be to the proposition team's inevitable permutation of your counterplan. In this case, the proposition team will no doubt argue that you can and should distribute malaria medication using both the USA and the World Health Organization. While the proposition team is probably right that you *could* act through both agents, they are not necessarily right that you *should* act through both agents. You are questioning net benefits. What are some arguments you can make against this permutation? For the most case, you have already made them. If you can show that there are affirmative reasons *not* to prefer the proposition team's agent of action, then all of those reasons function as *disadvantages to the permutation*. That is, they are reasons that the permutation (just like the plan) causes bad things to happen. All the reasons that it is bad to use the USA as an actor *still apply to the permutation*, thus the permutation is not net beneficial. Instead, it is better to prefer the counterplan alone than the combination of the plan and the counterplan.

Agent counterplans are a very useful tool for opposition teams. The above example shows how you can argue for agents other than the USA, but the same basic method applies to all agent counterplans. When thinking about agent counterplans, you should be creative. Consider using different agencies within the same government. For example, if the proposition team advocates using the Federal Bureau of Investigation, you might recommend that the plan be done by the Central Intelligence Agency instead. If they say the plan should be done by the legislature, think of some reasons why the executive branch or the judicial branch might be a superior actor. One way to effectively master agent counterplans is to come up with a list of common agents of action. Then generate arguments about why each is a bad agent in general as well as in some specific areas of public policy. Finally, generate arguments about why each is a good agent in the same categories. This way, you will always be prepared to counterplan with an alternate agent.

No discussion of agent counterplans would be complete without a section on what we call the **states** or **sub-national governments** counterplans. These are a specific subgroup of agent counterplans that try to delegitimize the need for federal action by showing that sub-federal action is superior to the proposition team's reliance on the federal government. This counterplan originated in policy debate in the USA as a way to test the affirmative's (proposition team's) use of the U.S. Federal Government as an agent of action. Opposition teams can *counterplan* with state action, saying that action by the 50 states would be superior to federal action.

This type of counterplan can be used with great success when discussing other regions of the world. Opposition teams can argue that provincial, decentralized, or other nonfederal government entities should enact the plan's mandates instead of the federal government. To be net beneficial, these sub-national counterplans must show that federal action in the area of the plan is bad. Frequently, opposition teams running this counterplan will also claim that their policy is better suited to redress the proposition case's harm area because states or provinces are better positioned (via efficiency, experimentation, enforcement, or whatever) than the federal government to help those in need.

When you are defending the proposition, you will need to be prepared to defend your agent of action so that you don't lose debates to agent counterplans. To do so, you will need to have prepared at least three sets of arguments. (1) You need to be able to argue why *your specific agent is the best one for the task at hand.* (2) You will also need to have a variety of arguments against other potential agents. (3) You are wise to have a developed defense of your permutation argument. One thing to consider about permutations to agent counterplans is this: Frequently, it is the case that having two agents work at the same problem will produce a kind of *double solvency*; i.e., the permutation could potentially solve the designated problem doubly well. Consider the example of the USA vs. the WHO in malaria prevention. If both agents worked at the problem, it might be solved more quickly and with greater coverage than if either acted alone. The permutation could save more lives than either the plan or the counterplan alone. If you could win this argument, you could argue that the counterplan was therefore not net beneficial.

What would you say, as the opposition team, if the proposition team advanced this "double solvency" argument in defense of their permutation? Here, the debate gets more complicated. The important thing to remember is that you must *weigh the issues* and their associated *impacts*. We will discuss techniques for this process in the chapter on rebuttal skills. For this specific argument, you would do well to answer that the WHO will solve the problem well enough on its own, and that the potential risks of involvement by the USA in the project *outweigh*, or are more important than, the potential benefits of extra solvency.

## SUGGESTED EXERCISE:

Below we have listed a few common agents of action and a corresponding public policy area. For each agent, generate three arguments for why this agent would be a good actor in the specified area. Then come up with three arguments for why this agent would be a bad actor in the specified area. Provide as many specific examples as you can.

- USA - peace negotiations in the Middle East
- United Nations - peacekeeping operations
- Corporations - environmental pollution
- USA - War on Drugs
- Britain - sanctions on Iraq
- European Union - immigration
- World Trade Organization - labor law

## STUDY COUNTERPLANS

Often, proposition teams choose to advocate a course of action in an area where the existing research or available information is substantially unclear as to either the causes of the harms or the correct way we should proceed to redress these harms. This confusion happens all the time in complex issues of public policy. In these cases, a good option for the opposition team is to propose a *study counterplan*. The study counterplan is a generic counterplan that says that instead of acting in the specified area of the proposition or the proposition team's case, we should instead study the problem some more to find the most desirable course of action.

This counterplan is a great option for opposition teams, because it applies to a wide variety of propositions and specific proposition team cases. When you argue a study counterplan, you need to establish that there is great controversy over the area the proposition case deals with. You need to prove that a study might be the appropriate course of action to pursue in the harm area elucidated by the proposition team.

Public policy advocates routinely decide to study rather than pursue a more direct course of action. For example, recently in Illinois, the governor was confronted with the need to make a decision about that state's death penalty. Much new evidence revealed disturbing inconsistencies in the application of the death penalty in that state and others. In fact, several convictions had been overturned as new evidence came to light. Many critics argued that because of inconsistent applications and dubious due process protections, the governor should act to ban the death penalty in Illinois. Instead of taking this course of action, the governor decided to declare a moratorium on the death penalty and *study* its application to find a way to reform death penalty policies and procedures. This action is a real-life example of deferring to a study counterplan. The governor decided that he did not have enough information to make a decision about banning the death penalty, and *instead* decided to study the problem to reach the optimal solution.

When should you use study counterplans? There are two basic circumstances in which they are eminently useful tools for the opposition:

• solution optimization
• inadequate information for decision making

Initially, study counterplans can try and optimize a solution for the problem area outlined by the proposition team. When the proposition team confronts a difficult problem with a dubious solution, you should consider using a study counterplan. Argue that the counterplan is net beneficial because it will create the information necessary to choose the best solution for the problem at hand.

Study counterplans are also useful when you can show that the proposition team is acting on inadequate information. In most societies, even relatively open democracies, the information necessary to make an informed decision about a problem is difficult to find and often highly classified. All too often, debaters (just like journalists and other public policy opinion makers) simply do not have all the information they need to draw an informed conclusion about the topic at hand. If you can establish that this is the case in your debate, if you can show that the proposition team may *literally* not know what they are talking about, then you may be able to win that a study counterplan is the superior course of action.

You need to be careful and specific when writing the text of your study counterplan. In general, it is vital that you have an *actor* – a commission that will do the actual studying. You will also need to have a designated *length* for the study – usually, anywhere from six to 18 months, although it could be longer or shorter depending on your assessment of what is needed. Finally, you need to make sure that the counterplan mandates some sort of action at the study's end. If the proposition team's plan was to have the U.S. Federal Government abolish the death penalty, for example, your study counterplan might look a lot like this:

Counterplan:  The U.S. Federal Government should immediately impose a moratorium on the death penalty. A blue-ribbon commission should be appointed to study how the death penalty is applied, with special attention paid to inconsistencies in due process and ethnicity-based application. This study will last 18 months, and subsequent policy action will be based on recommendations of that commission. Opposition speeches will clarify intent.

Notice the last sentence, "opposition speeches will clarify intent." It is a useful phrase to include at the end of any counterplan text, because it creates leeway for the opposition team to interpret their counterplan in light of any objections or requests for clarification that the proposition team might offer.

As a proposition team debating against a study counterplan, you have a few options. Initially, you should always defend your course of action with as much specific and recent information as you can. Try to show that there is no need for a study – that you have enough relevant information to make the decision now. You should also argue that study will take too long and fail to resolve critical harms that are happening right now. Try to show that there is an affirmative reason to adopt your proposal *now*, rather than waiting for a potentially inconclusive and tediously boring study to reach a dubious conclusion. Finally, you should argue that the results of the study will be biased. Ask the opposition team who will be on the commission. Ask them who will appoint these members. Argue that their so-called "blue-ribbon" commission will most likely reflect the dominant paradigm – precisely the thing your plan tries to combat.

As the opposition team, plan in advance for your answers to these questions and arguments. On the issue of specification about the commission's content, consider directing the same questions back at the proposition team. Ask them who will be implementing *their* plan and how those people will be chosen. Insist that your counterplan be held to the same standards of specificity as the plan.

## SUGGESTED EXERCISE:

Imagine that you are debating on the opposition. The proposition team's plan says that the government should build a large, centralized, underground storage facility for nuclear waste. You think you can prove that there is a substantial risk that such a facility might cause lasting environmental damage. You decide to argue that the government should study these potential consequences before deciding on a course of action. Write the text for your counterplan, using the above example as a model.

### DELAY COUNTERPLANS

Public policies do not simply come into being *ex nihilo* (Latin for "out of nothing"), just as they do not spring full-grown from the heads of the progenitive propositional team. Every public policy has an implementational stage whereby its mandates are actually carried out by the various government or private functionaries whose job it is to implement public policies. Some implementation works better than other implementation. Consider how many international treaties, for example, are inadequately enforced or not enforced at all – the United Nations Declaration on Human Rights is, in theory, a mainstay of international law, yet is almost never enforced in any meaningful way. When the leader of a nation issues an executive order, many questions still remain as to how and when its dictates will be actualized.

These implementation considerations are fertile ground for all kinds of opposition arguments. Many policies, though noble ideas, are more likely than not simply to remain under-enforced, under-funded, or simply not implemented for any number of reasons. Perhaps the elite establishment has a vested interest in seeing that their money or power is not redistributed. Perhaps there are latent or well-entrenched biases in a culture that will ensure that change running counter to those biases will proceed slowly, if at all. How a policy is implemented is often just as important as the specific content of that policy itself. There are several types of counterplans that compete not on specifics *in* the proposition team's plan (i.e., in the *text* of their plan), but on the circumstances under which that plan might come to be implemented or adopted.

One important consideration for policy adoption is *when* a policy is implemented. Sometimes, policies are simply delayed due to exigent circumstances. Legislators may wait to put some economic policies into effect while there is a recession. Spending priorities may be frozen or reoriented in an emergency. Sometimes, policies are delayed due to external political circumstances. A president may wait to implement a policy until a critical constituency is developed or until there is enough popular support to ensure that the policy will be carried through.

Consideration of *when* is the basis for a type of counterplan known as the *delay counterplan*. A delay counterplan suggests that the judge or audience withhold implementation of the proposition team's plan until a specific time or condition named by the opposition team. For example, the opposition could argue that a policy to raise taxes should be delayed until the next fiscal year, so that consumers and businesses would have time to adjust to the economic transition. A similar policy of delayed implementation was used to decide when the euro would be introduced as currency.

Delay counterplans can also *condition implementation* of the proposition team's plan. That is, they can argue that the plan should not be adopted until such time as certain political or social conditions have been met. These counterplans are very useful. Imagine that a proposition team argued that the global community should lift sanctions against Iraq. As the opposition, you could counterplan to lift sanctions against Iraq only when Iraq has agreed to allow United Nations weapons inspectors in its borders and secure sites. This delay counterplan conditions implementation of the plan on the fulfillment of some external situation.

You can see that these counterplans are similar to study counterplans in that both institute delays of implementation. The important difference is that study counterplans do not commit to what specific course of action will be taken at the end of the period of study, while delay counterplans simply postpone implementation of a specific plan.

Delay counterplans, as in the above example of conditioning sanctions, compete based on *opposition expectations about implementation*. In debate, often we say that the opposition should have a reasonable expectation that they will be able to clash directly with the proposition team's case. This theoretical basis for almost every topicality argument is widely accepted among judges and debaters alike.

This counterplan competition argument can be extended to questions of plan implementation in a few ways. First, as an opposition debater, you can argue that you should be able to assume that the proposition team's plan is being advanced *unconditionally*. If this is the case, then conditioning or delaying the plan, as the counterplan does, is certainly fair game for the opposition. If the proposition team, for whatever reason, says that they are in fact advancing the plan conditionally, you should take advantage of this opening for humor. Ask them what conditions they are putting on the plan and when, exactly, they were planning to inform you of these hidden conditions so that you could debate them. Point out that these same tactics are often used by used car salespeople, who lure you into the showroom with promises of low prices only to jack up the prices later, using previously undisclosed costs. This argument strategy is known in the business as the "bait and switch," as the proposition team is luring you in to debate one type of policy, only to switch the target on you once you've committed.

Second, you can argue that in formal debates, we presume the consideration of the proposition team's plan in real time, meaning that the question for debate is whether their proposal should be adopted at the conclusion of the debate. Therefore, it is incumbent upon the proposition team to prove their proposal should be adopted immediately ... *not* whenever they get around to it, or when the stars are in the right arrangement, or when swallows return to San Juan Capistrano bearing the corpse of Jimmy Hoffa, or when any other number of external circumstances resolve themselves.

Delay counterplans are certainly controversial among people who think about formal debate theory. It might surprise or frighten you, for example, to see the opposition team arguing a counterplan that appears to contain your whole plan. This kind of reaction is normal. Take solace in the fact that there is by no means a consensus on the legitimacy of this type of counterplan. Whatever your position on the legitimacy of the counterplan, however, you will still have to know how to answer it when you debate it as a proposition team member.

In many ways, you should answer this kind of counterplan in the same way as a study counterplan. Your first line of defense should be a set of arguments about why the plan should be done now rather than waiting. Talk graphically about the lives that will be lost or the rights that will be violated while the opposition team would have us sit around, twiddling our thumbs, waiting for the designated time of implementation.

You should also be prepared to debate counterplans that condition plan implementation. One of the best ways to answer these counterplans is to argue that the condition set by the opposition will never be met. In the Iraq example mentioned earlier, you might simply contend (based amply on past experience) that Iraq will never agree in good faith to such a condition. Given that fact, you should add, the opposition's counterplan will never actually end up lifting sanctions. Then, you should reiterate the need to lift sanctions. Explain the horrific impacts that sanctions have on the people of Iraq. Try and convince the judge that it is better to go ahead and act to remediate these horrible consequences than to wait for some far-fetched condition to be met, given that the condition will most likely never be met in any case.

## CONSULTATION COUNTERPLANS

We will discuss one final type of generic counterplan, although there are many more. *Consultation counterplans* are a type of implementation counterplan that mirror the delay counterplan in many ways. A consultation counterplan argues that we should consult another relevant actor as to whether or not the proposition team's plan should be implemented. That alternate actor is therefore given a kind of veto power over the adoption of the proposition team's plan. If the alternate actor says yes, the plan is adopted. If the alternate actor says no, the plan is not adopted.

Let's say that you are debating a proposition team that advocates the following plan: NATO should expand its membership to include the Baltic states. This plan is ripe for a consultation counterplan. When you try to find grounds for a consultation counterplan, think to yourself: what actors might be angered or otherwise substantially hurt by adoption of the plan? In this case, the obvious answer is Russia, a nation that has in the past made threats about what might happen if NATO were to expand without explicit consultation. As the opposition team, you might counterplan this way:

> Counterplan: NATO will consult with the Russian government on the issue of expansion to include the Baltic states. Implementation of expansion plans will be made contingent on Russia's explicit approval. Opposition speeches will clarify intent.

You should argue that the counterplan is net beneficial because it does not anger Russia. In this situation, it would be appropriate to argue some sort of NATO-Russia relations disadvantage off the case, claiming that this disadvantage is a net benefit to the counterplan. What do we mean by this?

Counterplans can often compete on the basis of what we call *external* net benefits. These net benefits are usually disadvantages to which the plan links but the counterplan does not. In this case, you could probably argue convincingly that the plan would anger Russia substantially because, by not consulting them, it would send a message that Russia was cut out of the communications loop or was otherwise not substantively important enough to be consulted on the matter of NATO expansion. We say that the counterplan *solves* or *avoids* the risk of the disadvantage link because it does engage in active consultation, as opposed to the plan, which continues to act in a unilateral and (dare we say it) profoundly headstrong manner. The consultation counterplan thus competes based on external net benefits.

Otherwise, the counterplan competes in much the same way as the *conditional implementation* variant on the delay counterplan we discussed earlier. It simply puts a condition on implementation of the proposition team's case: *If* this external actor says "yes," *then* we will implement the plan. You can defend the counterplan theoretically in many of the ways listed above. Be creative with your consultation counterplans. Think: who would be the interested actors in this policy calculation? Consider, for example, that the World Trade Organization is involved in monitoring all kinds of domestic and multilateral regulations. Perhaps they should be consulted about the possibility of new regulations to ensure that those regulations will not be struck down.

You may be skeptical of this kind of counterplan at first. What permutation jumps immediately to mind? At first blush, it seems that the proposition team could just argue a permutation whereby one could consult Russia and then do the plan. As the opposition team, you should argue that this permutation still links to the disadvantage and *potentially* links more than the plan action alone. Consider: If NATO were to consult Russia and go ahead with expansion regardless, it would be a textbook case of bad faith negotiation. After such a meeting, why would Russia ever trust negotiation with NATO again? Such an incident could poison the well of good feelings between NATO and Russia, and potentially impede all future possibilities for constructive and cooperative communication. In this respect, the permutation may accrue the link to the NATO-Russian relations disadvantage considerably more than just the plan alone: The plan just does not consult, while the permutation consults in a knowingly fraudulent manner. The permutation is not real consultation. It is merely notification, and should be treated as such.

When you argue for the opposition with a consultation counterplan, you need to remember to establish that the plan does not (and cannot, for the same reasons discussed above as to why a plan cannot be conditional) itself provide a potential veto power to any other entity.

When you argue for the proposition against consultation counterplans, you need to remember not to let the counterplan steal your case. Sound like perplexing advice? Consider the way in which this and other counterplans function. Smart opposition teams will try to steal as much of your case as possible. This "theft" is good defensive strategy. To get the most edge against the proposition team, smart opposition teams will try to co-opt as much of the proposition team's plan and advocacy as they think they can reasonably get away with. *Exclusionary counterplans*, which we will discuss later, are the culmination of this drive. The strategic advantage of the consultation counterplan and others of its ilk is that that they co-opt most (if not all) of the proposition team's case. The counterplan will probably end up doing the plan, but will wait to do so until the relevant actors have given their consent.

Practically, for the proposition team, this means that the opposition will be able to argue that all the reasons that the plan is a good idea are now reasons to endorse the opposition, because: (1) The opposition counterplan solves the harms and advantages outlined by the proposition team; and (2) The counterplan accounts for the risk of a link to the disadvantage that the proposition team's plan necessarily accrues.

What to do if you are the proposition team? The wisest course of action is usually to argue that the counterplan will not be able to do the plan because the relevant actor will say *no* in consultation. This strategy may seem dangerous, because you are in effect conceding the link to the net benefit disadvantage. In the Russia example, this proposition team strategy would involve conceding that the plan would anger Russia. It is tempting, as a proposition speaker, to try and have it both ways in this situation. Don't be a sucker. Instead, heavily contest the impact to the disadvantage and then argue that the impacts to the case advantages outweigh any potential risk of angering Russia. The alternative is far worse. If you let the opposition get away with a decent possibility that their counterplan will implement your plan's mandates, they're probably going to win. At the end of the debate, the counterplan will probably solve the case advantages and avoid the disadvantage, while the plan will only solve the case advantages and definitely link to the disadvantage. In order to avoid this high-risk rebuttal situation, you should instead disarm the opposition by arguing that Russia will say no and that the counterplan will never in fact implement the plan mandates. Then, all you need to do to win the debate is to prove that the impacts to the case outweigh the impacts to the disadvantage.

Notice that the consultation counterplan applies especially well to very small proposition team cases whereby the proposition team does not have very large advantages to weigh against the risk of the opposition's comparatively large external net benefit.

## SUGGESTED EXERCISE:

Below find a list of potential actions. For each action, pick an actor to consult about that action and explain why they should be consulted. In effect, you are here writing a consultation counterplan and constructing a disadvantage to non-consultation. Explain why that actor should be consulted and what might happen if they were not consulted. Be specific.

- environmental regulations
- setting wage standards
- immigration reform
- elimination of racial profiling
- pulling out of the World Trade Organization

## PLAN/CASE SPECIFIC COUNTERPLANS

We have discussed several types of generic counterplans. You may have figured out by now that even the label "generic" is misleading for these counterplans, which must always be substantially adapted to the proposition case they are designed to defeat in any given round. A second type of counterplan is a *plan or case-specific counterplan*. These counterplans are adapted very specifically to respond to the mandates or advantages of the proposition team's case. These counterplans fall into three basic categories: counterplans that compete based on solvency, counterplans that neutralize advantages, and exclusionary counterplans.

Initially, opposition teams can argue counterplans that compete based on substantial, exclusive, solvency differentials. These counterplans usually go in the so-called *opposite direction* of the proposition team's plan. For example, if the proposition team argues that more government regulation is the best solution to environmental pollution, an opposition team might productively argue that a superior solution would be a deregulation counterplan. There is in fact a substantial debate about the comparative virtues of government-based as opposed to market-based solutions to environmental problems. When you debate on the opposition, you should consider arguing deregulation as a productive solvency-based counterplan as a response to regulation cases, and vice-versa. The advantage of such a counterplan is that it goes in the opposite direction of the proposition case's mandates and becomes a competitive alternative. On the opposition, you can make a good case for why deregulation addresses the given harm better than regulation. The exercises below encourage you to come up with your own arguments to substantiate both sides of this debate.

The important thing to remember about this sort of counterplan is the debate about the permutation. What is the logical proposition team permutation? It is to both regulate and deregulate to solve the harm. On the opposition side, you should argue that this permutation is incoherent and infeasible – one could not conceivably regulate and deregulate the same area at the same time. Argue that the judge must choose one option, and then try to prove that deregulation is the superior option using the method already demonstrated earlier:

- Show that their plan is bad. In this case, show that regulation is a bad solution, perhaps because it causes bad external consequences or simply fails to solve the problem.
- Show that your counterplan is good. In this case, prove that deregulation accrues multiple advantages and solves the problem better than regulation.
- Weigh the potential costs and benefits. In summation, show the judge that, on balance, deregulation is the superior alternative because it redresses more significant harms than regulation.

This counterplan is not the only one of its kind. Other examples of comparisons include: unilateral vs. multilateral action, criminal vs. civil penalties, or compulsory vs. voluntary incentives.

A second type of case-specific counterplan is designed to neutralize advantages to the case. In formal debate, we call this *counterplanning out advantages*. This practice is different from all of the other types of counterplans mentioned in this way: *When you counterplan out advantages, you are not necessarily trying to make your counterplan compete.* What does this puzzling claim mean? We have just spent several pages trying to teach you how to make your counterplans competitive.

Sometimes counterplans don't necessarily have to be competitive. Consider that at the end of the debate, a judge draws up a kind of balance sheet to determine what each side has won or lost. In a debate where the proposition team won their advantage, and the opposition team won their disadvantage, that sheet might look something like this:

Proposition Team:           Opposition Team:
Advantage                   Disadvantage

What if you could neutralize the proposition team's advantage? In that case, you would doubtless win because you would succeed in tipping the balance sheet in your favor. This is why the opposition sometimes counterplans out advantages. *When they do so, they argue a counterplan that solves the proposition team's advantage, thereby capturing it for their side.*

Imagine that the proposition team argues a case that says that the government should provide single-payer health insurance for all potential recipients. Their advantage claim is that such a policy would increase research and development on the part of private industries because the market would be bigger. On the opposition, you could counterplan to neutralize this advantage by saying that the government should fund additional, public, research and development. This counterplan would solve the advantage, ensuring that *both sides* accrue the research and development advantage. The important thing to realize when employing this strategy is to make sure that your counterplan avoids the link to the disadvantage. In this case, the disadvantage might be that single-payer health insurance is bad because it hurts the private insurance market. Your counterplan avoids this disadvantage, setting up the following judge balance sheet:

| Proposition Team: | Opposition Team: |
|---|---|
| Advantage | Advantage |
| | Disadvantage |

Opposition most likely wins, because they also solve the proposition team's advantage, yet avoid the insurance industry collapse disadvantage. The interesting thing about counterplans that neutralize advantages is that they don't really have to be competitive in the traditional sense. The proposition team can certainly permute the counterplan, but such a move won't really get them anywhere, since both teams will still accrue the same advantage even after the permutation.

To avoid these counterplans when you argue for the proposition, you need to make sure that your advantages are *germane* to your plan. That is, you need to do your best to ensure that your plan is the only way such advantages could be achieved.

From an opposition perspective, this kind of counterplan is eminently useful for countering the flood of proposition team advantages that are often only barely related to the proposed plan. Feel free just to counterplan them out to neutralize the advantages. Some judges may say you can't argue more than one counterplan. In this case, consider consolidating your counterplans so that you only have one counterplan with three or four different mandates.

## Exclusionary Counterplans

A final type of case-specific counterplan is the *exclusionary counterplan*. A fairly advanced type of counterplan, it is an extremely powerful weapon for the opposition. Sometimes proposition teams will argue plans with several different mandates or components. You may have arguments against some, but not all, of their mandates. In this case, you might want to consider using an exclusionary counterplan. An exclusionary counterplan endorses some, but not all, of the proposition team's plan. This type of counterplan competes on based on arguments about why the excluded parts of the plan are bad. Exclusionary counterplans are a way for the opposition to focus the debate back on areas they might be more familiar with, or areas they feel are more advantageous for them to discuss.

Public policy makers endorse exclusionary counterplans all the time. For example, when the U.S. Congress was debating new air pollution and emissions regulations for automobiles, they were considering adapting sweeping reforms applying to all vehicles. Then someone proposed light truck exemptions from that legislation. The legislation with the exemption was, after some debate, adopted.

As an opposition debater, think of exclusion counterplans as "the plan, except..." In order to win that your exception is net beneficial, you have to win a disadvantage related to the specific topic or item that you exempt from their plan. Let's say that the proposition team argued the following plan:

The U.S. Federal Government should restrict the export of all pesticides currently banned for use in that country.

You might happen to know that some of these pesticides have uniquely beneficial aspects for the economies of other countries. The Mexican timber export industry, for example, is extremely reliant on the pesticide chlordane to kill termites in their lumber stacked for export. Also, DDT is very useful for malaria eradication. You could exempt one or both of these pesticides in your counterplan:

> The U.S. Federal Government should restrict the export of all pesticides currently banned for use in that country except for chlordane and DDT.

The net benefits to your counterplan would be arguments about why it would be good to continue limited exports of chlordane and DDT.

As a proposition team, your best defense against exclusionary counterplans is good, careful plan writing. Don't write mandates into your plan that you aren't prepared to defend. In this pesticide example, it might have been wise not to use the word "all," as this word arguably gives the opposition team plenty of ground to argue their exclusionary counterplan.

## SUGGESTED EXERCISES:

1. Make three arguments that show why government regulation is the best way to solve environmental problems such as air and water pollution.
2. Make three arguments that show why deregulation and its subsequent reliance on corporate action is the best way to address environmental problems such as air and water pollution.

## FINAL NOTES ON COUNTERPLANS

This chapter has by no means exhausted the available theory on counterplans and responses to counterplans. As a way of concluding our examination of counterplans, we wish to address a few other issues related to their strategic use. First, we will talk a bit more about the proposition team's practice of permutations. Then, we will address the issue of counterplan advocacy: Can you have more than one counterplan? What happens if a counterplan is proven to be noncompetitive?

Recall that permutations test the competition of a counterplan. That is, they test whether the counterplan does, in fact, provide a reason to reject the proposition team's plan. There are a couple of important things you need to keep in mind about arguing permutations:

**THEY MUST INCLUDE THE WHOLE PLAN.** It might be tempting for proposition teams to remove parts of their plan to which the opposition has made compelling arguments. This kind of permutation is called a *severance permutation*. A severance permutation contains only part of (rather than all of) the proposition team's plan. We use the word "severance" because this kind of permutation *severs*, or removes, part of the proposition team's plan.

Severance permutations are generally thought to be unacceptable because they do not actually prove that the counterplan is not competitive. The counterplan is a reason to reject the whole plan as initially presented. Just because you could combine *part* of the plan with the counterplan, it does not therefore follow that the counterplan does not compete with the plan.

Some people also argue that severance permutations are unfair to the opposition. These people argue that the proposition team should not have the ability to change their plan in the middle of the debate, because the opposition team has already predicated their strategy on the original presentation of the plan.

**PERMUTATIONS DO NOT, HOWEVER, HAVE TO INCLUDE THE WHOLE COUNTERPLAN.** This is a common mistake made by debaters. A permutation should include the whole plan and *all or any part of the counterplan*. Why is this? Consider the following scenario:

You are debating for the proposition, defending a plan to reform national library acquisition policies. It's a small plan, but an effective one. The opposition team counterplans to ban reform of national library acquisition policies *and* to provide comprehensive national health insurance.

The counterplan bans the plan and does something else. Uh-oh.

How can the proposition team win now, given that they can't combine the plan and the counterplan? The answer is simple. The proposition team's permutation should advocate the *whole plan* and *part of the counterplan*, in this case, provide comprehensive national health insurance. Otherwise, opposition teams could always just counterplan to ban the plan and do something else, an unfair advantage for that side, to be sure.

PERMUTATIONS DO NOT HAVE TO BE TOPICAL. This should be a common-sense adage, given what you already know about the function of a permutation. Permutations are a test of the competition of the counterplan, and not *necessarily* a policy option advocated by the proposition team (although some proposition teams will, from time to time, reserve the right to advocate their permutations, usually in response to some perceived or actually egregious advocacy shift by the opposition team). Thus permutations do not have the same on-face topicality burdens as the proposition team's plan. Consider also that if permutations had to be topical, *all nontopical counterplans would automatically be competitive*, quite a disadvantage for proposition teams.

There are a few leftover questions to consider when arguing and planning to argue counterplans on the opposition side.

CAN YOU RUN MORE THAN ONE COUNTERPLAN? Of course you can. There is no logical reason not to. Counterplans test the viability and desirability of the proposition team's case. There is no reason to limit the opposition's ability to contest the proposition team's case. Some judges may disagree with this, however. In this case, consider consolidating your counterplans into one, multi-pronged, policy initiative. However, be careful of biting off more than you can chew. Counterplans tend to complicate debates greatly. Multiple counterplans can do so exponentially. Don't put yourself in a position for the last rebuttal where you are defending multiple, confusing policy options. You probably won't be able to cover all the relevant issues, and the judge will most likely think you are incompetent for biting off more than you can chew.

WHAT HAPPENS WHEN A COUNTERPLAN IS FOUND TO BE NONCOMPETITIVE? This is an important question. There are two schools of thought on this issue. One school believes that once a counterplan has been argued, the opposition team is stuck with it for good or for ill, much as a proposition team should be stuck with a bankrupt plan.

We do not necessarily agree with this way of thinking about counterplans. Recall that the purpose of a counterplan is to test the desirability and opportunity cost of the proposition team's case. If the counterplan is found not to be an opportunity cost of the plan, it can simply "go away;" that is, the opposition may feel free to abandon its advocacy of the counterplan. This is said to make the counterplan *conditional*. Arguments advanced in debates are often called *conditional*; which is to say that they may be dropped at any time without repercussion to their advocates. Usually this phrase is used in the context of *conditional counterplans*, which can be dropped if undesirable without forfeiture of the debate.

Many people have argued that conditional counterplans are illegitimate and unfair, because they force the proposition team to invest considerable time in responding to the counterplan, at which point the opposition may simply abandon the counterplan. While this plea for fairness is understandable, in many ways it misses the point of what it means to argue a counterplan. A counterplan is always "just a test" of the proposition team's plan.

When the proposition team argues against a counterplan, they are contending that the counterplan is not relevant in the debate because it does not run *counter* to the plan. Thus, if the opposition team chooses to abandon the counterplan, they are essentially admitting their agreement with the proposition team's claim: that the argument is no longer relevant to the debate. Of course, in debate, any irrelevant argument can be removed from debate without penalty.

Further, all arguments in debate are conditional in the sense that they may be dropped or discontinued at any time. If you made a series of attacks on the proposition team's stated harms initially, and then decided not to extend those arguments in your rebuttal speech, would you then be making those arguments conditionally? The answer is yes. All arguments are *conditional* because all arguments are advanced provisionally, accounting for the chance of satisfactory refutation.

As you can see, there are many difficult questions you will have to face directly related to questions of counterplan theory. Nevertheless, we believe that it is important for debaters to learn to use and answer these powerful and relevant opposition team tools.

# CHAPTER 9:

# OPPOSITION STRATEGY – CRITIQUING

## INTRODUCTION TO THE PRACTICE OF CRITIQUING

Through our relentless pursuit of colorful similes, we have already told you that arguments are like automobiles, dinner invitations, small monkeys, and cans of ham. Arguments are also like houses in that they rest on foundations. Recall that in the chapter on argumentation we detailed how arguments are constructed: They have supporting premises, warrants, and data. Complex arguments, like the kind made by the body of a proposition team's case, are composed of many different, smaller arguments that (hopefully) unite to make a cohesive whole, much like the robots that assemble to form Voltron. A proposition team's case, therefore, rests on a fairly broad foundation composed of other arguments and the support that those arguments rely on. While this broad foundation can render a case fairly stable, it can also be the undoing of a proposition team's case if approached correctly.

You may have had the occasion to play the popular block-stacking game Jenga. In Jenga, many small blocks are stacked on each other, cross-hatched to make an irregular square tower. Participants remove blocks until someone is unfortunate enough to remove the block that causes the whole structure to come crashing down. That load-bearing block is a fundamental, even critical, part of the whole structure of the tower. Many of the other blocks are essentially trivial, and can be treated as such. They can be added and removed with no cost to overall structural stability.

As with Jenga, so it is with arguments. All arguments make assumptions and leaps of reasoning. Some of the assumptions are more critical than others for the overall stability of the argument. Consider the following example: You are taking a class on ancient civilizations at your university. Your final paper assignment is to write a comprehensive report on one of the Earth's ancient civilizations. After weeks of hard work, you turn in your magnum opus – a history of Atlantis. The teacher fails you. Horrified by this turn of events, you go to her and ask why. She says that there *were* some things about the paper that impressed her. For example, she was excited and intrigued by your detailed and informed discussions of native Atlantean foods, dances, and cultural practices. She thought that your position on Atlantean civil-military relations was quite innovative. In fact, it was a spectacular paper. There was just one small problem: There is no such civilization as Atlantis. Oops. You made a fundamental assumption that turned out to be incorrect. (Jenga!)

Some assumptions, like the Atlantis assumption, are just plain wrong. Others are both wrong and dangerous. Imagine that you and a friend arrive in San Francisco for a sightseeing tour. You've never been to the city, but you hear that it's lovely. After leaving the airport, you rent a car and take the map offered by the attendant. Since you are a better driver, you pilot the car while your friend navigates. After a little bit of driving, you notice that the streets you are on don't quite match up with the streets on the map, but you assume that's just because you are lost. You are very lost. You are so lost, in fact, that while trying to get to Berkeley you drive into the Bay. As you are sinking, you realize the problem: The map you were given, that you assumed was correct, was in fact a map of Chicago. Oops. You made a fundamental assumption that turned out to be incorrect and dangerous. (Jenga!)

Debate arguments make assumptions that are incorrect and potentially dangerous all the time. But debate rounds are not (perhaps fortunately) like Jenga. It is very rare that you will be able to identify a single argument which, when pulled out and examined, will bring down the entire position of the other side. However, the investigation and criticism of fundamental assumptions is an invaluable part of debate for both the proposition and opposition sides. This notion may seem obvious, given that the gist of this book thus far has been to show the roots and assumptions of debate arguments and techniques of all kinds. The goal of this chapter is to show how the practice of critiquing arguments and their accompanying fact sets can be used as a strategic argument type for use in debate.

You have already learned that the most effective way to refute an argument is *not* by simply providing an assertive counter-claim. Arguments are most effectively refuted from within their own substance; that is, sophisticated debaters know that *arguments are best unraveled by focusing on the language, reasoning, underlying assumptions, expert testimony, interpretations, and proofs of the opponent*. We answer arguments like this all the time. When you answer a disadvantage, you attack its reasoning, testimony, expert testimony, and proofs. Whenever you argue against a proposition team's case, if you are making sophisticated arguments, you are doing much the same thing.

In academia or public policy analysis, the practice of criticism is almost ubiquitous. One important thing to remember about argument critique is that it is all about where you look, and from what perspective. You may have heard the old story about the three blind men who are called to examine an elephant. One feels its side and determines that it is a piece of luggage. Another feels its foot and says it is a stool. A third feels its tail and calls it a snake. They are all wrong, of course, but from their perspective they are correct. Our point here is not to vitiate radical perspectivism – after all, in this story at least we know there is an elephant and so are not in the least worried about the possibility of implementing policies based on these incomplete worldviews. In public policy decisions, however, it is not so easy to identify the elephant or even to know that there is an animal being examined in the first place.

The closest thing to an elephant we have in any formal debate, at least from the perspective of the opposition, is the presentation of the first proposition speaker. That presentation is not merely (if it can be considered to be so at all) a plea for endorsement of a particular proposal. Rather, it is a kind of text to be interpreted and analyzed. Every component of the proposition team's argument set is potentially up for debate in any number of ways.

This idea of speeches as texts is important, and one that is critical to understanding how the practice of critique works in debate. If the proposition team's case is a kind of text, it is therefore up for interpretation just like any other text. The proposition team's case should not necessarily be thought of as a set of presumptively true facts. It is, however, usually presented as such. This presentation should pose no great barrier to a critical opposition team who want to reinterpret the proposition team's presentation in a manner that will be conducive to their ultimate victory in the debate.

Let's see how critiquing is done in practice. When presented with a particular fact set, people from different intellectual traditions and perspectives will almost invariably look at it differently, with different results. These multiple perspectives can be an informative basis for engaging arguments with sustained critique. Let's take the example of the death penalty to see how this works in practice. Here's a description of a state of affairs, one that could very easily be a component of any number of proposition team cases:

> A man is arrested for killing someone. After being given due process, appropriate prosecution, and trial in front of a jury of his peers, he is found guilty of murder. Once his appeals have been rejected, he is executed.

Different critics will have different commentaries to offer in response to this description of a state of affairs.

A critic who argues from the perspective of the Critical Legal Studies (CLS) movement might point out that what this description leaves out is a critical examination of the part played by class interests in this whole process. She might point out that the poor or otherwise indigent are more likely to be arrested and indicted for any number of crimes, including murder. She might also call into question the seemingly neutral description of "due process" in this text, given the abundant evidence that suggests that economic disparities dramatically affect the quality of justice given to defendants in criminal courts. Among other factors, your net worth directly determines what kind of lawyer will defend you: an overworked public defender or a specialized private attorney. Finally, she might suggest that the jury was most likely *not* a jury of his actual peers. She might say that this description of the situation is, *at best*, misleading because in its omissions it inaccurately describes the situation. At worst, this description might be dangerous because it seeks to paint as neutral a process that is fundamentally unfair and unjust. Several fundamental components of the description have been substantively undermined by means of this criticism. The critic has shown that it makes faulty assumptions about the world (echoing the example of the Atlantis paper) and that its presentation is dangerously misleading (echoing the example of the map of Chicago). If she chose, the critic could probably make a convincing case for disregarding or rejecting the description on these grounds.

This exercise is what it is like to practice criticism in debate. When you focus on the underlying assumptions of your opponents' arguments, you are engaged in criticism of their arguments. The practice of critiquing arguments can have tremendous currency in contemporary parliamentary debating, and has quickly become a crucial type of argument for opposition teams. We will discuss how critiquing can be used by the opposition side in a debate and then conclude with some general advice about the practice of criticism.

When the proposition team makes their case, they are presenting a text for analysis and interpretation. This text usually consists of a few basic components:

- a description of the present state of affairs
- an explanation of how that state of affairs causes a problem
- a proposal (the plan)
- an explanation of how the proposal will remediate the given problem

• an explanation of how the proposal will remediate other problems

All of these components, as well as their various combinations, are potential grounds to be mined for criticism. On the opposition, you can criticize the proposition's text on any number of grounds. Three of these, though they are by no means exclusive or particularly distinct from each other, are the grounds of language, values, and thinking.

## LANGUAGE

Initially, you can address the proposition team's case by criticizing its language. Traditionally, we are given to understand that language is fundamentally neutral, a kind of "container" with no particular currency of its own. Many social theorists who argue that the language that we use does, in fact, create lived reality in many tangible ways have heavily criticized this perspective on language. Here are some questions to consider:

• Does it matter if you refer to a given nation as part of the "Third World"? From a certain perspective on global affairs, it certainly matters. The language of "Third World" assumes a hierarchy of civilizations and thereby creates assumptions of inferiority and superiority. It also implies that the nation in question and the rest of the "Third World" are fundamentally detachable from the other, numerically designated "Worlds" (wherever those are).
• What happens when you call someone an "alleged criminal"? All too often, the power of the word "criminal" overcomes its modifier "alleged" to type the individual in question as a presumed lawbreaker, whether or not that person has, in fact, committed a crime.
• What kinds of cultural and historical associations do we have with the word "black"? There are a myriad of ways that, at least in the West, "black" is a negative modifier – think about the "black arts," "black magic," or what it means to call someone "black-hearted."
• How do you talk about a civil disturbance? Do you call it a "riot" or an "uprising"? Is there a difference between the two? When we think about a "riot," we think about directionless, senseless violence and destruction

of property and lives. When we think about an uprising, we think about a specifically political event that is targeted to achieve social change or at least to "rise up" against some oppressive set of circumstances.

The worldview that holds that language is itself more or less meaning-less can and should be called into question by interested opposition teams. All too often, policy decisions are justified with and framed in language that may betray some of the more nefarious or at least puz-zling aspects of that particular policy action.

One good example of this is the language of "development." The idea of development implies a kind of ends-orientation, or *teleology* whereby one is proceeding from a state of affairs to the next logical state of affairs. Think about how we use the language of development in biology: Embryos develop organs, wings, legs, and heads according to their chromosonal design. In biology, the idea of development car-ries with it a kind of destiny as well as a destination – we proceed as we must, following a developmental plan, towards becoming fully-formed beings. The transplantation of the language of development from this biological context to the realm of human and (specifically) international affairs has some troubling implications for policymakers and those who would critically examine public policies.

Many, many public policies are framed using the language of devel-opment. In the USA, a good bit of foreign aid is funneled through the Agency for International Development (US-AID), a division of govern-ment that has the word "development" in its very name. Money and assis-tance is given (by the US-AID and by other agencies and other nations) to countries who are often explicitly referred to as "underdeveloped" or as "Lesser Developed Countries" (LDCs, in the dialect of international relations). These countries are understood to be in need of "develop-ment." What is, exactly, to count as "development" is an interesting ques-tion. Development is understood to be exemplified by the so-called "developed" countries – those countries, including Europe, Japan, and the USA, which have reached their fully formed status. The implication is that some countries need development because they are not like a set of other (industrialized, consumer-based) countries.

There are many who critique the deployment of this language of "development" to describe and attempt amelioration of social problems. It is said, in the first place, that the language of "underdevelopment" misunderstands the nature and causes of real harms in specific parts of the world. What is the cause, for example, of high infant mortality? Is it because there are not enough well funded medical facilities in a given nation? Or is it because that nation is not enough like its "developed" cousins? These questions matter quite a bit for the business of interpretation and criticism. It could be, for example, that the way the problem is framed obscures other ways of thinking about it while lending an air of legitimacy to the proposed solution. The language of "development" might be said to betray a fundamental misunderstanding of the present system and its concomitant harms on the part of the policy advocates, while *at the same time* dangerously obscuring other, more trenchant, problems and their causes from further examination. Further, if the harm is misunderstood, then how can the proposed solution be said to "solve" it in any meaningful way? "Solve *what*?" you might ask. "If we have proven that you don't have any idea what the problem is, then what possible currency could this appeal to solvency have?"

There are also (at best) tautological and (at worst) sinister aspects to using "development" to help "underdevelopment." Critics of the language of "development" have argued that the idea of "development," inherited and refined as it is from the legacy and practice of colonialisms and imperialisms, is itself responsible for many of the most trenchant problems in so-called "underdeveloped" countries. From this perspective, it follows that using "development" aid to alleviate the problems of "underdevelopment" might be a bit like using sewer water to clean an open wound. In practice, development assistance often fails to achieve its stated goals. It has often been said to perpetuate dependency on donor states, further impeding economic and social self-sufficiency. In this respect, development assistance may achieve the *opposite effect* of what its advocates intend – not creating development at all, but rather furthering the supposedly abject state of "underdevelopment."

It is probably easy to imagine a proposition team using the language of "development" to justify their proposal. They might propose giving food and farming aid to some nations defined as "developing." They might call the aid "development assistance." They might even talk about the responsibility held by all "developed" nations to help along their less-privileged cousin states. The proposition team would have a harm – famine. They would have a plan – development aid. They would try to show that their plan dealt with the problem.

As an opposition team, your work would be cut out for you. You could argue that the case's implicit and explicit relationship with the language of development reveals some fundamental flaws in the proposition team's reasoning and presentation. You could argue that:

a) They fundamentally misunderstand the problem, and thus their statements of harms should be disregarded.

b) This misidentification of the harm undercuts any appeal to solvency that they might make.

c) Their proposal is part of the problem rather than part of the solution.

d) Their proposal will at best be unable to ameliorate the problem. At worst, their proposal will simply make things worse rather than better. Thus, there is a net solvency turn for the opposition.

Of course, you would want to flesh these arguments out by giving much of the analysis and explanation offered above, but the gist of your argument should still be fundamentally clear. Should you choose to criticize the proposition team's embrace of a difficult or objectionable type of phrasing, value, or thinking, you will usually try to make all of these arguments (a-d) as evaluative statements that detail why your criticism matters.

When you critique the proposition team's case, you will have to prove at least two things in order to win the debate on your criticism. You will have to uncover a fundamental assumption of the proposition's case, and you will have to use that assumption to win the debate. How is this done in practice? If you choose to structure your criticism (using subpoints labeled A, B, and C, for example), there are as many ways to structure your argument as there are potential criticisms to be made in a debate round. Generally, you will need to prove at least the following components of your argument:

- The proposition team makes assumption X.
- Assumption X is bankrupt (or dangerous, or patently silly, or shamefully weak) for the following reasons...
- Because we successfully criticize Assumption X, we win the debate because...

Notice that the evaluative arguments a-d above would fit nicely (with appropriate explanation) under the third component, since all are reasons why the criticism functions to undermine and turn back the proposition team's case.

We are reluctant to advance a specific *model* for advancing critical arguments. As you might have gathered by now, they are a bit different from previous kinds of opposition arguments you have encountered. However, one outline you could use to make the critique of "development" argument is this:

A. The proposition team frames and advances their policy using the language of "development." They propose giving food and farming aid to some nations defined as "developing." They call the aid "development assistance." They even talk about the responsibility held by all "developed" nations to help along their less-privileged cousin states.

B. The language and concept of "development" is bankrupt and dangerous.
[explain]

C. Because we successfully criticize the language and concepts of "development," we win the debate because:
1) They fundamentally misunderstand the problem, and thus their statements of harms should be disregarded.
[explain]
2) This misidentification of the harm undercuts any appeal to solvency that they might make.
[explain]
3) Their proposal is part of the problem rather than part of the solution.
[explain]

4) Their proposal will at best be unable to ameliorate the problem. At worst, their proposal will simply make things worse rather than better. Thus, there is a net solvency turn for the opposition.

[explain]

This is just one suggestion for how this argument could be advanced in a formal debate. You could certainly flesh it out or cut it down. You could also de-structure the argument, turning it into a more unified attack without explicit structure. We show how the argument works as a structured phenomenon only to show the relationships and flow between its components.

## VALUES

In addition to criticizing the language of the proposition team's proposal, you can also criticize the assumptions it makes about values. We have a tendency to think about values as abstract entities without a direct relationship to policy choices. This tendency is a fairly dangerous way of thinking about values: They are not just disembodied concepts like "dignity," "freedom," "justice," "liberty," "order," "security," "democracy," and "safety": They are also the prime movers for our policy and lifestyle decisions. In the chapter on topic interpretation, we discuss the relationship between values and policy choices. It is, in theory, possible to think about a value in the abstract, but you can't think about a policy without reference to values.

How can you productively criticize the proposition case's allegiance to particular value structures? First, you need to pinpoint a fundamental value that seems to inform the proposition team's case. Then, you need to criticize that value. Finally, you need to show how your criticism of that value proceeds to undermine or unravel the proposition team's case. In this respect, value criticism is very similar to criticism based on the language of the proposition case. Let's walk through an example to see how this works.

The proposition team opens their speech by detailing a problem that exists in the present system: There is tremendous violence in the Middle East, specifically violence between Israelis and Palestinians.

They then present a specific proposal: The USA should deploy peace-keeping troops to the Gaza Strip and the West Bank to help quell the violence. Finally, they argue that the presence of these troops will deter and prevent conflict, thereby keeping the peace.

This presentation is ripe for criticism from the perspective of a philosophy of nonviolence. You could argue that the entirety of the proposition team's proposal relies on an implicit belief in the value of violence, and is thus inconsistent on its own merits and according to its own value system. Consider that the harms detailed by the proposition team all have to do with a deploration of existing armed conflict between Israelis and Palestinians. The understanding here, at least according to the proposition team, is that violence is something to be avoided and prevented, or at least stopped. As an opposition debater, you can concede these fundamental harms and argue that the proposition plan fails to redress them and in fact might make the problem much worse. The proposal, after all, *deploys the military*, assuming that it is right or acceptable or even feasible to use force to make peace, an assumption that is contested by hundreds of years of thinking about non-violence and the practice of non-violent resistance.

One critical question to ask of the proposition case's solvency claims is this: How is it, exactly, that the presence of troops serves to deter conflict? The answer, of course, is that the troops signify and embody a threat of further force. This threat, it can be argued, is itself a kind of violence: A regime that keeps the peace by means of threats is itself an intrinsically violent arrangement, and one that forecloses the possibility of other social arrangements by constantly threatening that more violence will erupt if adequate deterrence is not maintained. On the opposition, you can argue that the proposal is inconsistent within its own stated hierarchy of values. The fact of this inconsistency alone, however, is not necessarily a sufficient reason to reject the plan. You must also show how the proposal fails on its own terms. One way to do this might be to show that the presence of troops will only escalate the level of conflict rather than ameliorating it — as has been the case in the U.S. intervention in Somalia, Russian intervention in Afghanistan, American intervention in Vietnam, Cuban military deployments to Angola, and British troop deployments in Northern Ireland. Foreign military intervention has a nasty habit of upping the ante for insurgent forces intent on victory. There is, therefore, a decent possibility that the plan will make the problem worse.

You might also voice a principled objection to the use of force, thus advancing a kind of *value abjection* to the proposition team's proposal. Using an adaptation of the model given above, your argument might be structured something like this:

A. The proposition team's case relies on the use of violence. They deploy troops to the Middle East and argue that those troops will be good because they will deter conflict. Deterrence, however, is just code for threatening behavior.

B. The idea of using violence to stop violence is bankrupt and dangerous.

[explain]

C. Because we successfully criticize the proposition team's use of violence, we win the debate because:

1) The plan double-turns with the harms. If they are right about violence being bad, then they lose the debate because their proposal is intrinsically and necessarily violent. Their proposal is part of the problem rather than part of the solution.

2) Their proposal will at best be unable to ameliorate the problem. At worst, their proposal will simply make things worse rather than better. Thus, there is a net solvency turn for the opposition.

[explain]

Note that the parts where we have written "[explain]" are the places in the argument outline that you will need to fill in to make the argument complete. This kind of value critique tries to show that the proposition team's value claims are at odds with their specific proposal.

Another kind of value critique investigates the proposition team's values for inconsistencies. Our value concepts are often so broad that proper investigation can reveal troubling internal inconsistencies. Take the example of "liberty," for example. Although just about everyone supports "freedom" in its abstract sense, they rarely support it without qualification. Few human societies, for example, recognize that there is a universal freedom to kill (although some reserve this power for the state exclusively, as in the example of the death penalty). This value means that "freedom" is generally only accepted with the qualification that one has freedom as long as it doesn't interfere with the freedom of others. This qualification may make sense in the abstract but often makes little sense in its social application. In a desert society, your freedom to consume fresh water necessarily conflicts with the freedom of others to consume fresh water. There is thus an inevitable conflict of rights inherent in the very concept of liberty.

When debating on the opposition, you will frequently encounter proposition cases that claim to protect "liberty" or "freedom" as abstract values. One way you can counter this kind of case is to argue that although the case is in favor of liberty, there is no liberty they can really identify as a value, since the very concept of liberty is itself internally inconsistent and thus fundamentally incoherent. Consider also that the way we are made out to be volitional, fundamentally free "subjects" is also the way that our punishment and incarceration is enabled. It is assumed that if we can take responsibility for committing crimes, then we can be punished for those crimes. The conditions of our subjectivity are, arguably, also the conditions that allow our subjugation.

A third kind of value criticism shows the conflict between two incommensurable values. In our discussion of impact comparison, we talk briefly about the relationship between the values of liberty and equality. These two values are often in conflict in society. Ask yourself: Are we free to discriminate in a university or business setting? After all, these institutions are often privately owned. If we are to support liberty unconditionally and at all costs, we would have to also support the right of business owners and university presidents to discriminate against whomever they chose. This practice of discrimination, however, is seldom tolerated in societies that support equality.

In these circumstances where values are in conflict, you need to construct and defend a value hierarchy in which you argue that one value is a dependent, diminished, inferior value compared to others. You might argue that equality is more important than liberty because of the historical exclusion of minority groups and because the failure to provide equal treatment amounts to a denial of citizenship to those victims of discrimination. This denial of citizenship could be said to quash the liberty of those victims of discrimination, thereby justifying your use of a hierarchy of values to de-justify the proposition team's value-based case.

All of these are ways of arguing against the values that inform and structure the proposition team's case. It is important to note that when you argue against the case and its values, you are *not* arguing against the values held by the proposition team members themselves. After all, it is unlikely in the extreme that you even know what values they introduce, let alone which of those values might match up with those present in the arguments they advance. Our point here is to entice you to think more about how values are applied in a policy context. Liberty interests can provide us with any number of freedoms in civil society, but can also allow for child pornography or sex tourism, so they are not necessarily an unqualified good.

You may have already noticed that the distinctions between language and value criticism are less than well-defined. The examples we have used make this pretty clear: the criticism of the discourse of development is also, intrinsically, a criticism of the values embraced by the proposition team's case. Likewise, the criticism from the perspective of non-violence may employ instances of proposition team language to substantiate its contention. You might talk about how the language of "deterrence" is a code for threatening posturing, as in the case of nuclear deterrence planning (which brought us such appealing concepts as "Mutually Assured Destruction" and "winnable nuclear war"). You could also criticize the use of the language of "peace" as assuming the absence of war, when in fact the deployment of troops and the maintenance of a system of martial law are hallmarks of a state of war. Finally (but by no means exhaustively), you might criticize the language of "peacekeepers" as a kind of paradoxical characterization that functions as a convenient cover for disguising missions of war. The distinctions between critiques of language and value are less than clear.

## THINKING

A third kind of criticism relies on critiquing the kind of *thinking* that informs and structures the proposition team's presentation of their case for the motion. This type of criticism can and probably should incorporate elements of value and language critiques in focusing on the systems, patterns, and assumptive habits of thought that make the proposition team's case possible in the first place. This is arguably the most sophisticated kind of criticism one can advance in debate, yet it is also the most loosely defined.

When you critique the thinking of a proposition team's case, you are essentially saying that the *way they are thinking* about their problem, solution, or both is essentially bankrupt or dangerous. This conclusion might be true for any number of reasons. Perhaps their perspective on an issue is outdated, biased, or fundamentally incomplete. Maybe their method for approaching the problem fails to take into account critical factors that would, if accounted for, radically change their approach and its results. Perhaps, because of blinders or other learned socio-cultural incapacities, they misidentify the causes of the problem they attempt to solve. We will walk through a few examples of criticisms of thinking to show how this might work in practice.

You can productively refute the proposition team's case by criticizing the way of thinking that makes it possible in the first place. We are taught in science and social science classes to think of methods of approach as more or less neutral. We just *think* about a problem or a fact set, rather than apply some kind of specific (let alone potentially nefarious) ideology to it. Methods of thinking, particularly in science, have been traditionally understood to be fundamentally neutral. But, as we have already established, the perspective of approach does in fact greatly change what it is that you see when you examine a given fact set or argument. Many theorists have argued that our methods and ways of thinking should be subject to the same kind of criticism as their results.

One public policy issue that pops up often in debates is the problem of population control. The conventional narrative about the world's population problem is fairly predictable and standardized, and goes a little something like this: there are simply too many people on the planet and, therefore, there are not enough resources (food, fuel, drinkable water, television, Pokémon cards, etc.) to go around. This problem is getting worse all the time, as resources (with the help of technology) at best only increase arithmetically, while population increases geometrically (A maitre d's worst nightmare, perhaps: "Malthus, party of 2?" "Malthus, party of 4?" "Malthus, party of 16?"). Population is the problem, according to this way of thinking about the issue. If the number of people continues to grow, then there will not be enough resources to go around and people will starve, or else they will fight each other for control of valuable resources, or else they will starve while they fight each other for control of valuable resources. The proposed solutions therefore attempt to remedy this by doing something about population, usually by dispersing some combination of family planning techniques. This solution is said to deal with the problem very neatly: if there are fewer people, then there will be more even distribution of resources.

Many people have advanced compelling critiques of this way of thinking about the problems of population control and resource allocation. It is said that this conventional narrative fundamentally misunderstands and thereby grossly mischaracterizes the real causes of resource shortages. Think about existing global resource distribution patterns. It is the case that a vanishingly small percentage of the world's population uses a gigantic percentage of the world's available resources. The average European, Japanese, Canadian, or U.S. citizen, for example, uses a vastly larger amount of resources than the average Guatemalan or Somali citizen. It may be the case that there are not enough resources to go around, but it is important to ask *why* this is so. Perhaps there are not enough resources to go around because of fundamentally unjust patterns of allocation and *not* because of population.

If this is the case, we must ask a follow-up question: Why, then, are resource shortages blamed on population excesses rather than on the excessive and unjust consumption patterns practiced by a certain segment of global society? Critics suggest several motives for this shift in blame. It all has to do with assumptions that permeate the way the problem is analyzed. For example, it is not necessarily in the interests of thinkers in industrialized nations to be critical of their own consumption habits. Also, there is a certain naturalization that occurs whereby we assume that existing patterns of distribution and consumption exist, have existed, and are therefore more or less inevitable and not necessarily fair game for substantive questioning. This assumption may mean that the proposed solution – providing for family planning and fewer people – is part of the problem insofar as it not only fails to address the real causes of resources short-ages but also serves as a rationalization for continuing the practices that have created the problem in the first place.

By this point, you can probably see how this critical dispute might play itself out in a debate. The proposition team makes a case for increasing family planning aid. They say that there is a problem: too many people, not enough resources. They say there is a solution: fam-ily planning and population control. They say that their solution addresses the problem: It reduces the aggregate number of people.

Given the arguments made above and others you generate yourself, you could easily construct a critique of the thinking that informs this case. You might say first that the way the proposition team has described the problem is fundamentally flawed. You could admit that there are, in fact, existing and looming resource shortages, but that the proposition team misidentifies the reasons for these shortages. This misidentification means that the proposition team's harms contention is functionally void. You can also argue that as a presentation it is inherently dangerous in that it leads us to disregard the real problems of discriminatory resource distribution and rationalized overconsumption by greedy industrialized nations. Your reinterpretation of the text of this contention shows that it is dubious at best, and at worst is nothing more than a bit of transparent propaganda designed to prop up the ruling class.

You could then proceed to criticize the solution proposed by the proposition team. You might say, as we have said with the "develop-ment" argument, that their misidentification of the harms undercuts any appeal to solvency they might make: "Solve *what*?" "How does family planning solve discriminatory resource maldistribution?" You could also argue that the plan is part of the problem rather than part of the solution insofar as it is complicit in maintaining the existing state of affairs that causes the harm in the first place. Finally, you could argue that the thinking that enables the case is so fundamentally flawed that their solution could make the state of affairs worse rather than better. Using the model we've modified for the other critique arguments, you might frame your initial opposition argument like so:

A. The proposition team's case relies on a particular way of thinking about the population problem that is wrong and dangerous. [explain]

B.  Because we successfully criticize their thinking about resource allocation and population control, we win the debate because:

1)  They fundamentally misunderstand the problem, and thus their statements of harms should be disregarded.

[explain]

2)  This misidentification of the harm undercuts any appeal to solvency that they might make.

[explain]

3)  Their proposal is part of the problem rather than part of the solution.

[explain]

4)  Their proposal will at best be unable to ameliorate the problem. At worst, their proposal will simply make things worse rather than better. Thus, there is a net solvency turn for the opposition.

[explain]

Sound familiar? It should. The format we're using is more or less the same — all you need to do is fill in the details depending on your particular argument and the specifics of their case argumentation. Critiques of thinking, done properly, can nullify every aspect of a proposition team's case.

Your endeavors at criticism need not be so grandiose or far-reaching, however. You can target criticism to just respond to specific parts of the proposition's case, e.g., you might just criticize the reasoning or thinking that enables their solvency contention or one of their advantages. The important thing to remember about critiquing is that it is not an argument type that is set in stone. Critiquing, in essence, remains the same as our initial explanation: uncover a fundamental assumption of your opponents' argument and use that uncovered assumption to win the debate.

## RESPONDING TO CRITIQUING

Disadvantages and counterplans are specific argument types with predictable components. Thus we are able to offer fairly predictable and stable advice to proposition teams regarding a basic method of answering these kinds of arguments. When you are debating against a disadvantage, for example, you will answer the link, the uniqueness, and the impact. When you debate against counterplans, you will try to show that they do not compete or are not net beneficial. Critique arguments are not as stable and predictable as disadvantages and counterplans – they are not an argument type, *per se*, but are instances of a practice of criticism. There are, thus, no generic answers that we can offer for critique arguments, and we advise you to be very suspicious of people who say that they can. (As the old proverb goes: "Beware of debate coaches bearing 'wrong forum' arguments.")

The best advice we can give you is to *think*. Take the opposition's argument seriously and try hard to answer it on its own terms while still using the brunt of your case as leverage against it. Remember: Critique arguments will usually try to take your case and turn it against you.

When you think about the opposition's critique argument, try to consider it in policy terms. Identify the way in which it is consistent with rather than in opposition to the case. Let's say that you make a case for limiting the government's power in a particular area. The opposition criticizes your approach because they say that you focus inappropriately on the state rather than thinking in opposition to a state-centric view of policy problems and their solutions. In this instance, you should argue that the opposition's criticism is fully consistent with your case presentation. You should say that there is no way to eliminate the state other than to have the state eliminate itself.

Many critique arguments are ahistorical. That is, they presume that there's been no thinking about the issue prior to the debate, when it's possible that in fact the proposition team *has* considered the subject of criticism and has decided to introduce the plan *based on* that consideration rather than in spite of it. Let's look at an example. Imagine that you make a case for the proposition by advocating increased environmental protection. Your advantage claim might be that adoption of the plan would save many human lives. In response, the negative team might critique your case's alleged complicity with *anthropocentrism*. Anthropocentrism is a view of the world that is centered on humans. Many environmental advocates, particularly those affiliated with the so-called "deep ecology" movement, criticize a human-centered approach to environmental issues. Anthropocentrism is said to be detrimental to environmental philosophies and policies because it promotes the idea that the nonhuman world is only valuable insofar as it is useful to protect human life, a point of view that is arguably at the center of the current environmental crisis. The opposition team's criticism, therefore, is potentially very serious – they say that you are only protecting the environment to save humans and thereby replicating the central error of previous environmental policy.

What should you say? You should say that you have certainly considered the serious issues of anthropocentrism. You could argue that you do, in fact, favor policies that protect all matter (not just humans, that is). It is, perhaps, just that the particulars of *this* case happen to protect humans. The criticism is therefore ahistorical and has no foundations for its criticism of the ideas associated with the case.

The critique arguments outlined in this chapter are fairly sophisticated. They are also, alas, not necessarily representative of the majority of critique arguments that appear in debates. As a competitive debater, you will hear many substandard disadvantages, counterplans, and critique arguments. To this end, we want to offer a few general things to consider when debating critiques:

It is *vital* that you figure out, *before* you answer the opposition team's critique argument, what the implications of their criticism are for your case. In other words, if they win their criticism, why does it therefore follow that they win the debate? After the opposition's presentation of their argument, if you cannot discern why the critique is a reason to reject your case, you should *ask* using a point of information. This way you will be able to debate the implications of the criticism.

Often the most vulnerable part of any opposition critique argument is its implications. Any assumption of any argument can be criticized, but only the most fundamental assumptions of a proposition case are essential to ensuring the case does not collapse. Remember Jenga? If the opposition team only criticizes non-essential or non-fundamental assumptions of the proposition case, the structure will remain intact and chances are you will still be able to win that your case achieves a clear and decisive advantage over the present system.

Some opposition critique arguments may have only a tangential relationship to your case, and you should point this out. Some teams will make a point of criticizing a broad system of thought – i.e., colonialism, statism, patriarchy, capitalism — of which the proposition case (if they are complicit at all) is only a small part. The opposition team will argue that the case should be rejected because of its complicity with this larger system of thought. In these cases, you should certainly maintain that your case is barely, if at all, related to the overall philosophy being critiqued, and that even if the opposition is right that capitalism (for example) is always bad, it does not therefore follow that the plan is bad. Call this error in reasoning what it is: the fallacy of division. Pressure the opposition team to apply their argument specifically to the mechanics and contentions of your case. Instruct the judge not to vote on the argument until the opposition meets at least this minimal burden of specific proof.

Use your case. We talked about the need to use your case as a weapon to fend off or turn disadvantages earlier. You should also use your case to fend off or otherwise respond to critique arguments. Use your case to demonstrate the comparative advantages that adoption of the plan would accrue. Challenge the opposition team to show that the consequences of adopting the plan would be worse than the harms that would be redressed. Use empirical examples of harms and solvency to show that the way you're thinking about the world is, in fact, sound – the opposition team's loudest protestations about social theory aside.

Above all, don't panic. Read up on social theory and various perspectives on national and international issues. Be ready to debate about such things as political realism, feminist international relations theory, critical race theory, queer theory, anarchism, post-colonialism, socialism, and the critiques of globalization. Be conscious of the perspective you employ when you design your case and be ready to defend it as well as its most fundamental assumptions. Just as you design your case to preemptively answer common disadvantages and counterplans, so too should you design your case to preemptively answer common critique arguments. Anticipation is one of the hallmarks of successful debaters on both sides of a proposition and of any experience level.

# CHAPTER 10

# PARLIAMENTARY
# POINTS

## INTRODUCTION

P arliamentary points–points of information, order and privilege-
–distinguish parliamentary debating from other forms of inter-
scholastic and intercollegiate debating. In parliamentary
debates, a debater may make a point while another person is speaking.
The "interruption" of a speech by a parliamentary point, delivered
either to the speaker holding the floor or the judge, is unusual in contest debating. In other debating formats, speaking opportunities are
limited, by rule or convention, to presentations that do not interrupt
debaters during the presentation of their speeches.

Parliamentary points provide opportunities for interactive debating. Points of information, which are available in most parliamentary
debate formats throughout the world, create a space for the debaters to
challenge arguments or ask questions of a speaker. Points of order or
privilege, which are used in several parliamentary formats, particularly in North America, allow debaters, in collaboration with a ruling

from the judge of a debate or the designated speaker of the house, to establish the rules for the introduction or removal of arguments from the debate.

Points of personal privilege and points of order are infrequently introduced in a debate, even in the parliamentary formats authorizing their use. Points of information are a regular part of most parliamentary debates and are an important strategic tool for competitors.

## POINTS OF INFORMATION

A point of information (a. k. a., "POI," pronounced as P-O-I) is a brief statement or a question to an argument claim, example or other point that is being made by a speaker. The point must be concisely made–a debater is typically given 15 seconds to successfully conclude a point. A point of information, unlike the point of order or personal privilege, is directed to the person speaking rather than to the judge or designated Speaker of the House.

In the American parliamentary debate format, points of information are permitted in the first four speeches–the constructive speeches also popularly known as the Prime Minister Constructive, Lead Opposition Constructive, Member of Government Constructive and Member of Opposition Constructive. Points of information are not permitted in either rebuttal speech. In addition, parliamentary points are not permitted during "protected time," the first minute or the last minute of a speech that gives the speaker an opportunity to introduce and conclude a speech without distraction or interruption.

The timekeeper, often the same person serving as the judge of the debate, a designated Speaker of the House or a person selected as timekeeper, should signal that the opening minute of a constructive speech has been completed, typically using a knock on the table, clap of the hands or other noisemaking but not attention-getting device at the end of the first minute and at the beginning of the last minute of each constructive speech. Points of information are permitted only between these two signals. In the British parliamentary debate format, points of information are permitted during any of the speeches, but there is a minute of "protected time" at the beginning and conclusion of each speech as in the American format.

Points of information are requests for the speaker holding the floor to yield time for a statement or question from the opposing side. For this reason, the time for a point of information counts against the allotted time for the speaker holding the floor. For example, if a speaker is delivering a seven-minute speech and a person on the opposing side requests a point of information at the first opportunity (one minute after the beginning of the speech or, in other terms, with six minutes of the speech remaining) and the point is accepted, the time will continue to run. If the point is made in 15 seconds and the speaker replies to the point for 15 seconds for a total of 30 seconds committed to the point of information ("but I participate in debate because I thought there would be no math"), the speaker holding the floor will have five minutes and thirty seconds remaining in her speech.

There are a number of local conventions and subtle differences regarding the presentation of a point of information. To make a point of information, in a conventional or generally acceptable form, you rise and face the person speaking, indicating an intention to speak by signaling with a gesture, typically an extended hand, or by offering a verbal sign, (saying, for example, "Point of information," "Information," or "On that point.") The person speaking holds the floor during the time of her or his speech. The speaker may take the point of information or refuse the request for a point. The speaker might quickly acknowledge and agree to take a point (for example, "I'll take the point," or more simply, "Yes.").

If the speaker accepts your point of information, you make your point and sit down. Additional or "follow-on" statements or questions by the debater making a point are out of order. After all, the speaker only recognizes you for a single and brief point of information, not for a sustained commentary, detailed interrogation, or multi-part question. On the occasions in which a speaker accepts an informational point, the speaker should carefully listen to the point and make a decision to answer it or ignore it (more on strategic replies to points of information below).

A speaker should be patient during the presentation of a point of information. Although points of information ought to be brief, a 15-second point of information may seem like a significant disruption to a speaker who has much to say and little officially permitted speaking time for it. In other words, the recipient of a point of information is often, unsurprisingly, impatient with an opponent's presentation of a point. To the interrupted speaker, it always seems to be the case that the amount of time taken to make a point greatly exceeds the 15 seconds allowed by rule or convention for an informational point.

This "crisis of temporality" reigns in parliamentary debating contests, despite the fact that it is surely rare for a point of information to last for a full 15 seconds, let alone exceed that time. Interruptions of a debater's point by the person to whom the point is addressed are as unwelcome as the prolonged point. (A recommendation: Parliamentary debaters might experiment to better understand the officially or socially approved amount of time for a person on an opposing team to make a point of information. For example, you might pinch yourself, or otherwise perform a painful but non-invasive or permanently scarring quasi-medical procedure, for a timed 15-second period. Or, as a G. Gordon Liddy-like thought experiment, you might imagine holding your hand over a candle flame for the same fifteen-second period. It would be difficult to believe that any debater engaged in such experiments would believe that fifteen seconds constituted a brief or insignificant time.)

The speaker might also refuse to take a point of information. A speaker might dismiss points of information with a brief phrase (e.g., "Not at this time" or "No, thank you.") In some locales or parliamentary debating formats, a more curt or brusque dismissal is possible. A speaker might reject a point of information with a quickly and strongly expressed "No" or may not even respond orally, but alternatively gesture with a downward wave of her or his hand to indicate that a debater rising for a point of information should sit down. If the person speaking declines to accept the point of information, you must sit down immediately.

Points of information are directed to the opposing team in a debate. "Friendly" questions, supportive comments, and other asides or prospective points to one's partner or, in the British format, to another team arguing the same side of a motion, are not permitted. Each speaker in the debate should both make and accept points of information. If you fail to make any points, it will seem that you are incapable of challenging the legitimacy of the ideas of your opponent. Additionally, in formats with six or eight competitors, you might fail to engage the majority of the participants or the more salient ideas in the discussion. In other words, you might not appear to be actively engaged in the debate.

If you decline to accept any points of information it may appear to the judge and the audience that you fear the opponents or their arguments. On the other hand, if you accept too many points of information, you might appear to lose control of your speech. The distraction and continuous interruption might undermine the many good arguments you might want and need to present to sustain your team's position in a debate. As the English-Speaking Union's guidebook explains: "Offering points of information, even if they are not accepted, shows that you are active and interested in the debate. Accepting them when offered shows that you are confident of your arguments and prepared to defend them. A team that does neither of these is not debating."

## STRATEGIC USES OF POINTS OF INFORMATION

Points of information are a powerful tool for the effective debater. They direct the judge's attention to the more germane issues of the debate. They provide opportunities for dynamic and direct clash with opponents. Informational points are opportunities for displays of wit, humor, and style.

### MAKING STRATEGIC POINTS OF INFORMATION

STATEMENTS OR QUESTIONS? Parliamentary points may be statements or questions. In much of the world, debaters routinely use statements or questions as points of information, choosing either a declarative or interrogatory form, as the circumstance requires. In the USA, the National Parliamentary Debate Association has codified the use of informational points as statements or questions:

A debater may request a point of information—either verbally of by rising—at any time after the first minute and before the last minute of any constructive speeches. The debater holding the floor has the discretion to accept or refuse a point of information. If accepted, the debater requesting the point of information has a maximum of 15 seconds to <u>make a statement or ask a question</u>. The speaking time of the debater with the floor continues during the point of information.

A statement is a preferred form of parliamentary point, if you can use either a statement or a question to make a point. A declarative claim reveals command of the facts and argument debate. A question more likely indicates your lack of knowledge about one or more issues and appears as a request of the speaker holding the floor for information. A question, therefore, places the person making a point in an inferior and unfavorable position relative to the person holding the floor, and exerts a powerful persuasive influence on judges and audiences alike about which side is winning.

Too many debaters use a somewhat tortured method of converting statements to questions for the purpose of making a point of information. For example, a debater might make the following claim:

> Speaker: "The application of the death penalty is an effective deterrent to capital crimes. Research for decades has consistently shown that states with capital punishment have lower murder rates."

You might choose to reply with a statement:

> Respondent: "On that point. [The point of information is accepted by the speaker holding the floor] That same research indicates that states that actually use the death penalty have growing rates of capital crimes and that states with an unused death penalty have decreasing murder rates."

This point of information challenges the factual claims of the speaker, entirely undermining the legitimacy of the argument claim that the death penalty deters crime. In fact, it is a proof of the opposite position, namely, that the application of the death penalty might actually increase the safety risk to the public.

You could also "convert" the authority of this declarative point of information and press forward with the following interrogatory:

Respondent: "On that point. [The point of information is accepted by the speaker holding the floor] Isn't it true that states that actually use the death penalty have growing rates of capital crimes and that states with an unused death penalty have decreasing murder rates?"

The latter question simply does not confront the speaker's facts in the same way as the former point of information. The question here seems to indicate that the respondent is unsure of the facts and requires information from an opponent. The speaker is called to reiterate or otherwise confirm a portion of her speech. The answer to this question is tediously obvious to anyone who has observed even a few parliamentary debates. The predictable answer to the respondent's question:

Speaker: "Of course that isn't true. As I noted, the opposite is the case."

The transformation of powerful statement to weak question has a number of negative consequences for the debater making the point. In this circumstance, it fails to undermine the legitimacy of the speaker's argument claim about the deterrent effect of the death penalty. In fact, it reinforces the point made by the speaker, that is, that the death penalty deters murder, a fact supported by years of social science research. The speaker is able to support her own claim in a way that no judge would ever miss. It is initially noted in her speech and subsequently supported during a point of information.

In addition, the question increases the difficulty for the opposing side to effectively refute the argument claim at a later point in the debate. The respondent has seemingly undermined her own credibility—the question reveals a lack of knowledge about the deterrence issue. It appears to indicate that the respondent is not sure whether the death penalty is an effective deterrent to capital crimes. The question appears to indicate that the respondent might be searching for a weakness in the speaker's case but has been unable to find one.

It would be difficult to establish an equally credible argument regarding your knowledge of the deterrent effect of capital punishment after asking a question indicating you might not be sure of the requisite facts. In a debate, the credibility of the speaker is essential to an understanding of the factual material. In this sample, an opposing team's subsequent argument about the deterrent effect of the death penalty would have little leverage against not one, but two, authoritative claims by the speaker. And one of those authoritative claims would have been heard during an interactive portion of the debate– one of the infrequent opportunities for the debaters to "square off" and confront each other about the debate's facts. In this circumstance, a judge would be hard-pressed to agree with the respondent.

## APPLICATIONS FOR POINTS OF INFORMATION

There are five primary purposes for points of information. Points may be used to understand the issues presented by an opposing side, clarify the core issues of the debate, evaluate factual material, advance your own arguments and undermine your opponent's arguments.

SEEKING UNDERSTANDING. A point of information can be used for understanding. In a debate, it is necessary to appreciate the arguments from the opposing side. It is not possible to make tactical decisions regarding argument selection, speech organization, and refutation without first identifying the key issues of the debate, including the arguments initiated by opponents. It is not possible to answer arguments with which you are unfamiliar or uncertain. Points of information are available to establish a mutually shared knowledge base for informed debating.

Informational points may be used to examine a motion's interpretation, the scope of a proposition plan or opposition counterplan or counterposition, the nature of argument and debate theory, agency operations, the technical details of products, services and policies, and more. Examples for each of these follow:

• "The notion for the debate is 'Bury it.' Could you explain how the recovery of DNA from exhumed corpses supports the motion?"

- "Your plan establishes that the United Nations ought to use peace-keeping forces to more effectively implement the requirements of the Universal Declaration of Human Rights. Would you employ military forces for every violation of human rights, regardless of location, degree of the problem or the prior intervention of other peacekeeping forces?"

- "Please describe, in a known human language, what it is you mean by the phrase 'dispositional intrinsicness counter-permutation?'"

- "The World Health Organization is responsible for international smallpox eradication. What is the WHO's position on eradication of the smallpox virus at remaining sites and how is it carrying out that policy?"

- "I understand your claim that a 'suture,' as explained from the synchronic gaps in a signifying chain, might lead to narrative dismemberment. What I don't understand is your subsequent claim that the suture effect on a hypertextual subject in the international binding of the docuverse might lead to diachronic discourse closure or link function fragmentations. Please explain the latter."

Points of information may additionally clarify or simplify the issues of a debate. Debates are not occasions for disagreeable people to exchange unpleasantries for an hour, in order to temporarily protect family, friends, colleagues and neighbors from their acute social dysfunction, personal insecurities and pathologies. Debates involve elements of disagreement but they surely include areas of agreement as well.

ESTABLISHING AGREEMENT. The clever debater (you) will want to successfully identify issues of agreement in a debate. This tactic can reveal the inadequacies in an opponent's argument (the argument may be based on faux difference, a near-classic argument fallacy). It might also refocus the salient issues of difference in the respective arguments of the debating teams, enabling the judge to better understand the arguments that support the (potentially) winning side. It is in the interest of each participant to mark points of agreement.

In a debate on the motion, "This House prefers liberty to equality," a generalist claim by the opening proposition speaker might profoundly influence the outcome of the debate if not carefully checked by an opposing debater with a point of information regarding agreement. "Liberty" is hardly a simple concept with a singular understanding. There are many conceptions of liberty, some at odds with each other.

The opening proposition speaker might not clearly delineate the various understandings of "liberty" (as if such a condition could be met in a seven-minute speech without divine intervention). Although this might be a fine strategy for the proposition team (providing considerable argument room to maneuver in their speeches, manipulating the text of the debate for their advantage, as they cleverly adapt their arguments in the later speeches to account for the parries and thrusts of even a talented opponent), it is clearly against the interests of the opposition team to play the same game.

The opposition team must do something to focus the discussion on a limited set of ideas that might be successfully refuted in the allotted time. Agreement – established with a point of information – may be the solution. If the opening speaker seems to support a unifying example of liberty interests throughout her performance (say, for example, the independence of the individual citizen from state interference), it may be to your advantage, as a representative of the opposing team in the debate, to seek agreement with that expressed perspective of liberty and "seal the deal" with a convincingly agreeable point of information.

• "Point of information. [The point of information is accepted by the speaker holding the floor] "Can we agree that liberty, in this debate, should be exclusively understood as the independence of the individual from control, direction, or manipulation by the state?"

Agreement by the parties in the debate is more likely to "fix" the argument positions of the teams. In other words, it is unlikely that a team will succeed with a "bait-and-switch" tactic, i.e., offer an abstract initial position, receive the opposing side's argumentation on the point, then shift the discussion to a new and strategically modified argument. This tactic is commonly known as a "shift" in a debate and, despite the consternation shifting argumentation causes its victims, it remains a common tactic. Agreement establishes a mutually agreed basis for debating. The clarification with a point of information makes this agreement apparent to your debate judge.

Such an agreement, confirmed by a point of information, compels attention to a particular set of issues in the debate, namely those "other" arguments that remain in dispute (those ideas about which there remains disagreement). Since neither side can make effective claims influencing the outcome of the debate with argument points that may also be claimed by an opposing team, debaters must inevitably address the germane issues about which they disagree. Any argument supported by more than one team fails to create a substantive clash between the sides of a motion that might give one of the teams a superior position in the debate (see section on uniqueness in disadvantages). Points of information that clarify issues of agreement therefore remove issues from a judge's consideration so that the debaters might concentrate on more important and decisive matters.

EVALUATING FACTS. Interesting claims about history, government, economics, politics and culture are often introduced in parliamentary debates:

- "There are fifty nations in NATO."
- "It is not possible to have unemployment and inflation at the same time."
- "The most underdeveloped European country is Hawaii."
- "The United Nations was established in 1850, at the conclusion of the First World War."

The listed claims are, quite obviously, inaccurate. (If they are not inaccurate to you, perhaps you were the person uttering one of these lines in a recent debate. You should now know that you were, indeed, factually incorrect.)

There are other, less obvious, factual inaccuracies in many debates. Many debaters claim to represent the factual world (at least the non-quantum one) with a knowledge base that includes a healthy dose of misinformation, half-truths, gossip, rumors, innuendo, hearsay, official government or corporate propaganda, quasi-royal decrees, slander, puffery, eyewitness accounts, hyperbolic realities, voodoo simulacra, carnie wisdom (not to be confused with Carnie Wilson), folk psychology, reporting from the Fox News Corporation, psychic hotline notations, tarot pronouncements or a personal belief system. On some occasions, there are even false claims in debate topics. (Adonis is the god of vegetation, not love!)

Points of information are a superb opportunity to examine the "information" of a debate. You might question the veracity of opponent's fact-sets, reconsider the historical record or analyze the relevance or import of noted examples and exceptions.

ADVANCING YOUR OWN ARGUMENT. A successful debater might be able to advance her own argument during points of information with a little bit of help from her friends. Advancement is best accomplished with a cooperative point, i.e., one that avoids the confrontational, strident, skeptical or accusatory tone often accompanying points of information in the over-heated, electrically charged adversarial crock-pot that is modern parliamentary debate.

As most interrogators are aware, an unfriendly question is easily anticipated and often resisted by witnesses. Many points of information are decidedly unfriendly:

- "Point of information. [The point of information is accepted by the speaker holding the floor] You, madam, are deceiving the good ladies and gentlemen assembled, not to mention the judging panel. As sure as I have an active brain wave, there are fifty nations in NATO."
- "On that point. [The point of information is accepted by the speaker holding the floor] I knew Jack Kennedy. I worked with Jack Kennedy. And you, sir, are no Jack Kennedy."
- "On your reinterpretation of Mein Kampf. [The point of information is accepted by the speaker holding the floor] Will you continue to persist in this national socialist vision, or are there other ideas that you will advance in the debate?"

Many other debaters take a contrary and directly opposite stance to the argument points presented by a speaker, with little meaningful consequence for the individual advancing the point of information. This confrontational stance essentially leaves the person making the point in the same position as before their 15-second utterance. The point does not matter at all, at least as substantive commentary:

> Respondent: "Point of information. [The point of information is accepted by the speaker holding the floor] You claimed that increased prosecution of drug offenses will reduce drug use. That is not the case, nor has it ever been true."
>
> Speaker: "A new regime of criminal penalties will indeed work. And here are the reasons as to why..."

A better strategy might be a "leading" statement or question, designed to encourage your opponent to speak at length on an issue, rather than have your adversary simply resist the point. (You can catch more with a pinch of sugar than a plague of flies, or something like that. It is in the Old Testament somewhere, or so it is rumored, gossiped, or told by carnies and psychics.)

To advance a point of information, which might advance your argument in the debate, you should appropriately anticipate the issues that will be presented. Argument anticipation is a key to successful debating. Anticipation is important in all competitive contests – athletics, board games such as chess and backgammon, card games, and other academic competitions (Model United Nations, academic decathlon, public speaking contests, etc.).

Your success in competitive contests presumes that you will identify the potential moves that an opponent might make and effect counters to those moves. In an athletic contest, for example, one might anticipate a physical move by an opponent and use a feint or misdirection to avoid her. In a board game, such as chess, victory is typically predicated on a player's ability to anticipate the direction of play eight, nine, ten or more moves in advance. In debates, consistent success requires anticipation of the issues that will be argued in the contest. Effective debaters should "know," with some degree of confidence, many of the issues that will be introduced in a debate before the opening speech.

How can a debater anticipate opponents' issues and, subsequently, their own replies to those arguments? It is a relatively simple matter. You should initially consider the arguments that you will introduce in the debate. Then imagine the manner in which your opponent will respond to each of your arguments. Ask yourself the following question: "What will my opponent say when I make this argument in the debate?" The answers to this question will successfully reveal many of your opponents' arguments.

Once you have identified the likely rejoinders to your arguments in the debate, it is then necessary to consider the moves you will make to answer those claims. At this point, ask yourself the following question: "What will I say when they present their answers to my first arguments?" This, of course, will provide the appropriate arguments to address the replies to your initial argument set. It is then possible to repeat these two relatively modest, yet vitally important questions to account for all the speeches of a debate.

In this way, a debate can be "scripted" before it starts. Scripting does not mean the elimination, or even the serious reduction, of extemporaneous debating. After all, it is extraordinarily rare to anticipate all of your opponents' arguments. Opponents, although too often despised or feared, are hardly that transparent. A number of unanticipated issues will surely enter the overwhelming majority of your debates. At the same time, "scripting" or argument anticipation abets the debater who is able to address the concerns of the opponent (and the judge) before the debate starts.

Advancing an argument through a point of information relies on argument anticipation. In a debate, you will successfully anticipate some of your opponents' arguments and prepare your answers to them. You would like to make sure that you are able to introduce your arguments with necessary legitimacy and credibility.

You should craft a point of information, which will "enable" your opponent. In other words, your point will appear to be friendly, inviting your opponent to respond. The point will get your opponent to speak. In fact, your opponent will not just speak to the point – your opponent will "embrace" the properly worded friendly point. Like many relationships, however, there is something "funny" about the friend.

The point of information, as an example of advancing your own argument, bonds the point to the speaker in the speaker's own words. It is a dysfunctional connection, to be sure, but one created and nurtured by your opponent. For the speaker receiving the point, there is no escape from her newly announced co-dependent relationship and, like many relationships with a hint of dysfunction, it will not take long (just until your next speech) to reveal to those assembled that there is a serious and lurking problem.

In the following example, we will presume that the proposition team has presented a case advocating that the federal government of the USA should significantly expand its school breakfast and lunch program, providing nutrition supplements to needy children:

Respondent: "Point of information. [The point of information is accepted by the speaker holding the floor] But the federal school breakfast and lunch program doesn't provide a comprehensive diet. It doesn't even include dairy, does it?"
Speaker: "Yes, it does include dairy. It provides all the necessary components of a daily nutritional supplement."

In this example, you, as respondent to a speaker holding the floor, have introduced a point of information that has encouraged the speaker to say precisely what is needed to advance your arguments indicating that:

1. Dairy products exacerbate the incidence of childhood asthma;
2. The inclusion of dairy products reduces immunity to bacterial infections. As dairy farmers add antibiotics to livestock feed to protect their herds, the medication is passed, through the consumption of dairy products, to consumers and the addition both generates antibiotic-resistant strains of germs and increases the tolerance of the immune system to particular drugs, reducing antibiotic's effectiveness; and
3. Many children, particularly those of African or Asian descent, are lactose intolerant. A "dairied" diet is insufficiently culturally sensitive, unhealthy and inedible for many of the

children for whom the federal school breakfast and lunch program is designed.

These issues, anticipated before the debate, are secured with a point of information. The proposition speaker, in reply to the point of information, has established a clear relationship between the plan of action in the opening speech that endorses a significant increase in the federal school breakfast and lunch program, and a diet that includes dairy product. This relationship, or "link," is more than enough to serve as a foundation for the opposition arguments listed here, as well as many more. The opposition is now in a superior position to advance its own interests in the debate because a point of information encouraged the opposing side to speak on an issue, albeit in a predictable way.

UNDERMINING YOUR OPPONENT'S ARGUMENT. We will preface this section on applications of points of information in order to note that this last task, undermining your opponent's arguments, is the most challenging of all. Points of information are different from the Spanish Inquisition or Salem Witch Trials. For example: no dunking. The opposing side must have the approval of the speaker holding the floor to make a point. Only one point may be made – there are no opportunities for a series of questions or an open forum. The speaker may choose to answer the point or might dismiss the issue from the other side entirely. In addition, speakers are notoriously skeptical of debaters making points of information and are ready to resist any unexpected (even well-anticipated) point. In other words, the person making a point of information is not in a strategic position to elicit a confession, admission or disclosure from the speaker. It is highly unlikely that a person making a point will be able to rhetorically disrobe a speaker.

There are, however, some opportunities to effectively counter the claims of the speaker. These include challenges to the logical construction of arguments, the presentation of counterexamples or the critical examination of fact sets.

A challenge to the logical construction of an argument (an investigation of causality or the revelation of an argument fallacy, for example) might undermine the extant argument point by the speaker. In a debate on the need for development assistance in the form of capital development projects in the Sudan to spur economic growth and relieve human misery, the opposing side might offer the following point:

> Respondent: "On the Sudan. [The point of information is accepted by the speaker holding the floor] The proximate cause of human misery in the Sudan is a multi-year drought and a civil war between Christian and Muslim factions. Development assistance, particularly capital intensive projects, will do nothing to forestall hunger and disease from lack of potable water. These new projects will only increase the violence of the civil war, as participants struggle for the few incoming dollars."

Using points of information to undermine an opponent's argument is a worthy tactic, but a difficult one to accomplish in serious debates.

## AVOIDING THE "RULE OF THREE"

This is a misnomer. There is no "Rule of Three." Some debate coaches teach as if such a rule exists. It does not. Let us clarify: In parliamentary debate, there is no "Rule of Three." No such rule. Number of "Rules of Three" in parliamentary debating – zero. For those readers still uncertain about this issue, we will conclude with the following, "THERE IS NO RULE OF THREE."

Why, then, is it important to discuss a non-existent rule? Perhaps in a wistful manner that echoes belief in Oz or Atlantis, some debate coaches do believe the rule exists. So do a number of judges. Unfortunately, some debaters perpetuate the myth of its existence. It is, therefore, important to understand what it is and how one might avoid it.

Some debaters, coaches, and judges, primarily but not exclusively in the USA, believe that a speaker holding the floor is obliged to accept three, but no more than three, points of information. Some of them extend the faux rule in this way: They believe that a team may attempt only three points of information during speeches. Neither is accurate.

ART, ARGUMENT AND ADVOCACY

Debate teams may attempt any number of points of information during the non-protected time of opponents' speeches (after the first minute of the speech and before the last minute of the speech). You are not limited in any way in the number of attempts. No parliamentary debate community places a restriction on informational attempts because the speaker holds the floor and must approve any points of information. The speaker may accept or refuse points in a strategic manner during her presentation. The speaker controls the introduction of points of information from opponents and does not need the institutional protection of a formal rule.

In practice, debaters in the USA train their judges and coaches in the "Rule of Three." Debaters are likely to reply to points of information this way:

- "I will take your first question."
- "I will take your second question."
- "I will take your third and final question."

This overly rehearsed and mechanically delivered set of responses offers poor instruction to inexperienced judges. To begin, the listed replies presume that points of information are interrogatories. Wrong. As discussed above, points of information may be either statements or questions (and clever debaters would, for noted reasons, prefer the point of information as a statement.)

This approach also makes the error that the speaker holding the floor controls the number of attempts that might be made by the opposing side. Although the speaker is able to accept or refuse points, he or she is not authorized to dictate the number of attempts made by another team. The opposing side may, if desired, continue to make attempts. The fact that a speaker holding the floor might decide to preemptively refuse later points during her speech does not mean that there will be no meaningful need for informational points. The speaker might present confusing arguments, inaccurate facts or technical details of a product or public policy. Any of these circumstances or many additional issues of controversy and concern could prompt an attempt by an opposing team.

Too often, points of information are poorly presented. The statements or questions meekly quibble with the argument claims and evidence of a speaker. In these circumstances, it is in the interest of the speaker to accept more than three points because it reveals her superior argument ability or demonstrates her model debating skills. It does not make sense to arbitrarily limit the number of points of information to "three," when taking more points will help improve the odds of winning or gaining favor with the judge for higher individual marks.

In parliamentary debating, particularly regarding points of information, "three" is definitely not a magic number. Debaters should be free to raise points and accept or refuse them at will. Practice and debate convention might suggest that taking three points during a speech is good form but this is in no way an obligation of any debate institution or format.

## MANNER DURING POINTS OF INFORMATION

ATTITUDE. Debaters should present information in a clear, relatively dispassionate manner during points of information. This recommendation applies equally to the person making the point and the speaker holding the floor. Debates are, by nature, adversarial. Competition, particularly at renowned invitational or intervarsity tournaments, including national or world championships, potentially increases participants' anxiety and tension between teams. Points of information, because they constitute an interactive portion of the debate, are an occasion for desperate, hostile, or confrontational stances that might spill over into open conflict. Debaters must keep in mind that points of information are not an opportunity to vent frustration on the opposing side. Rather, they are an occasion for further communication with the judge(s).

A debate judge is likely to hold both parties (the person making the point of information and the speaker holding the floor) responsible for the breakdown of effective communications during points of information. It is unwise to antagonize the judge with unreasonable, petty, immature, mean, or small-minded behavior. An appropriate understanding of the role of communication in debate ought to remedy judges' behavior.

As in any setting, communication in debates is effective when the message is delivered to the appropriate decision-maker. In the overwhelming majority of debates, the decision-maker is a single judge or a panel of several judges. There are exceptions, including decisions by a vote of the full audience assembled in a debating chamber, combination of experienced or officially–selected judges or an internet or other broadcast audience. In other circumstances, the audience may be the actual decision-maker, even if there is a panel of judges with the responsibility to adjudicate the debate. Debaters should make every effort to provide information to the decision-makers and should largely ignore the effectiveness of their communication with their opposing side. This is not the same as the old adage "Never argue with an idiot." Your opponents might be quite respectful, honorable and intelligent. It is simply the case that the opposing side is not in a position to issue the final verdict on the merits of your arguments in the debate and you would not want them to do so even if they could. It will be a conflict of interest.

It will undoubtedly be the case that there is little satisfaction in speaking with an opposing side in a debate. For one thing, they **oppose** you. Your appeals to their rationality, humanity or general decency are likely to fall on deaf ears. They are extraordinarily unlikely to concede the debate to you, even in dire circumstances for them. It is inevitably the case that any communicative appeal to the opposing side will be less than gratifying.

Of course, direct communication with the opposing side may unleash the dogs of war. Little good can come of interpersonal conflict with other debaters. You should be careful to avoid any openings for this unpleasantness.

Instead you should focus attention on the person or persons actually making a decision on the outcome of the debate – the debate judge. The presentation of a point of information, although directed to a speaker holding the floor, is an opportunity for supplemental information to the judge. The superior debater should employ points of information that will use (in this case, exploit, besmirch, manipulate or make dirty) the other side, treating them as foil, patsy, dupe, or pawn as you make effective efforts to communicate with the judge (examples follow later in the chapter). The suggested approach – information to the judge rather than to the speaker holding the floor – is more likely to reduce hostile or impotent communication during attempted points.

GESTICULATION. Local conventions will determine the forms for the presentation of a point of information. These forms include, but are not limited to, the following. A person attempting a point of order will:

- rise.
- rise and say "Point of information."
- rise and extend an open hand.
- rise and extend an open hand and say "Point of information."
- rise and extend one open hand, while placing the other hand on her head.
- rise and extend one open hand, while placing the other hand on her head and say "Point of information."
- rise and extend one open hand, while placing the other hand on her head and say "Point of information." At the same time, the debater must position either foot on the shoulder of her partner, strike a match and touch her belt buckle not once, not twice, but thrice. Rumor has it that a pony is involved somehow.

Unnecessary, inappropriate or anachronistic gestures can confound an audience. Several of these forms are at odds with local cultural practice and history. Several others might fit a particular space, time or zoo facility but are poor intercultural models. (The latter examples constitute obscene or offensive gestures in some regions the world. Other gestures, for example, the less and less popular maneuver involving placing a hand on the hand to hold in place an invisible powdered wig, seem out-of date and out-of-place. Okay, okay, we get it. You are a little teapot.)

The selection of the form of presentation of a point of information is an appropriate escalatory tactic for those occasions when you want or need to make a point and the speaker holding the floor continues to refuse your attempts. The initial attempt of an informational point ought to be minimalist – the person making the point should rise and make no other verbal or physical moves. If the point is refused, the second attempt should be more demonstrative, e.g., the person making the point should rise, saying "Point of information" in a clear, loud but measured tone. If the second attempt is also refused, the third attempt might add an extended open hand, a gesture clearly asking, perhaps imploring, the speaker to recognize you.

These verbal and physical escalations make it apparent to the judge that the speaker is ignoring your attempts at making a point. The judge will not think less of your performance if she identifies that the failure to make a point is at the speaker's exercised discretion and not because your attempts failed. The judge may also hold it against the speaker for her refusal to engage you.

If your first attempt in the debate throws in every statement and gesture in the known POI world – hands outstretched and on head with an additional verbal cue that you are delivering a "point of information," (the latter comment evidently announced to provide a contrast with the other moments during opponents' speeches when you rise to strike an awkward or eccentric pose) you have eliminated your ability to engage in escalatory tactics (as fatal in parliamentary debating as it is in high-stakes international negotiations or nuclear deterrence posturing). Save the ballet for those times during opposing side speeches when a point of information **must** be made.

**HUMOR AND HECKLING.** Yes, by all means, do it. But be careful. When required, negotiate the issue with judges before competition or a round of debate begins. All judges admire wit, cleverness and humor. Many prefer heckling. Some, however, believe heckling is boorish, crude and disruptive. Please discuss the issue of heckling during points of information with judges, area coaches, and fellow debaters if you are unfamiliar with the local debate conventions or the judges.

There are different heckles that you might successfully employ during points of information. Let's face it. Speakers holding the floor are, at best, reluctant witnesses. They have decidedly pained or unfavorable reactions to most points of information. They do not want disruptions during their all-too-important arguments and they certainly do not want successful challenges to their analytical reasoning or factual claims.

There is an even more serious problem for the successful competitor. Parliamentary debate is a team event. There are as few as two and as many as four teams in the overwhelming majority of the world's parliamentary debating contests. If your opponents detect that you are a superior debater to your partner or the members of another opposing team, and that you display a flair for the incisive and witty remark, it is likely that you will have few of your attempts at informational points accepted. More likely that your partner (not a dullard but not as brilliant a competitor as you) or, in the British format, a representative of the other team on your side of the motion, will make successful attempts. The other debaters will make an effort to "freeze–out" the talented debater, answering questions or responding to statements from the weaker participants (debate is about looking good relative to opponents, after all). Heckling the speaker, not in lieu of but in conjunction with attempts at points of information might be the only option for you.

Heckling of this type takes the form of a request for a point of information. Typically, debaters providing a verbal cue for their point of information will offer one of two popular expressions:

- "Point of information."
or
- "On that point."

It is possible to vary the language of the attempt, subtly including an argument in a brief statement, that is, three- or four- word verbal announcement of the point. A classic heckle. You might say the following in an attempt to make a point regarding your criticism of the factual foundation of an opponent's argument:

- "Point of reality."

Perhaps you are tired of your opponents' business-as-usual, conventional restatements of government decrees and pronouncements as the final word in public policy. It is possible to attempt a point of information with the following:

- "On that official propaganda."

**227**

Likewise, you might begin a point after listening to an opponent prattle on about the dangers of unsupervised artists or treacherous journalists:

• "On your impression of General Pinochet."

In these cases, it does not matter if the speaker holding the floor accepts or refuses the point. If the speaker accepts your point, you will make it. If the speaker refuses the point, however, the damage is still done. You have made an argument about the credibility of the information or the speaker and the judge will take that claim into consideration (perhaps in a subconscious or unconscious way, if not an obvious one). This tactic allows a debater to make a point even in those circumstances when the point of information is refused.

Another effective strategy for heckling during points is to heckle the reply from the speaker holding the floor to your point. To briefly review, the speaker will only recognize you for a single point. No commentary. No multi part questions. No follow-up questions or cross-examination. Certainly, no dialogue. How, then, is it possible to have the final word on the point, avoiding the ever-so-cute replies from speakers as they signal that they are never troubled by any issue brought to them during a point of information ("I am glad you asked that question." "There you go again." "Oh, you could not be more wrong.")?

The short answer: a brief heckle as they conclude their reply to a point of information. It might be executed in this manner:

On the motion "This House would use force to make peace," an opening speaker for the proposition might argue for military intervention by the United States of America to promote nation-building and deter military aggression.

> Respondent: "On that point. [The point of information is accepted by the speaker holding the floor] The United States of America should never engage in military intervention. It produces local and regional violence and undermines stability. The experience in Vietnam proves it."
>
> Speaker: "If there is a clearly stated military mission in collaboration with international support, as well as nation-building and

humanitarian aid, intervention can work. The Marshall Plan, which included military forces to provide security and stability in Western Europe at the conclusion of the Second World War, combined with development and humanitarian assistance, promoted a progressive and independent Europe."

Respondent: [as she seats herself] "Same inputs, different results, in Somalia."

This tactic may prove to be a particularly effective one. It offers an effective reply to the point made by the speaker holding the floor. (It advances clash and an additional example in the debate). But it does so much more.

In the typical case, the opposing side makes a point of information and the speaker holding the floor offers a reply. If the speaker is has the requisite intellectual dexterity of the substantial majority of parliamentary debaters, the point is effectively countered. This is not a neutral position. Due to the linear nature of debating contests (a steady line of call-and-response to argument points), judges tend to consider the authority of arguments from the last word on the subject (all other things being equal, of course. According to a number of participants in debate communities, judges' easy reliance on the authority of opinion from the most recent utterance of a debate speaker is not related to the linear construction of debate argumentation but to the absence of mid- and long-term memory of judges. The authors do not approve of this sort of criticism of judges. As the authors, as well as debaters everywhere know, many judges also have serious shortcomings regarding short-term memory.)

What does this tactic mean in the course or outcome of a debate? The speaker holding the floor has an **edge** relative to the person making a point of information. A satisfactory reply by a speaker, even a near-satisfactory reply, is usually enough to win the point for the speaker in the eye, heart, mind or other fleshy organs of the judge. A successful heckle from a respondent might, therefore, effectively counter the tendencies of judges to favor speakers.

In addition, a respondent's heckle leaves the speaker with a thorny problem. If the speaker replies to the opponent's commentary, she has probably spent much too much time on the point. The point then constitutes a genuine distraction for the speaker, undermining the points to be made for an effective speech. If the speaker does not respond to the heckle, an effective reply might **win** the point for the respondent.

## RESPONDING TO POINTS OF INFORMATION

To be brief, be brief. Points of information should not distract from the message of the speaker. Even relevant points may not be require much of an answer. They may not have sufficient import or significance. They may be relevant to the discussion but irrelevant to the issues of proof for or against a motion.

Be brief but be clear. Let the judge know that you understand the objection or question and that you have presented a fully satisfactory rejoinder. Do not return to your speech if the judge is not convinced of the reply—she will continue to think of (perhaps obsess over) your reply, reducing your ability to effectively communicate the next set of info-bits in your speech (you want the judge to actively think along with your presentation in real-time, not focus on past content.)

Avoid the rhetorical traps of the maladjusted speaker. Abandon the "Rule of Three." Avoid rejecting points by saying "Not at this time." (It only encourages your opponent to rise moments later. "Is this a good time?" Or moments after that. "Is this a good time?" "Not at this time." Or nanoseconds after that. "How about now? Is this a good time?" "Not at this time.") It is quite obviously better to say, "No." Direct. Clear. Evident. Don't worry about hurting their feelings. And if they are that sensitive, they probably needed the push to therapy. So be proud of your work, you Samaritan.

Take points during argument transitions. This tactic minimizes the distraction of the point. First, complete your argument. At the conclusion of your argument, pause, just briefly, to create some rhetorical space for a point of information. (You are, in effect, inviting a point of information at this time, at your convenience.)

Before the introduction to your next major point, if an opportunity presents itself, take a point.

- Respondent: Point of information.
- Speaker: No, thank you. [The speaker holding the floor refuses to take the point. The respondent sits and the speaker continues with her presentation.] In conclusion, the risks of chemical and biological weaponization and proliferation are today greater than the risks associated with the use of more traditional weapons of mass destruction and terror–nuclear weapons. I will now take your point.

This tactic effectively controls the delivery of points of information to those times in the speech with the least distracting or confusing effect. It is often the case that the respondent, the person making the point, has forgotten the informational point by the time she is called to stand and deliver. Making your opponent seem forgetful and ineffectual is a real plus:

- Respondent: "Point of information."
- Speaker: "No, thank you. [The speaker holding the floor refuses to take the point. The respondent sits and the speaker continues with her presentation.] In conclusion, the risks of chemical and biological weaponization and proliferation are today greater than the risks associated with the use of more traditional weapons of mass destruction and terror–nuclear weapons. I will now take your point."
- Respondent: "That's okay. I don't have a point."

Those responding to points of information should prepare retorts to objectionable, obstructionist and other distractions. As previously noted, there are circumstances in which the adversarial nature of the format is confused in the minds (?) of some competitors – they become more aggressive and anxious with points of information as the interactive opportunity for vengeance. (Old debate proverb: If you come home during a point of information seeking revenge, dig a grave for two.) Humor is not necessarily the result of these interpersonal confrontations – tension and conflict are more likely. Be prepared and judicious. It is easy to antagonize an opponent, as well as the judge and assembled audience, with an opportunistic and caustic comment. Any such reply should loosely abide by dictates better associated with the history of just war theory: It should be defensive, reactionary, and proportional.

- "Please sit down. We would all like to stay awake for a few more moments."
- "Please sit down. You satisfactorily embarrassed yourself last time."
- "No, thank you. I am trying to protect your dignity (or credibility)."
- "There are some things that go without saying. Would you mind being one of them?"

Points of information are often the ally of the speaker holding the floor. It is possible to dismiss the point as an empty gesture from a confused opponent or to use the point to your strategic advantage (i.e., almost any direct and effective reply is counted as a victory). You might be able to consider the point a "straight line," using a reply as the "punch line" to make light of an opponent or her ideas.

These tactical advantages are available to you because you hold the floor. The point of information is a valuable but limited tool. Speakers have the time to respond to even well-expressed points and should be ready to do so.

## SUGGESTED EXERCISES:

1. Take daily press clippings or an article from a weekly periodical on a public policy issue or other substantive matter. Make photocopies of the document and distribute to each of participant. Have each of the participants analyze the story and propose areas of critical investigation. Can the information be challenged for its historical, economic, social, cultural, political or other commentary? Have students explain their criticism of the issue or press commentary of the issue.

   This exercise trains students in critical evaluation of factual information. An examination of opponents' facts is the basis for the majority of points of information.

2. Present a case study or historical example. Have students ana-

lyze the example. Have students identify counterexamples or supporting examples for the case study.

This exercise provides a model for one of the more effective counters as a point of information–the disagreeable example. The opposing side in a debate, using a point of information, might be able to entirely undermine any abstract claim or cleverly expressed theory with powerful empirical counterexample. These examples are certainly necessary when your opponent has his or her own effective examples.

3. Take a passage from a speech or have a debater present a three- or four-minute extemporaneous speech on a narrow motion. All others assembled will prepare a point of information and make attempts to enter them during the brief speech.

   This exercise provides real-time training in the creation of points of information. It also teaches floor management for the speaker, who will inevitably receive a significant number of points of information but will need to maintain her composure and effectively deliver one or two substantive arguments.

4. Create two teams of equal numbers of debaters (the exercise works best with four to six debaters per side). Have a debater present a seven-minute speech on a narrow motion. The teams then alternate sides, delivering points of information in turn. Each debater has to make a point within a set period of time (typically, 15 or 20 seconds). No points may be repeated. If a debater is repeats or is otherwise unable to make a point, she is removed from the competition. Debaters are removed for frivolous points as well. At the conclusion of the speech, another round begins with the remaining competitors. The last side with participants wins the contest.

## POINTS OF ORDER AND PRIVILEGE

Unlike points of information, those parliamentary points directed to the opposing side in a debate, a point of order or point of privilege involves a rules or convention violation and is directed to the Speaker of the House for an immediate ruling. These points are included in the rules of American parliamentary debating and some other debating formats but they are excluded from the British parliamentary format and many other parliamentary debate forms.

The speaker holding the floor does not have the option to refuse or accept these points; consequently, these points do not count against his or her speaking time. The timekeeper stops time during a point of order or privilege and resumes the time at the conclusion of the ruling on the point by the Speaker of the House.

## Points of Order

A point of order when there is an alleged formal violation of the debate's rules. You may rise on a point of order when a member of the opposing team violates a rule. As there are few rules in parliamentary debating, points of order are usually reserved for the presentation of a new argument in rebuttals or when a speaker goes over his or her time limit.

To make a point of order, the person rises from her seat and interrupts the speaker holding the floor, typically saying, "Point of order." The timekeeper stops the clock and the person states the point to the Speaker of the House, explaining the rules violation. Local convention primarily guides the administration of these points but one of the following is likely to occur:

• A judge listens to the point and issues a ruling on it.
• The speaker holding the floor immediately begins to debate the point and directs this information to the Speaker of House. Nonetheless, many debaters do not adhere to any stipulation that points of order are not to be debated. The majority of judges seem to encourage a reply regarding the point from the speaker holding the floor. After brief argument from both sides, the judge issues a ruling on the point.
• The judge (or designated Speaker of the House) might question the person making the point, analyzing the information pertaining to the rules violation. In this circumstance, the judge will not permit commentary on the point from the side receiving the point of information but may function as proxy for that side or as Grand Inquisitor, care-

fully considering the merits of the point before issuing a ruling.

At the conclusion of the point of order or subsequent argument on the point, the judge will issue one of three rulings:

- "Point well taken."
- "Point not well taken."
- "Point taken under consideration."

If the judge rules, "Point well taken," the person making the point wins it, meaning that the opposing side is, in fact, in violation of the rules. The offending speaker should immediately cease his or her violation. If the issue involves a new argument in the rebuttal speeches, the speaker should abandon the new argument and move to another reply or a different point of contention. If the speaker is over their allotted time, he or she should hastily conclude their speech.

A judge may use successful points during the deliberation of the outcome and assignment of individual speaking scores. It is rare, indeed, that a successful point of order will tip the balance of the debate for a team based solely on the merits of having won a point. Winning a point of order is unlikely to trump the substantive information from the major speeches in a debate. Success with several points of order, however, might indicate to a judge that one side is unable to engage in effective argumentation without introducing a considerable number of new issues in the rebuttal speeches. This factor may influence the judge's final deliberation.

It is more likely that successful points of order will improve the individual speaker points of a person advancing these winning challenges and may reduce the points of a speaker who violates the debating rules.

Points of order may be instrumental to the outcome of debates in a different way. These points function as "gatekeepers"– they permit access for some ideas and exclude others from the discussion. Your well-taken point could exclude a new argument from a speaker on the opposing team that might do great damage to a potentially winning argument for your side. Likewise, a successful point might end a speech from a debater in need of additional (and illegitimate) time to decisively answer your arguments. Points of order can influence the substantive matter of the debate and the debate's outcome.

If a point is "not well taken," the person making the point has lost the issue. The ruling from the judge or designated Speaker of the House means that the speaker is not violating the standing rules of debating and may continue with her speech. A judge may hold repeated failures of points of order against the person making them.

The introduction of points not well taken is a serious matter. Points of order are usually reserved for rebuttal speeches (the single most common violation of the rules is the presentation of new argumentation in rebuttals). Rebuttal time in the American parliamentary debate format, for example, is approximately one-half of the allocated time for the constructive speeches. The rebuttal speakers must review the entire debate in that brief time and cogently express the final winning points for their side. Any interruption or distraction is disappointing to the speaker and its mere presence may influence the outcome of the debate.

Points without merit may do as much damage as a well-taken point, as they sufficiently intrude on a brief but critically important speech. As a consequence, judges are more likely to have a strong negative reaction to failed points of order and may take appropriate and hostile actions, such as factor the failed points into their decision making or reduce the individual speaker points.

In more and more contemporary debates, judges issue rulings to take points "under consideration," meaning that a judge will not issue an immediate ruling on the point. The judge will wait until the conclusion of the debate and evaluate the point at that time. The point will be one of many factors in the judge's deliberation, which, in most debates, is private. The debaters may never know how the judge dispensed with the point of order.

The reason that judges take points under consideration is that it is often a challenging endeavor to make an immediate ruling from the chair. In some cases, a ruling is evident. If a speaker has eight minutes to make a speech and has used nine minutes and a person on the opposing side offers a point of order and states that speaking overtime is against the rules, it is quite a simple matter for a judge to issue a "point well-taken" ruling. It is a more complex consideration, for example, for a judge to listen to a debate featuring dozens of arguments and examples for 30 minutes or more, and, with only a moment for deliberation, issue as decisive and fair ruling regarding the "newness" of an issue.

New arguments in rebuttals can be vexing issues. Judges often want to get the decision right. At the very least, they do not want to make a public pronouncement that is clearly "wrong." It is better decision for many judges to devote some time for deliberation on points of order.

What do you do when a judge announces "point taken under consideration?" This decision presents challenges for speakers. For example, you are delivering the final rebuttal speech in a debate. You present an argument that you believe is a logical extension of an argument from your partner's earlier speech. A member of the opposing team rises on a point of order, stating that your position is a new argument. You are permitted to respond to the point and the judge patiently listens to both the point and your reply and then states: "Taken under consideration." What to do? Should you continue with that portion of your speech as if you have won the point? The judge has not stopped your presentation by issuing a different ruling. But what if the judge ultimately decides in favor of the point of order? In that case, your argument will be ruled out of consideration. You will have then wasted important time in your final stand discussing an issue that will play no role in the outcome of the debate.

Should you dispute the point of order itself after a non-committal "taken under consideration" ruling is issued by the judge? Is it appropriate to answer the argument of the point of order by trying to establish that your argument was a logical extension of a previously established issue when your speaking time resumes? Will the judge think you are taking advantage of your opponent, that you are arguing the point of order after the judge has closed argumentation on the point with her ruling?

This confusion may be a reason to dispense with the point of order altogether. Judges or designated Speakers of the House increasingly decide the issue in private and after the debate has concluded. New arguments, both those marked in a formal way during the course of the debate and other new arguments identified by the judge, are almost always excluded by the judge during deliberation. Judges do not want to include new rebuttal arguments in their decisions. They do not believe that the presentation of new issues so late in the contest adds to the quality of the debate nor is it fair to the participants on the other side (the victims, if you will, of this dastardly tactic or debate malfeasance). Because judges are already predisposed to ignore new arguments, it is evident that debaters do not genuinely require the protection of this particular parliamentary rule – the point of order.

Of course, debaters do not get much protection anyway, if the judge issues a "point taken under consideration" ruling. As previously described, this ruling only confuses the matter and confounds the debater, leaving the speaker with unsavory options during a speech with little time and lots of important work to do. Points that distract participants from effective summaries of the contest's salient issues are probably not worth keeping.

## POINTS OF PERSONAL PRIVILEGE

A point of personal privilege suggests an egregious personal violation by the opposing team in a debate and may be another case of an unnecessary parliamentary point. It is about bad behavior. It is not a rules violation per se.

You may rise on a point of personal privilege during an opponent's speech in two circumstances: (1) The speaker holding the floor has made boorish, crude or insulting remarks directed at you or (2) Your position has been seriously misstated by the speaker. Like a point of order, a point of personal privilege is directed to the judge or designated Speaker of the House for a ruling. All other general guidelines regarding points of order apply, including the administration of the point of personal privilege. In response to a point of personal privilege, one of the following will occur:

- A judge listens to the point and issues a ruling on it.
- The speaker holding the floor will immediately begin to debate the

point with the person accusing her of a rules violation. After brief argument from both sides, the judge issues a ruling on the point.

- The judge (or designated Speaker of the House) might question the person making the point, analyzing the information pertaining to the rules violation.

A point of personal privilege is not available as a parliamentary point in many debating formats. Even when expressly authorized by the rules, it is quite infrequently employed. It is almost never used to counter crude commentary from an opposing speaker. You do have points of information and speeches to respond to any venting or hostility from your opponent in the debate and we do not recommend a response in kind to boorishness. It seems a bit extreme to unbosom yourself to the judge and request the chair's protection, a rhetorical defense shield, from your opponents.

A point may also be made to avoid a misstatement from the opposing side. Misstatement from the opposing side? This also seems unlikely. Compared to many public speakers, including professional speakers, debaters are articulate, organized, and cogent. Speeches include a certain amount of redundancy to make a comprehensive argument (if the analysis of an issue is unclear, the supporting historical or empirical example or other evidence usually is sufficient to sort it out). There is little likelihood of a misstatement so fundamentally at odds with a presentation that it needs to be met with a parliamentary point.

Points of personal privilege are sometimes used to produce a tactical advantage. An experienced debater might argue that an opponent's refutation to her argument claim is nothing other than a "misstatement" of the issue. She would then seek a ruling on a point of personal privilege to effectively eliminate an argument reply. But debating includes the manipulation of the rhetoric of an opponent. A misstatement is not very different from, and may be precisely the same thing as, a powerful rejoinder. Points of personal privilege may exploit the judge to accomplish that which a debater ought to do on her own, namely, argue issues effectively with the opposing side.

Points of order and personal privilege are troublesome additions to parliamentary debating. Although it is possible to use them judiciously to address select and important violations of rules or conduct, they are seldom employed in that manner. Common rulings from the chair (e.g., "taken under consideration") amplify problems with these points. Debaters would do well to limit the use of these points to extraordinarily serious breaches of rules or conduct, those rare violations that could profoundly affect the outcome of a debate.

# CHAPTER 18

# SKILLS

## PERFORMANCE AND SPEAKING FUNDAMENTALS

Parliamentary debaters must be good public speakers. It is not enough to merely have the right argument at the right time. To be persuasive, you must present your arguments with authority and credibility. You must win over the good will of your audience. How can you accomplish this? Public speaking, like argumentation, is more of an art than a science. Good public speakers have many practices and habits in common; however, they also embrace their own unique and individual styles. Think of the good public speakers you may have seen or heard. Barbara Jordan and Winston Churchill were both powerful, inspirational speakers. They had different ideas and different persuasive techniques. They sounded and gestured differently. Their speeches were organized in different ways to different effects. Yet both were able to motivate groups of people to act on their propositions.

Public speaking is an exercise in both content and performance. You may have the best arguments, the best examples, and the best evidence to substantiate your side in a debate, but if your performance is poor, you may still fail to persuade an audience. Just as you should research and think critically about your arguments, so you should practice and think critically about your performance.

Initially, you should endeavor to speak clearly and at an appropriate volume. Speakers who mumble or otherwise mutter incomprehensibly may puzzle or annoy an audience, but will rarely be able to persuade them. Just as you should not mumble under your breath while speaking, so too should you not YELL AT THE JUDGE AT THE TOP OF YOUR LUNGS. Audiences do not like to be berated or otherwise lambasted by speakers. Try to use an appropriate volume when speaking. Articulation is also important. If you want to be understood, try not to run your words together or otherwise fail to pronounce clearly.

A good speaking performance requires good delivery. You will have to use vocal variety, appropriate gestures, and good word economy to effectively deliver your speeches. By "vocal variety" we mean that you should vary the tone, pitch, rate, and volume of your speech to cultivate and maintain the audience's interest. Few things are more likely to induce instant sleepiness than a speaker who delivers her presentation in a monotone.

You will also need to use appropriate nonverbal communication. We do not only communicate with our voices. Our bodies and their constituent parts are also vital tools for communication. Some debaters are notorious for using overly expressive gestures – they wave their hands about in a manner more appropriate for guiding airplanes into their gates or practicing semaphore. If your hands seem to be substantively out of your control or serve to fan or otherwise air-condition the room, you should rethink your use of gestures. We recommend that you gesture sparingly, using your hands to emphasize important points or transitions, and not as a metronome to keep time during your speech. Be conscious of how you use your hands – consider using a three-part gesturing method whereby you first get ready to gesture, then you gesture, then you put your gesture away in a graceful manner. Do not hold a pen or other object in your hand while you speak. It appears to be a security blanket and communicates to the judge that you are insecure about speaking. Such props are also distracting. Some debaters, holding a ballpoint pen during their speech, will unconsciously and repeatedly click the point in and out while they speak. It is this kind of behavior that drives judges to an early grave, or at least to civil commitment.

Do not pace, shuffle, watusi, or otherwise move your feet in a distracting manner. Try to plant yourself and remain planted throughout your speech (although subtle, slight, natural movement is of course acceptable). Debates are enough like tennis matches without the audience having to constantly follow you with their eyes. Some debaters try to implement a method of using steps to signal transitions. Do not do this. It is distracting and appears amateurish. The judge will be left wondering why you cannot restrict your waltzing to the dance floor. Our point here is certainly not that dance has no place in debates; but use it judiciously and not simply as a nervous or otherwise misguided habit. Our best advice for nonverbal communication is to appear confident at all times. Do not cross your arms or appear to hug yourself. Remember: You are good enough and smart enough.

Make good eye contact. If you are nervous about your speech or about public speaking in general, you are not alone. Most people rate public speaking among their top fears. Do not stare at your notes, the ceiling, or just over the judge's shoulder while you speak. You should make eye contact with the judge or audience during your speech. If you have trouble doing this, you should consider practicing in front of a mirror. By making eye contact with yourself, you can make eye contact with other people. A bit of advice on this front: If you are speaking in front of an audience, particularly a large one, you should try to make eye contact with individuals at different positions in the crowd rather than simply scanning the crowd with your eyes. The scanning strategy can leave a crowd feeling as if you have looked at them but made eye contact with no one.

Often, debaters will look at their opponents while they are speaking. This is a terrible idea and is generally considered to be an amateur mistake. You are not trying to convince the other team of your side of the issue. Even if you are the most gifted debater on the planet, they are unlikely to agree with you – it is, after all, their job to oppose you. You are trying to convince the judge or audience. Therefore, you should look at the judge or audience. Looking at the other team while you are speaking can also put you at a major disadvantage, because you seem to invite points of information. If you appear to be insulting or otherwise criticizing the other team in a direct manner, they will invariably pop up repeatedly for points of information. Just as you should not look at the other team while speaking, so you should not address the other team directly by prefacing your arguments with "you..."

- "You just don't say anything about this disadvantage of ours."
- "We're crushing you on this argument."
- "You bring shame on this House."
- "You are ridiculous, wrong, and absurd. You are abusive. You don't have a prayer of winning this debate."

If you engage in this kind of chest-pounding, you will most likely get what you deserve. You should not only avoid addressing the other team as "you;" you should also avoid hostility at all costs. Of course, good-natured jibes and other heckling, as we saw in the last chapter, are vital parts of parliamentary debate. Debate is adversarial, but debaters should not be adversarial with each other.

It is particularly important that you are never adversarial or hostile toward your partner. EVER. Even if you are convinced that your partner is the worst debater in the history of the activity; even if you are prone to compare yourself to Job for being saddled with such a terrible rock, you should NEVER, EVER talk badly about or behave in a disrespectful manner towards your partner. Your relationship with your debate partner is professional. You must conduct it in such a manner. Never discuss conflicts with your partner with anyone except your partner or your coach, and always in private. Meanness to your partner will make you look like the worst sort of jerk, damage your competitive prospects, and undoubtedly hurt their feelings.

Sometimes debaters conflate hostile behaviors and confident behaviors. The two could not be more different. Hostile debaters are mean, rude, irritable, and often so insecure that they must make others feel badly in order to feel good about themselves or about their performance. Confident debaters display forthrightness in explaining ideas. They speak in a convincing way and command attention without having to demand attention with cruelty or by lambasting their competitors and colleagues. You should always appear confident, calm, and collected in debates, even if you are losing. Be careful that you do not inadvertently invite opposition to your arguments by engaging in nervous behaviors like lowering your voice or trailing off at the end of your sentences.

In the long run, effective debate and public speaking necessitates efficient and effective word choice. There are two critical considerations for debaters in this area: word economy and word choice.

## WORD ECONOMY

In a formal debate, you must labor under time constraints. Speech time is always limited by the rules set by your particular format, so you need to choose your words carefully. Debaters who exhibit good *word economy* use the minimum number of words necessary to present their arguments. Economical word choice allows them to present the maximum number of independent arguments and examples possible in their limited speech time. If you use a lot of filler words, you will not be using your speech time to its maximum advantage.

Think about how you speak in everyday conversation. You will find that you use lots of filler words that do not contribute to your statements. In America, people often use "like" ("And then I was like, dude, we're *totally* turning your case advantage;" "Like, are you going to eat that burrito?") or "you know" ("So, you know, I was wondering if you, you know, wanted to get some coffee or something?" "This movie is completely, you know, terrible."). Interjections, such as "um" and "er," are also used.

Debaters use these filler words plus all kinds of other, more debate-specific, filler words and phrases. They punctuate their thoughts with phrases such as:

- "remember" (Used once, it's completely suitable, even desirable.

Used repeatedly, it's highly annoying, massively redundant, and a terrific waste of time: it takes a whole second to say, and if you say it 15 times in a speech, you are in effect sacrificing 15 seconds of your speech time.)

- "Ladies and gentlemen" (Yes, we know – sometimes you need to use this combination honorific to address your audience, but there is no need to punctuate so many of your sentences with it. Everybody knows you're just saying it when you don't know what you're going to say next.)

- "in fact" (This phrase places in doubt the speaker's overall grasp of the facts by the 30th time she has used it. She does, perhaps, protest too much.)

You most likely use all these verbal fillers and many more. What's worse, you may not even realize that you, like just about everyone who has ever debated, have bad word economy habits. Try to diagnose and repair these bad habits. We suggest that you tape yourself debating – videotape, if possible, and then pay close attention to how you phrase your arguments. Once you diagnose a word economy problem, it is relatively easy to solve. If you remain conscious of the word(s) you are trying to fix, you will try to avoid them normally. Practice speaking more slowly and deliberately, and focus on the individual words as they come out of your mouth.

## WORD CHOICE

Just as you should use an economy of words, so too should you respect the admonition offered in *Indiana Jones and the Last Crusade* and "choose wisely." In the section on impact assessment, we will explore more how important it is to use vivid language to persuade judges and audiences. In debate, we talk a lot about the concept of "power wording." The words you use will shape the reality that the judge perceives. Do you describe a decline in the stock market as a "correction" or a "crash?" Do you describe discrimination by the state as "inequality" or "slow-motion genocide?" Is a military invasion a "police action" or a "war?" Consider that your words matter, and directly affect how your arguments will be perceived. Strong wording will always make your arguments seem more credible. There is one caveat to this rule, though: If you routinely use "power wording" to frame arguments that are obviously weak, you will lose credibility. For further reference on this subject, see: "Wolf, The Boy Who Cried."

There are many other word choice decisions you can make in debates to improve your effectiveness as a speaker. For example, consider using selective repetition to emphasize your most critical arguments. Specifically, quote your opponents when appropriate. Often you can take their dubious statements and turn them to your advantage.

The words you use reflect how you and your arguments are perceived in the debate. In order to be a decent human being, avoid prejudiced bias in appeals that target some groups at the expense of others. In order to be an effective debater, avoid exclusive language. Use inclusive language instead. Make appeals to sympathy rather than stereotypes. People think highly of themselves – if you can convince the judge or audience that innocent people are persecuted, that decisions are arbitrary, that there are conspiracies or issues that affect them of which they have little knowledge, then the judge or audience will believe that the harm might happen to them.

As a final note, always be considerate of the physical circumstances in which you are performing. If you are speaking from behind a podium, don't put your hands on the podium and keep them there. Try to move out from behind the podium at least once during your speech to dispel the audience's suspicion that you are some sort of talking head. You will need to learn how to use a microphone, if you don't know already. Don't speak too close to or far away from the microphone, or you will massively distort your natural speaking voice. Speak into the middle of the microphone so your "p's" don't pop. When speaking in front of a camera, keep your gestures inside the frame of your body. Use exaggerated speaking, including louder and clearer delivery so the sound isn't muddy. You will also need to glance at the camera rather than stare at it – the audience will also expect you to make more eye contact with your opponents in a televised debate than in an audience debate.

## HUMOR AND HECKLING

Parliamentary debates are engaging and dynamic events. Unlike most formal speaking engagements and other forms of academic contest debating, they are designed to encourage speech interruption from the opposing side of the motion (for example, points of information) and the assembled participants and audience (with verbal and non-verbal heckling).

In all formats, humor and heckling play important roles in parliamentary debate's dynamism. Humor has striking persuasive power in an oral presentation. It motivates the audience to engage in critical listening. The audience, including judges for the contest, wants to be entertained as well as informed. Debates go on too long for a dull recitation of facts.

Humor not only connects the speaker with the judge and audience but it enhances the credibility of other arguments in a presentation. The use of humor is popularly associated with higher-level critical thinking skills and intelligence. (This is the case despite the fact that the field of humor includes forms that are decidedly not funny – the pun and the practical joke are examples. These weak attempts might, at best, amuse an oaf, or, in the plural, oaves.) This association of humor and wit with intellectual sophistication reflects favorably on a speaker's other, and frequently rational, lines of argument.

Debaters should prepare to use humor in the same way they might prepare to express an opinion on historical, political or social events. Research and practice are keys to the effective use of humor in speeches.

There are hundreds of texts providing reference material for humor. Dictionaries of humorous quotations are available. Websites collect the malapropisms of political figures and celebrities Periodicals such as *The Onion* (www.theonion.com) offer models of humor, including, in its headlines, the elements of surprise, satire, and irony.

- SURPRISE: Man Accidentally Ends Business Call with 'I Love You'
- SATIRE: Depression Hits Losers Hardest

• IRONY: Sculptor Criticized for Turning Women into Objects

The hardest working people in show business are stand-up comedians, who toil for many hours to craft minutes of material. Debaters do not need to devote similar effort, but some preparation is required. Debaters are not expected to make the same kind of presentation as a comedian. For this, debaters ought to be thankful. Debate audiences, starved as they are for any sort of entertainment, are a receptive crowd for subtle wit and drollery. It is not necessary to be "laugh out loud funny" to be a hit in the debate world.

A speaker should use humor at the beginning of her speech, certainly within the first 30 seconds. Early use encourages critical listening on the part of the assembled judges and audience as they eagerly await the next funny bit. It doesn't have to come until two or three minutes later, at the point of the speech at which they believe you might have already exhausted your treasure chest of jokes. Some wit or cleverness toward the end of the speech is also appreciated: Merely a few clever lines, some prepared in advance and some extemporaneous comments rising from the clash in the debate, should suffice for an entertaining speech.

Debaters should consider the circumstances of the format and the conditions in which they would use humor. Here are examples:

SPEECH INTRODUCTION
"I delivered this speech once before in a prison. I apologize to those of you who have heard it before."

ON THE CASE PROPER
"For every problem, there is a solution that is simple, neat, and wrong." -H. L. Mencken
"'I am from the government and am here to help you' is only slightly less trustworthy than I'll respect you in the morning."
"I suppose this is their idea of progress: We are going in the same circle, only faster."
"That is an argument with few equals – only superiors."
"On a less serious note, my opponents claimed…"

"The plural of anecdote is not evidence."

"If ignorance is bliss, ladies and gentlemen, I would like to introduce you Mr./Ms. Happy."

Heckling, the interruption of speeches with verbal commentary or nonverbal signals from those individuals who are not recognized as the speaker at the time, is a welcome part of parliamentary debating in many parts of the world. It is, however, an issue that debaters should negotiate with the judge or understand from local community norms. Some perceive heckling as disruptive or rude behavior. You will want to know if your heckling performance is a welcome addition or likely to produce calls for security guards.

Heckling can be supportive. It is common practice for debaters to knock with their knuckles or slap their hand on a table or bench to cheer particularly well reasoned ideas of colleagues. (They might also cheer, for that matter, the rhetorical blunders of opponents.) Much heckling is negatively inspired and directed to the speakers on the other side of the motion. Debaters are likely to call "Shame" on an opponent who misrepresents facts. These heckles can be effective at getting the judge to focus attention on a clever insight (an argument turn, for example) or a serious mischaracterization of an opponent's speech (e.g., a cry of "Shame" when an opponent insists that you failed to discuss a salient point that you believe you decimated with several outstanding arguments). You should be judicious about heckles, because their frequent use undermines their effectiveness. The judge is aware that you support your partner or the other team on the same side of a motion. General support for other speakers on your side only iden-tifies your use of heckling as non-strategic, perhaps boorish. Judges are quite aware that you believe that your opponents are wrong when-ever they challenge your ideas. The repeated cry of "Shame" loses its authority if it comes to mean that you disagree with the opposing side of a debate.

Other heckles can be effective. A counterexample or brief expres-sion (no more than two or three words) that makes a complete and powerful argument may sufficiently disrupt a speaker's presentation. If a speaker, for example, suggests that United Nations peacekeeping forces are ineffectual in managing conflicts, a single counter – "Cyprus" – might require a further explanation from the speaker to satisfactorily express her point to a judge.

Heckling is distinguished from barracking, which is general disagreement with the claims of a speaker ("No, no, unh-unh, nyet, no, nein, never, not at this time, no, absolutely not..."). A heckle should express a coherent argument in a concise manner without fundamentally disrupting the pace and delivery of a speech. Debaters should research and prepare for heckling in the same way they would prepare to use humor. They should also prepare counters to boorish hecklers. Some examples follow.

REPLIES TO HECKLERS
"I would like to help you out. Which way did you come in?"
"Yes, I am sure we all remember our first beer."
"If I have said anything to offend or insult you, please believe me."
"There are some things that go without saying. Would you mind being one of them?"

## DEBATING IMPACTS

One thing that differentiates successful debaters from their less accomplished colleagues is the ability to assess and explain impacts. In this section, we will discuss some common criteria for assessing impacts and then proceed to offer some pearls of wisdom (which is not to describe you, gentle reader, as swine) about explaining impacts in a way that makes them seem tangible and realistic.

To debate effectively, you will need to learn how to weigh and measure impacts using an array of criteria by which you can assess the relative importance and significance. One of the interesting things about debate is that the criteria for what is to count as significant are always up for debate. Do not assume that you, the judge, and the other debaters agree on what is important for the purpose of evaluating the debate. Even in a non-confrontational situation, you could most likely not agree on a flavor of ice cream. Far better to stake out the battle for what is to count as significant early and often in the debate. Contrary to some popular coaching advice, weighing arguments is not and should not be confined to the last rebuttal (though it is certainly essential to that speech). What follows is a list of some common criteria you can use to compare and contrast impacts (and also, not coincidentally, all kinds of other arguments, argument components, food choices, television programs, vacation options, and elective surgeries).

## NUMBER OF PEOPLE AFFECTED

This is one of the simplest impact yardsticks you can employ. It seems almost maudlin to say that some things affect more people than others, yet debaters routinely forget to use this basic calculus. If your case for the proposition claims to save millions of lives by preventing war, pestilence, famine, plague, or an ABBA reunion tour, then you should probably mention at some point that your plan will save a lot of lives. This tactic becomes particularly important when the opposition argues a disadvantage with a substantially smaller impact than that of your truly gargantuan advantage.

## DEGREE OF HARM INFLICTED

The number of people affected is rarely, however, adequate criteria by itself. You also have to ask yourself what *happens* to those people. Otherwise, you would have to say that it would be worth it to summarily execute ten people if it meant that 50 would not have to wait in line for the bus. You also need to assess the degree of harm inflicted on the potentially hapless victims of the present system and the disadvantage (for example). The aggregate "size" of an impact is usually evaluated with reference to *both* the number of people affected and the degree of harm (or maiming, polyester, Ricki Lake, etc...) they must endure.

## PROBABILITY/RISK

Of course, it is not enough simply to assess the "size" of an impact: All too often, debaters ignore this basic dictate and fetishize impacts of great size and magnitude. Probability *must* figure into any even remotely sophisticated impact calculus. It is an integral part of our everyday decision making, after all. We decide, for example, to cross the street on a daily basis despite the low-probability, high-impact possibility that we might be run over by a bus. We make this decision because we think the probability of such a collision is a *low risk*. Risk is a very important concept in assessing impact debates. As a debater, a judge, or both, you will routinely have to assign *risk* to particular arguments in debates. A convenient formula that some people use to determine the real risk of something is "**Risk = Probability \* Impact.**" While we are adverse to the mad proliferation of quasi-mathematical formulas that purport to describe everything in our society these days ("War = Peace," "Social Value = Income \* Good Looks"), we do find a particular charm in this equation.

In the case of your potential surprise meeting with a wayward bus, we could assess the risk using this kind of formula: The probability is very low, and the impact high, so we see the risk as negligible. We could tinker with this formula as it suited us. For example, if the street you needed to cross was routinely rife with runaway traffic, the probability of getting hit would go up and you might have to think seriously about how much you *really* need to cross that street. You can also change perceived risk by boosting the impact. Let's say that we could somehow convince you that there was a very small, but real chance that if you walked across the street you would set into motion a chain of events that would lead to human extinction. Here we've got an almost incalculably large impact combined with a small risk. What do you do? Do you decide that you'll just skip that street altogether? Or do you write us off as insane and take the risk anyway?

It is important to think about questions like this because you need to think about how average judges and audience members see and evaluate risks in their own life. So much of our understanding about risk assessment creeps into debates unannounced; better to assign nametags so no one stands around looking awkward at the punch table.

## SYSTEMIC VS. ONE-TIME

Impacts, like gelatin desserts and other taste treats from the critical "hooves" group, come in a vast range of types and palatabilities. One useful way to categorize impacts is as either *systemic* or *one-time*. A one-time impact is just that: an impact that will only happen once. If you argue that the proposition team's case to regulate genetically modified organisms (GMOs) will cause a trade war or a shooting war, that is a one-time impact that may or may not outweigh the case advantages depending on their relative established magnitude.

Systemic impacts, on the other hand, occur continuously, either throughout time or space or some Star Trek-ish combination of both. Many environmental impacts are systemic, e.g., the presence of PCBs and dioxins in water can cause cancer, deformities, and death for many generations. So we can say, for example, that in a particular region there are a hundred incidents of cancer per year due to contaminated air or water. *Over time*, this impact adds up to be a tremendous amount of disease and death. It is critical that when you argue systemic impacts, you impress upon the judge or audience that the *cumulative effect* is quite staggering. It's not as if, for example, the Great Lakes will spontaneously clean themselves.

In the final rebuttals, impact debates quite often reduce to a comparison of systemic versus one-time consequences. You need to call these risks by name and compare them explicitly for the judge:

> "The opposition team says that our pesticide regulations will cause a trade war and that this *may* lead to a shooting war. Even if they're right about this dubious claim, we still win this debate because our case advantages are bigger over time. The continued effects of dangerous pesticides will cause tens of thousands of deaths over time. This is certainly a larger consequence than a minor fistfight over sneaker imports."

The debate over continuing sanctions on Iraq is a good example of how this kind of impact comparison works in public policy forums. The argument for continuing sanctions is, basically, that the probability and impact of Iraq developing weapons of mass destruction is very large. This (more or less) one-time impact is thought by some to trump the systemic impacts of sanctions, which include mass starvation and the death of tens of thousands of children every year. Whether or not you agree with this calculus is another thing entirely.

## PRIOR CONSIDERATION

In some debates, impact comparison and assessment will involve a debate about competing ethical or moral frameworks. One team may argue that their impacts must be considered before evaluating the opposing team's impacts. One classic, recurring example of this phenomenon is the "life vs. rights" debate. Let's say that the proposition team defends a case that puts a stop to racial profiling in the USA. They argue that this profiling by race or ethnicity is a violation of human and constitutional rights and should be rejected because of its latent racism. The opposition team argues, in response, that a ban on racial profiling will greatly hamper law enforcement agencies' ability to fight crime and terrorism, leading to loss of life and property. How should we compare these impacts?

A smart proposition team will argue, in essence, that the ends of a policy do not justify its means of implementation. That is, they will say that the government's obligation to protect rights is a *prior consideration*. In order to win the debate on their terrorism disadvantage, the opposition team will have to show that the debate should be resolved using a *consequentialist* calculus. Consequentialism, often conflated with utilitarianism, is a doctrine that the moral rightness of an act or policy depends entirely on its outcome or consequences.

We do not intend here to rehash the last several thousand years' worth of thinking about political and moral philosophy in order to clarify the difference between consequentialist and non-consequentialist perspectives on policy making. It will, however, greatly behoove you to read up on these perspectives so that you can defend both sides of this debate. Consider preparing a critique of consequentialist reasoning, which can be very useful, particularly on the proposition side, if many of your pre-prepared cases have small advantages or impacts.

## INDEPENDENT VS. DEPENDENT

Some impacts are said to be dependent on others to achieve their full force. How would you compare, for example, the relative importance of equality and liberty? One way would be to explain that equality is dependent on liberty. Consider that equality is (generally speaking) the equitable distribution of freedoms, resources, opportunities, or happiness. In order to ensure equality, you could say, we must first have liberty, resources, opportunity, or happiness. Others say (in a very simplistic manner, to be sure) about weighing loss of life against loss of rights that rights are useless if you are dead.

## "MOST GRIEVOUS ERROR"

Some impacts are said to be so unbelievably catastrophic (usually nuclear war or global climate change) that even a negligible risk warrants action to prevent them. If you look again at the risk equation above, you'll see how this works. If the impact is infinite, then any non-zero probability multiplied by infinity still adds up to be an infinite risk. See, math class isn't so tough. If this calculus seems a little odd to you, though, you're not alone. Even though the consequences of nuclear war or global climate change are potentially inconceivably horrible, it does not therefore follow that they are literally infinite. Further, this example clearly demonstrates the ultimate fallibility of the risk equation. Useful though math formulas are in debate (which is to say not very much), they are no substitute for good, well-reasoned argument. If we could just calculate our way through the dilemmas of human affairs, we would have no need for debate (or perhaps language) at all.

## "TRY OR DIE"

A cousin to the "most grievous error" argument, the "try or die" argument has become immensely popular in debate in recent years. The phrase "try or die" is a kind of slogan that appears with alarming frequency in proposition team rebuttals as an attempt to justify implementation of the plan. Here's how this argument works: The proposition team tries to show that there is a gigantic problem in the status quo. This is the "die" part of the equation. The proposition team is trying to establish that we're all going to die (not literally *all* of us, nor will it necessarily involve our *deaths*, per se – perhaps just a light maiming;

the idea is to show that a catastrophic impact is inevitable in the status quo). The "try" part of the equation is the part where you decide to endorse the plan, even if you are unsure whether it can actually remediate the detailed harm. Thus the rhetorical trope of "try or die": The proposition team tries to convince the judge that they might as well *try* the plan since the consequences of not solving the problem would be so unbelievably huge. This rebuttal technique, while startlingly effective, is generally recognized to be the last resort of proposition teams with poor solvency arguments and dubious plans.

## SUGGESTED EXERCISE:

Below find several pairs of competing impacts. Using the techniques above, compare them. You could, for example, argue that one is bigger than the other in scope or magnitude. Perhaps one is systemic while the other is one-time. Pick one of the pair and show why it is worse than its companion impact. Then show why the reverse comparison is true.
- economic growth vs. environmental degradation
- warfare vs. poverty
- individual rights vs. social welfare
- earthquakes vs. flooding
- nuclear proliferation vs. biological weapons proliferation

## EXPLAINING IMPACTS

Do it. Explain your impacts. Do not assume that the judge or other debaters involved will see them as the tragic, grievous circumstances that you perceive them to be. Recall that in the chapter on argument theory we mentioned Aristotle's concept of *pathos*, which is appeal to the emotions of the audience. To consistently and successfully win debates about impacts, you must appeal both to the logic and emotions of your judges. All too often, debaters simply fail to explain their impacts in a way that makes them tangible to the judge. It is *not enough*, for example, to say that your plan is a good idea because it ameliorates poverty, or stops inflation, or cleans up the air, or bans bad toupees, or even because nine out of ten dentists endorse it. To make an impact persuasive, you must flesh it out. Personalize it. Help the judge visualize the potential consequences of not voting for your side. Judges like to vote for plans that seem realistic and beneficial. In this way, they are just like average consumers, who want to purchase products that they are reasonably certain will solve an immediate need. Understanding this aspect of judge psychology will enable you to adapt your arguments accordingly.

Most debates are, in fact, won or lost on good impact assessment and explanation. We've already given you some tools to use in comparing your impacts against those of the other team. But comparison is no good without a concomitant explanation of exactly what the judge "gets" when she votes for your side. For example, you *could* just say: **"The plan is good because it brings people out of poverty. This outweighs their economy disadvantage."** *Or*, you could say:

> "Hundreds of thousands of people, many of them children, are starving or malnourished in our country right now because of endemic poverty, and few of these have any hope of surviving to make a meaningful life for themselves. Imagine what it's like to live like this – no food, no shelter, no clothing, constantly wracked by disease. Then, imagine what a tremendous boon the plan would be. Income redistribution would give these families a real chance at life and would, over time, save millions and millions of lives by lifting a whole segment of society out of poverty. The opposition team would have you believe that economic considerations come first, but this is the same economic system that is literally *built on the backs* of the same people the plan is trying to help. So corporations lose some money? So what? That's a small price to pay to lift up the most indigent among us."

The speaker is making the same basic argument as "The plan is good and outweighs their economy disadvantage," but she uses a variety of verbal and persuasive techniques to make the argument more tangible by building on it. When we exhort you to explain your impacts, we mean *just that*: Explain your impacts.

If you have trouble with this process, try thinking in terms of "because." Begin with an impact claim like this one: "Ozone depletion is bad." Then expand on it by using a series of "because" statements:

> "Ozone depletion is bad ....*because*.... more UV radiation will reach the surface of the earth, and that's bad ....*because*.... many people will get skin cancer as a result, and that's bad ....*because*.... skin cancer is often fatal, and will become more fatal as UV intensity increases."

Try this process using the suggested exercise below to learn how to explain impacts. Remember – judges like to vote for some tangible risk or result. If you can convince them that your risks or results are more tangible, then you will win more debates.

## SUGGESTED EXERCISE:

Explain why each of the following impacts is bad. If you have trouble generating explanations, use the "because" method.

| | |
|---|---|
| floods | forest fires |
| global warming | opera |
| breast cancer | imperialism |
| sexism | inflation |
| drought | weapons proliferation |
| slavery | David Hasselhoff |
| imprisonment | cheese in a can |
| resource wars | famine |
| inequality | |

## TIPS FOR REBUTTALS

A lot of impact assessment happens (hopefully) in the final rebuttals of a formal debate, your last chance to impress the judge with your command of the issues at hand. Many debaters, perhaps echoing socially maladjusted behaviors learned in primary school, will try too hard to impress the judge ("Ooh, please pick me, teacher! I'm ever so smart!")

by trying to win every single argument in the debate. This strategy ignores one of the most valuable rebuttal techniques you can employ: the fine art of strategic concession. Good debaters know when to concede arguments to strengthen their overall position. In impact debates, you can use a version of strategic concession to solidify your winning position. The key phrases to use are:

"Even if we lose this, we still win because….."
"At worst, they're just winning that ….., but this still doesn't trump our position because……"

What these phrases have in common is that they *take seriously* the possibility that the other team might be winning some of the arguments in the debate. The "even if" argument is one of the most powerful phrases you can use in a rebuttal speech: "Even if they win this argument that our plan increases government spending, we're still winning the debate because we prove that spending is worthwhile"; "Even if we lose this particular advantage, we still win the debate based on the cumulative strength of our other advantages"; "Even if you think this link turn argument is tenuous, the fact remains that they haven't *ever* answered it." These are important phrases to use in rebuttal impact assessment.

## NOTE TAKING AND CRITICAL LISTENING

Good listening and note-taking skills are critical elements for consistent debate performances and successes. Since debate is, in large part, about refutation and responsive or reactionary argumentation, it probably goes without saying that in order to debate, you're going to have to learn to listen critically. Critical listening is different from simple listening. Simple listening is the process of hearing information and perhaps (if the speaker is lucky) storing it in your mind or notes. Hearing is passive. Critical listening is just what it sounds like: listening with an eye towards criticism. It is an active process of engagement with the speaker. You must be able to understand and evaluate your opponents' arguments in order to respond adequately and appropriately. Good listening, like good speaking, takes practice. We learn terrible listening skills in many parts of our lives as television and other media inculcate us into becoming passive receptacles of information. Work on concentration skills and try to avoid "premature evaluation" whereby you rush to judge a speaker's intentions and arguments before the arguments are fully articulated.

You *must* learn to take notes effectively in order to succeed in debates. There are so many arguments made in the course of a given debate that even if you have a particularly heroic and encyclopedic memory, your chance of recalling all of them is effectively zero. You probably have extensive experience in taking notes, but the note-taking process in the classroom or business arena is very different from the note-taking process in debate. When you are taking notes during a lecture at your college, for example, you are trying to write down as much of what the professor says as possible for later use. When you take notes in a debate, you need those notes for much more than effective recall. You also need your them for effective refutation. To refute an argument effectively, you need to refer to it before you refute it. This is the "they say…" part of the four-step refutation model.

In a debate, notes *track* the development of arguments. This is why we refer to the process of taking notes in a debate as *flowing*. Arguments flow (and often ebb) during the course of a debate, and refutations pile upon each other throughout speeches by both teams. For the American parliamentary debate format, we recommend that you use paper divided into six columns, like **table 1** on the next page.

Notice that we've put the second opposition constructive and the first opposition rebuttal into the same column. The proposition team must refute the content of both speeches in the same speech, so it's practical to put them in the same column.

Flowing is one aid that debaters use to help them practice effective refutation and direct clash. A flowsheet also allows us to track the arguments of the opposition so that we can answer them specifically and in order. When you flow, you take notes in the column appropriate to the speech. That way, you'll know what you need to refute when it's your turn to speak. When you take notes in a debate, you need to follow a few basic precepts listed below:

**ABBREVIATE WHENEVER POSSIBLE.** Debates proceed rapidly, with remarkable density of information and argument. It is not physi-

| 1st Prop Constructive (1PC) | 1st Opp Constructive (1OC) | 2nd Prop Constructive (2PC) | 2nd Opp Constructive/ Opp Rebuttal (2OC/OR) | Prop Rebuttal (PR) | Judges Comments |
|---|---|---|---|---|---|
| | | | | | |

Table 1

cally possible for you to write everything down that is said in a given debate. Therefore, you will have to be selective about what you choose to write down, and abbreviate when you do. Develop a list of abbreviations that works for you. Try using standard abbreviations for debate terminology – "CP" for "counterplan," "DA" for "disadvantage," "T" for "topicality," etc. Use abbreviations that make sense to you. Your notes are for your use and not for the ages.

**TRY TO WRITE LEGIBLY.** Although your notes are primarily for your own use, your partner may need to refer to them from time to time, so you should try to write legibly. We have also coached several debaters who occasionally cannot read their own handwriting. If this happens to you, take steps to correct the problem.

**DON'T STOP WRITING IF YOU GET LOST.** Sometimes, debaters will get confused about what their opponent is saying or what part of the debate they are addressing. The appropriate response is certainly not to stop writing, stare into the ether, or hide under the table whimpering. Just keep taking notes, lest you miss some critical argument or example. Woe betide the debater who loses a debate based on his or her opponent's lack of organizational skills.

**MAKE NOTATIONS OF "DROPPED" OR "UNANSWERED" ARGUMENTS.** If an opponent fails to answer your critical arguments, you will be able to tell at a glance by looking at the flow. Circle arguments that have gone unanswered so that you will be able to point out that the other side has effectively agreed with certain contentions you have made.

**PRACTICE ROUTINELY.** You will only learn to flow well if you practice. A lot. Practice flowing your classes, the evening news, radio broadcasts, or debate meetings. Use abbreviations and try to track argument references and refutations with arrows.

**USE JUST ONE COLOR.** Although many debaters and coaches advise flowing in multiple colors, we disagree with this practice. If you think of something spontaneously, you should be able to jot it in the appropriate column rather than waste valuable time switching pens.

**USE PLENTY OF PAPER.** Don't try to cram an entire debate onto one piece of paper. You will not only fail, but will also create a tremendous mess in the process. Use multiple pieces of paper. Many people use separate pieces of paper or separate sections of their notes to track the development of "off-case" arguments, such as counterplans or disadvantages.

**SPACE OUT.** Here we are not talking about the time-honored practice of navel-gazing; rather, leave plenty of vertical space between individual arguments that you write down. Space ensures that your flow will not become cramped and illegible later in the debate.

**USE RELATIONAL SYMBOLS TO TRACK ARGUMENT DEVELOPMENT.** If you make an argument in your speech that is subsequently refuted, you need to visually represent that refutation on your flow with symbolic notation. We suggest that you use arrows. This relational notation will help you with rebuttal summaries: "We said X, to which they said Y and Z, but Y and Z don't really answer X, and here's why…"

These techniques will help you take notes in any debate. However, note taking in four-team debates is a bit of a different enterprise and requires a different approach, as you might imagine. A judge should create a quadrant and make notes in each of the four sections for both speakers on that side. These notes should be used in consensus deliberation.

If you are on the opening team on either side, flow in the same manner recommended above for two-team debating, because you are primarily concerned with what the other side is going to say in the opening portion of the debate. If you are on the second team on either side, flow your debate with the other second team in the same fashion. However, also have notes about the procession of the first part of the debate whereby you highlight and condense key arguments from the first team on each side so that you can reference those arguments. We suggest assigning numbers to the critical arguments from the first part of the debate and then referencing the reiteration of those arguments by numbers on your flow.

## Suggested Exercises:

1. Have someone read aloud each of the five sample speeches from the chapter on case construction and negation. Practice flowing these speeches.
2. Practice flowing the nightly television newscast. Work to get down as much of the delivered information as possible by developing a series of issue-specific abbreviations.

## Judging Debates

One of the things that distinguishes debate from simple argument is that in debate, you are trying to persuade a third party – sometimes, many third parties, in the case of a panel of judges or an extended audience. In parliamentary debates, the judge is the person who is responsible for deciding who wins and loses a debate. Depending on the arrangements made in any particular debate, the judge may also be the timekeeper, moderator, or Speaker of the House. They may assign a range of points and rankings to individual debaters or teams of debaters. After a debate, judges will offer a reason for their decision. They will explain their decision on a paper ballot, to be distributed to the participating teams at the conclusion of the tournament. Judges may also provide an oral critique after the debate, in which they explain their thinking as to who won the debate and offer advice and criticism to the participating debaters.

Of course, not all debates are judged in a formal way. Many debates are audience-oriented events, where no formal decision is ever rendered or announced. When you are an audience member for any debate, you are still, in a sense, a judge. Even if the audience doesn't make a formal decision, they are still evaluating the participants' performance. So whether you end up judging formal, competitive, tournament debates or judging debates as an audience member, you will need to know some basic skills in judging.

If you are a competitive debater, we highly recommend that you try to find opportunities to judge debates yourself. You might volunteer to judge debates for younger students or to referee practice debates between other members of your squad. This experience is an invaluable teaching tool for aspiring debaters. All too often, debaters are known to while away time that could be productively spent in any number of other ways (waxing the family pet, designing a marketing campaign for lawn darts, or sweatin' to the oldies) telling story after story about the idiocy and base incompetence of the judges to which they have been subjected. These stories often run like an Inquisition narrative, whereby the poor, innocent debater is tortured for hours on the whims of someone who is quite obviously her intellectual inferior. To which we can only say, "Hey, try it yourself and see how difficult it is." Some of the best debaters we have known have turned out to be some of the very worst judges. Some of the best judges we know never debated or were not successful in competitions. Regardless of the humility benefits that judging experience might provide to you, practice in judging will be a great teaching tool: It will show you what it is like to be the Person at the Back of the Room.

Helpful advice to debaters: Respect your judges. Not only that, but go out of your way to be kind and polite to them, even when (or perhaps most especially) when you disagree with them. Consider that your judges are volunteering their time or working for little pay to listen to you debate and provide you with the most reasoned deliberation that they can muster. Without the involvement of judges, debate tournaments would certainly not happen. That said, it is inevitable that you will encounter judges with whom you will disagree. Your best response is to listen carefully to their decision and try to understand why they voted the way they did. Just as everyone has different political and cultural opinions, everyone has different opinions about how to decide who wins and loses a debate and why. It is not uncommon for two judges in the same debate to vote for different sides, or to vote for the same side, but for different reasons. It is also not uncommon to be thoroughly convinced that you won a debate, only to find out afterwards that your judge disagreed with your assessment. Some debaters treat judges as if they were only a passive receptacle for information or proselytizing, a dim view to take of judges, who should be treated as an active participant in the debate. Just as you may educate the judge about certain issues, they may in turn educate you about the practice of debating. Keep an open mind, and above all, do not behave in a cruel or otherwise objectionable manner. That judge may judge you again, and will almost certainly have some good advice that you can carry on to future debates. There are very few bad judges. There are, however, many judges with whom debaters fail to communicate. One of the reasons we learn how to debate is to communicate with a wide range of people. Learn to communicate with your judges.

The purpose of this section is to provide advice for future and present debate judges. Debaters should also read this section for insights into the practice of judging. Before we begin, we should reiterate that there are as many ways of judging debates as there are ways of debating. Judges should work to cultivate their own style and method of evaluating debates. They should work with debaters, rather than in spite of them or around them, to create a learning community from which all participants benefit.

When you judge a debate, you are normally asked to decide which team did the better debating and why. This team is said to have *won* the debate, usually through a combination of argumentation and presentation. It is important to remember that the team that wins the debate may not always be the better debate team – instead, they were the better debate team in the debate that you watched. Even the best world-class debate teams have critical slip-ups every now and again. You should endeavor to be fair and judge each debate based on its own merits, rather than on gossip, speculation, performances in past debate rounds, or other environmental factors.

Don't be nervous. It is easy to be intimidated by the enterprise of judging debates. You may feel unprepared or under-experienced, especially compared to the debaters, who may seem very professional and experienced. In reality, you are (no matter your experience level) perfectly prepared to judge a debate. Even if you have never seen a debate before, you can still render a thoughtful and informed decision based only on your engaged participation. Parliamentary debate is meant to be entertaining and accessible to judges and audiences of all experience levels, so even if you are a novice judge, you will fit right in. You will also learn to be a better judge as you watch and judge more debates. You have to start somewhere, so don't be intimidated. All you have to do is make the best decision you can make. You do not have to make the "right" decision – in debate, as in politics or ice cream selection, there is seldom a "right" decision *per se*. There are some decisions that are better for some people than others. (For example, the authors prefer pistachio or green tea-flavored ice cream. We recognize that these flavors may not go over well with others, but don't particularly care one way or the other about that.)

Everyone recognizes, though, that some decisions are better than others. Debaters have a tendency to be opinionated. Judges are also opinionated. In fact, just about everyone who has had even the rudiments of a critical thought (or the remnants of an incendiary talk-radio show) fermenting in their brain is likely to be opinionated about something. Holding opinions is normal, healthy, and in the interest of building lively communities. There is, however, a substantive difference between having opinions and forcing them on others at the expense of reasoned debate and discussion. We recommend that when you judge you make an effort to maintain an open mind about the arguments and examples being evidenced in the debate. Open-mindedness is not so much an issue of surrendering convictions as it is a matter of respecting the debaters' opinions and efforts. It is important to remember that parliamentary debate is switch-side debating. That means that, on occasion, you may have the opportunity to watch debaters defending a side contrary to what they (or you) might otherwise agree with.

What do we mean when we say that some decisions are better than others? A good decision is one that relies on a consistent, fair method of deliberation. A decision is "good" not based on the outcome – we certainly do not mean that the quality of a decision is based on who wins and who loses a given debate. In order to judge fairly, you need to keep a few things in mind:

- Identify your biases and resist them rather than surrender to them.
- Apply reciprocal standards for evaluating arguments. In other words, don't identify an error made by one team and hold it against them when the other team or teams make the same error. Make your judging standards relevant and fairly applied to all debate participants.
- Presume that the debaters are acting in good faith. Resist the temptation to read intention into their perceived mistakes. If a debater makes a factual error in the debate, she may not know that she is wrong. Do not assume, for example, that she is being deceitful or is in some way trying to put something over on you.

- Be patient. The debaters may, during the course of a given debate, do a good many things to annoy or otherwise irritate you. They are most likely not doing these things on purpose.
- Give debaters the benefit of the doubt about their choices – they may not make the choices you would, but that's okay. Debate isn't about ego projection on the part of the judge. Instead, it's an opportunity to create a rhetorical space where other bright critical thinkers can imagine, analyze, and innovate. If you do not give them the benefit of the doubt, you could end up stifling their creativity or substituting your sense of creativity for theirs.

Good decisions are reached fairly with appropriate and adequate deliberation on the issues and arguments that are presented in the debate. Good judges know and follow the rules of the particular format and tournament they are participating in. As long as you make a concerted effort to be fair and respectful, you will quickly learn the practice of judging.

How should you conduct yourself in a debate? We have already admonished debaters that they should not treat the judge as if she were merely a passive info-receptacle propped up at the back of the room with a pen and a ballot. Just as the debaters should conduct themselves appropriately towards the judge, so too should you conduct yourself appropriately towards the debaters. The following is a list of "Don'ts" for aspiring and experienced debate judges:

- Do not talk during the debate for any reason, particularly to friends ABOUT how the debate is going. Although you are a participant in the debate, your role should be primarily nonverbal until after it is finished.
- Do not use your debate as a "round off." All too often, some critics who are accustomed to judging policy debate use parliamentary debate as a respite, with consequent slovenly behavior toward the event, including failure to flow or painstakingly deliberate the event. This behavior is extremely disrespectful to the debaters who have carefully worked and prepared for the debate.
- Do not, particularly in international debating, penalize debaters who speak in accents other than your own. Take into consideration that, for some debaters, they may not be speaking in their native tongue.

- Do not usurp the role of the judge for personal whim or dictatorial edict (e.g., "you must use the words 'x, y, z' in the course of your speeches"; or "Tell an obscene joke and I will give you 30 points"). The course and content of the debate is not yours to dictate.

- Do not engage in partisan participation during the event (e.g., heckling, introducing and sustaining arguments during speeches, making points of information, voting for a side based on one's personal belief about the topic, etc.).

- Do not arbitrarily manufacture rules (e.g., "Points of information must be in the form of a question," "Parliamentary debaters are required to present a single value or criteria (sic)," "You need to have a plan and say the word 'plan,' in the Prime Minister Constructive," "All procedural arguments must be made in the first minute [first two minutes, first three minutes] of the Leader of the Opposition's constructive speech," "New examples are prohibited in the rebuttal speeches.").

- Do not write the ballot during the rebuttal speeches. This distasteful practice conveys a total disregard for the competitors and for the integrity of the process. Wait until after the debate to make your decision and wait until after the debate to write the ballot.

- Do not "cut" speech time to hasten the process of the debate. The debaters expect and deserve the full allocation of time.

- Do not ignore the rules to suit your own preferences. For example, you must always stop time for points of order and points of personal privilege.

- Do not fail to be serious about the debate. Sometimes judges will demand simplicity (e.g., "too tired" to listen to complex argumentation; did not get involved in parliamentary debate to hear "serious argumentation;" "just entertain me").

- Do not use marginalizing and discriminatory rhetoric or practice (anti-Semitic commentary; sexual harassment from compelled speech or judge behavior; voting against participants for fashion, hairstyle, body piercings, etc.). This rule should go without saying.

This list of "Don'ts" may seem long and foreboding, but it all boils down to a few basic precepts: Be respectful of the debaters and be fair in your conduct and evaluation of the debate.

Before the debate begins, the debaters you are about to judge may want to ask you questions about your "judging philosophy" or how you plan to judge the debate. Keep your answers brief, and try to be as instructive as you can to the debaters, who are genuinely inquiring about your disposition towards arguments that may be advanced in the debate. Normally, this questioning time is not built into the time schedule for a tournament, so don't use a lot of time if the debaters want to talk to you before the debate. Avoid overly generic answers that do not provide meaningful information to the debaters: "I vote on the flow." (Yes, everyone says that about themselves.); "Entertain me." (Look, buddy, this isn't Vegas); "I'm a policy maker." (Now, if only there were consensus about what that *means*); "Rebuttals are important." (Well, duh.). If you can't say anything meaningful, don't say anything at all. In the USA, these pre-debate questioning periods have become increasingly tedious and singularly uninformative. The time would be better used after the debate as an opportunity to educate the debaters.

When you go to judge a debate, you should always bring paper and pen. We encourage you to *flow* the debate, i.e., take notes in the stylized form described elsewhere in this chapter and adapted specifically to certain formats of parliamentary debate. Even if you do not flow in the traditional sense, you must still take notes. During the course of an average debate, many complex arguments are exchanged and refuted, and you will need notes to be able to follow and resolve these arguments for yourself and later in revealing your decision, either orally or on the ballot, to the debaters. No matter how reliable your memory, if you don't take notes, you risk missing some crucial example or answer that might aid in making the best possible decision. Good note taking will always help you decide who wins and how to best explain your decision.

Of course, the critical question is this: How *do* you decide who wins the debate? If we could offer a pithy answer to this question, we would be out peddling snake oil and certainly not laboring to produce a debate textbook. The simplest answer is that you should decide the debate based on the criteria offered by the debaters in the round. Every debate is about different issues, is conducted differently, and thus should be decided on its own merits. You will have to decide whether or not the proposition team has made a case for endorsing the motion for debate. The opposition team will make arguments about why the proposition team's case is inadequate or dangerous or otherwise misguided. You will have to evaluate the merits of these arguments and decide whether the proposition team's rejoinders are adequate and satisfactory.

During the course of the debate, debaters may offer different criteria for your decision. They may even address you directly, saying that you should or should not vote on a particular argument set or on certain kind of arguments. They are not trying to order you around; rather, this is common practice. They are trying to assist you and influence you in your decision making process.

After the debate is over, you should use a separate piece of paper to figure out your decision. Even if you think, at the conclusion of the debate, that you know conclusively who has won and who has lost, you should still take some time to check your calculations and assumptions. One technique that may help you is to draw up a kind of balance sheet for the debate. List the most important arguments in the debate and then go through your flow to determine which side won those arguments and why. Then compare the arguments to each other.

Do not decide the debate based simply on the *number* of arguments won by each side. You will also need to evaluate the qualitative significance of each argument on the overall outcome of the debate. Take this common scenario: The proposition wins an advantage conclusively, while the opposition wins a disadvantage conclusively. Who wins? You can't decide based on the information we have given you. To answer this question, you need to know the relative significance of the advantage and disadvantage. This relative significance can have both quantitative and qualitative aspects. You may be tempted to decide based simply on the "biggest impact." For example, you may decide to vote for the proposition team because they claimed to avert a war, while the opposition team was "only" able to prove that the government team's proposal would cause the deaths of thousands of children.

You also need to take into account questions of risk and probability when deciding who wins in complicated debates. In the above example, your decision would doubtless change if you decided, based on arguments advanced and won by the opposition team, that there was a very low probability that the proposition team's plan would be able to avert a war.

272

However, this does not mean that you should interject your own risk calculation into the debate at this point. If the debaters have *weighed* the round for you, i.e., if they have made the best case as to why their arguments outweigh or are more important than or more instrumental to the decision than those of the other team, you need to take that into account.

One common mistake that judges make is voting for the opposition team on the basis of partial solvency arguments. A partial solvency argument is an argument advanced by the opposition team that says the proposition team's case will not solve the problem *completely*, or that the harm or existing problem is not *quite* as bad as the proposition team claims it is. These are good defensive arguments for the opposition team, but they should *almost never* be reasons to vote for the opposition team. The only thing these arguments prove is that the proposition case is not as good as it was claimed to be. Big deal. It is rare indeed that arguments advanced in debates turn out to be just as triumphant as their authors predicted they would be. The proposition team can still win if their case can be shown to be *comparatively advantageous*; that is, if they can show that it is, on balance, some increment better than the present state of affairs.

Don't vote based on your personal opinion on the topic. Sometimes, when the topic is announced, you may read it and think that you know what the debate will be about. Often, the government team will choose a case that may be different from one *you* would have chosen. This choice does not mean that you should then disregard their case or use the opposition's topicality argument as a thinly veiled excuse to vote against the government team's case. You may also have strong opinions about the subject matter of the topic. Perhaps you are a committed opponent of the death penalty and have to judge a debate about this subject. You may find that your personal presumption lies with the team that opposes the death penalty, but do not hold the other team to a higher burden of proof. The teams do not have to persuade you *personally* of the correctness of their position; the debaters are debating each other and not you.

Track arguments as they proceed and develop through the debate so you can evaluate the debate in the fairest way possible. Some judges make the mistake of deciding the debate more or less solely on the quality of the final rebuttal speech. This is a mistake because the PMR needs to be evaluated both as a response to the opposition block's arguments and as a summation of the proposition team's final position. When deciding the debate, you need to figure out if the PMR dropped, or failed to answer, any opposition arguments. You then need to decide how to weigh those conceded arguments in the context of the other arguments in the debate.

Often you will have to consider dropped, or conceded, arguments and decide what to do about them. Some conceded arguments will not impact your decision. Others will. If an argument is conceded, it means you must assign the full weight of that argument to the side that argued it. This concession phenomenon should not mean that if a team concedes some arguments, they should automatically lose the debate. All arguments are not created equally. Some arguments can be safely ignored.

Other arguments may be introduced in the debate, only to have the team that introduced them later back down on their original claim. This is smart debating and is not a reason to look askance at a team. For example, an opposition team may advance a topicality argument in their first speech but not mention it again later in the debate. This behavior should be taken to mean that the opposition team has decided to admit (at least for this debate) that the proposition team's case is topical and concentrate their fire on other arguments. You SHOULD NOT then proceed to vote on topicality in this circumstance. If the opposition team has decided to drop this argument, you should drop it as well. It is common practice for opposition teams to argue a wider variety of arguments in their first speech than in their subsequent speeches. This tactic is called argument selection and is good debate practice. Do not penalize teams for not extending all of their arguments through the entire debate.

After the debate has concluded, you will have to decide who wins the debate and why. In American parliamentary debate, you will declare one side the winner and the other side the loser, usually based on the content of the arguments advanced in the debate. In international competition, you will evaluate teams based on the matter (substance) and manner (style) of their presentations. The norm is to give equal weight to manner and matter, meaning that the style of the presentation may actually trump a winning idea or a reasoned argument. When evaluating matter, judges should take into consideration the key issues in the debate rather than number of overall issues. When evaluating manner, judges should consider the effectiveness of delivery associated with the winning arguments as well as use of humor, use of and responses to points of information, and organization of the speech.

In British and international competition, the judge will almost always function as the Speaker of the House. In this role, you lead off the debate saying something like the following: "I call the House to order to debate the motion _____. I recognize the…" As their turns come up, you should recognize speakers (first speaker for the proposition, second speaker for the opposition, etc.). At important national and international events, you will have the option of adding more personal information about the debaters, such as the name of the speaker and their school. Generally, we advise you to be a minimalist about your role.

In some international debating, there is consensus deliberation rather than individual decision. In this consensus process, you should make an effort to build a genuine consensus – you may need to compromise on certain issues, and you will certainly need to make an effort to respect the opinions of others. The panel of judges issues a single decision, ranking the four teams 1st through 4th. For the purpose of tabulation, these rankings lead to point assignments – the team ranked first gets 3 points, second gets 2, third gets 1, and fourth gets 0.

In addition to deciding the winners of the debate, you will have to fill out your ballot and assign points and ranks to individual debaters. Speaker points are a measure of performance by individual debaters. Most tournaments give speaker awards, which are trophies given to individuals based on their aggregate point accumulation during the course of a tournament. Usually, you will be asked to rank the debaters on either a 30-point or 50-point scale, although there are other kinds of scales. You may choose to assign a *low-point win*. A low-point win is a circumstance where the team that won did not get the highest points. This circumstance arises occasionally, when judges feel that one team did the better job of speaking but did not win based on the arguments. We suggest the following guidelines for using these scales:

For a 30-point scale:
- 30: Almost no one should get a 30. A perfect score should happen every few years with a really brilliant speech.
- 28-29: Brilliant.

- 26-27: Strong, well above average.
- 25: Above average
- 23-24: Modest success as a debater
- Points below 23 should be reserved for people who are both unsuccessful as debaters and are also obnoxious and mean-spirited.
- Points should never drop below a 20, even if a debater was particularly bad. Lower points frequently exclude a debate team from elimination rounds, so if you give points below 20, you are saying that a debater has no chance of rehabilitation in any other debates.

For a 50-point scale:

- 50: See above regarding a 30. Should be reserved for the very best of the very best.
- 48-49: Incredibly brilliant.
- 45-47: Outstanding.
- 42-44: Well above average.
- 38-41: Good.
- 35-37: Good, but with one or more serious flaws.
- 30-35: Poor performance.
- Below 30: Similar to receiving points below 20. See above.

After assigning points and ranking the debaters, you will need to write your ballot. We recommend that you use the ballot space to explain the reasons for your decision. Why did you vote the way you voted? What arguments were most persuasive to you? Why? Give advice and constructive criticism to the debaters you watched. What did they do well? How could they improve their performance or their arguments? Try to use as much of the ballot space as you can. Debaters and their coaches save ballots, and often refer back to them as references and resources. Do not use writing the ballot as an excuse not to deliver an oral critique, however brief, to the teams that you judge. Whatever interaction you have with the debaters after the debate will always be more valuable than the comments you write on the ballot.

A final issue therefore needs to be discussed: post-debate disclosure. Should you, as a judge, reveal your decision and the reasons for your decision after the debate? The norms for judge disclosure vary greatly throughout the world. For example, the first six preliminary debates at the Worlds Championship are disclosed, while the last three are not. Until recently, there was no disclosure at the American National Parliamentary Debate Association championship tournament. We strongly support judge disclosure.

Disclosure encourages accountable and ethical decision making. In parliamentary debate, disclosure and post-round discussion serve an educational function. These practices offer the sole opportunity for new critics to consider the decision-making behaviors of experienced practitioners. This is a golden opportunity for judge training – it is lost when judges do not disclose. Judges do not have a sufficient chance to listen to peers critique a debate they have also witnessed. No space is created for the development of the critic's skills. This is akin to a convention that would prohibit new and relatively inexperienced debaters from observing more experienced participants. As a new judge, you will find that disclosure will help you learn quickly.

Furthermore, nondisclosure is not really an option: It does not exist. Judges reveal decisions at tournaments selectively – to friends, regional teams, successful national competitors, in trade with judges evaluating their own team despite tournament rules and directors' admonitions. It is not disclosure versus nondisclosure. The real issue is whether the community should sustain selective, unequal, and unfair disclosure or support universal disclosure. We encourage you to disclose your decisions and discuss them with the debaters. The educational opportunity that disclosure affords is unparalleled.

Some object to post-debate disclosure on the grounds that there is not enough time in tournament schedules for such interaction to occur. To this argument, we suggest that tournaments have an obligation to adjust their schedule to accommodate interaction time between debaters and judges. The educational benefit accrued from five ten-minute critiques by judges during the course of a day of five debates is more than worth the investment of fifty extra minutes by the tournament participants. Disclosure benefits judges, who learn and improve from the process. Debaters also benefit, as they get direct education and exposure to the thoughts of their judge in ways simply not satisfied by a written ballot.

# CHAPTER 12

# TOURNAMENT ADMINISTRATION AND TOPIC SELECTION

The debate tournament is an organized competition for debate teams representing academic institutions, debating clubs, language societies, or regional and national organizations. Each year, many dozens of universities, debate organizations, nonprofit groups, corporations, and governments sponsor tournaments.

Tournament forms include select invitational tournaments, those events limiting entry to a particular set of debate teams. Select invitational tournaments include round robin tournaments and qualifying tournaments. Round robin tournaments are limited entry events at which each team debates all or most of the other competitors in the contest. Qualifying tournaments require entering teams to pre-qualify for participation by demonstrating success at other tournaments, including local or regional qualifying tournaments. Some national championship tournaments require that entering teams qualify to participate in the event.

Debate tournaments may also be instructional seminars. This type of event is often scheduled by universities for novice participants, national and international debate organizations in conjunction with debate and argumentation conferences, or local debating clubs or leagues at the beginning of a competitive debate season. Normally, seminars feature debater and adjudicator educational seminars, a demonstration debate, an open forum on debating art and practice, and one or two competitive debates.

The most popular tournament form is the open invitational tournament, in which any eligible debate team may enter. The overwhelming majority of university-sponsored tournaments, as well as national and international championship events, are open invitational tournaments.

Expect eligibility requirements and other participation restrictions, even at open invitational tournaments. Many national championship tournaments limit participation to debate teams from the host country. There are academic restrictions at other events – some only permit undergraduate college students, while other events are open to undergraduate and graduate students. Some tournaments have language restrictions (debates are in Russian or English, or all debates are in the national language.) Some invitational tournaments prohibit hybrid team participation, meaning that teams comprised of students from different academic institutions or debating clubs may not enter. Other events place restrictions on participation from the host – some allow a host's teams to enter the event; others allow the host's teams to enter the event under the conditions that a team may not compete for awards; still others prohibit the host's teams from participating.

Tournaments may sponsor debate divisions for competitors with differing skills and debate experience. Competitive tournaments may sponsor an inter-varsity division for experienced debates, as well as a separate division for novice debaters. Some international events with debating in English may support separate elimination round debates or championship debate for participants with English as a foreign language.

Tournament hosts design events to serve competitive and educational needs. These goals can conflict. It is important that tournament hosts identify the appropriate goals for their events and design them accordingly. Tournament hosts should schedule events, if practicable, in cooperation with debate organizations and colleagues to minimize conflicts and increase debating opportunities for contestants.

## BEFORE THE TOURNAMENT

Debate tournaments may be simple affairs involving 10 to 15 debate teams and judges. They may also be very complex conferences with hundreds of competitors and additional hundreds of adjudicators and guests. Although the scope of arrangements and resources will differ from event to event, the minimum administrative arrangements are similar for all tournaments. A tournament director's responsibilities seldom vary, despite the change in the scope of her enterprise.

The following checklist includes the major elements of tournament administration and preparation:

### DECIDING TO HOST

The decision to host a debate tournament is a major undertaking for an individual or a small group. The decision should not be made lightly. Comprehensive planning, including prospective budgeting and tournament administration, ought to be completed before a public announcement inviting debaters and adjudicators to attend an event. It is better to anticipate problems, bottlenecks, and conflicts prior to a decision to host than to discover them at the time that guests are arriving at the airport, eager to participate in your tournament. Directors should, of course, consider the cost of awards, ballots, staff, guest judges, site expenses, office supplies, food, entertainment, lodging, and miscellaneous expenses in the prospective budget.

Running a simulation of a debate tournament, including the administration of the debates using tournament tabulation software, is useful as a staff training opportunity.

## ANNOUNCING THE TOURNAMENT

- Acquire contact information
- Arrange for a date and site
- Draft an invitation

The tournament director should initially acquire contact information for prospective attendees. Such information can come from mailing lists from debate organizations, tournament participant lists from directors in the region, and addresses of debate "listservs."

The director will need to arrange for a site and date for the event. She should coordinate a date for the tournament with local debate organizations and colleagues in the region. Preliminary contacts regarding the tournament will reduce the likelihood that other area debate events will be scheduled on the selected date.

The director should select the tournament site and begin preliminary negotiations for access to this site on the selected tournament dates. She should anticipate the potential number of participants and make sure there are sufficient rooms for debates. She should make arrangements for room access (unlocking doors, etc.) and any additional administrative support that might be required to manage the site.

If required, a tournament representative should contact national debate organizations for support information and counsel and ensure compliance with any administrative rules or guidelines for the debate events.

The tournament director should draft a letter of invitation for the tournament, including relevant details for guests. A sample tournament invitation letter is included in Appendix 2. The letter should be mailed to prospective attendees and debate listservs after the director manages the administrative tasks remaining in the tournament checklist.

## INFORMATION FOR TOURNAMENT GUESTS

- Schedule
- Transportation information

- Lodging information
- Meal information

Tournament guests require specific information when making a decision to attend a debate tournament and facilitate transportation to and from the event. Guests need to know the time they should arrive and depart the tournament. A tournament schedule is necessary for travel planning and should include the time for the opening ceremonies, first debate round, and the conclusion of the championship debate.

In our experience, too many debate tournaments are unable to complete events on schedule. The primary reason, it seems, is the tournament director's failure to set a reasonable schedule. Judges and debaters need time to move to and from the competition rooms. Some will get lost. If the tournament uses several buildings for the event, some individuals will get lost for each of the first two or three rounds of debate.

Judges may provide a "philosophy" or list of "preferences" prior to debates. In select debates, typically those debates for new competitors, there is a brief instructional or a question-and-answer period before the opening speech of the contest to familiarize participants with the specific rules for the event. A judge or panel of judges will need time to deliberate, privately or by consensus depending on the rules for the event, before reaching a decision and ranking the teams or listing a winner. The judge will take time to accurately complete a ballot for proper tabulation at the conclusion of the debate and make individual notes for speakers, offer written constructive criticism for teams, or explain the reason for the decision on the outcome of the debate on the debate ballot.

What does this mean? It means that more time is required for each round of debate than permitted in tournament schedules. Hosts should provide a meaningful schedule to guests and design it so there is time to adhere to it even if delays occur. Directors would be wise to add 30 to 45 minutes to the schedule, particularly after the first or second round of debate, to account for such issues as longer-than-anticipated instructional question-and-answer sessions, difficulties in finding competition rooms, and registration queues.

Tournament schedules and policies should minimize "hostage holding." In other words, a debate tournament should be designed to allow guests to attend the event and depart as quickly as possible after their elimination from the competition. Guests may, of course, choose to remain at a tournament for the duration of the event. Tournaments can be enjoyable social gatherings. The event's conviviality may encourage participants to continue to stay on. Many participants enjoy witnessing additional debates, particularly the later elimination debates in which the top competitors engage in highly skilled exchanges. These debates can be fine educational demonstrations for less experienced debaters, as well as sophisticated and enjoyable encounters. The choice to remain at a tournament site should be the guests' rather than that of the tournament administration. A debate tournament should assist guest departure in a convenient manner, a courtesy to those who may have traveled a distance to attend the tournament or may need to leave for any number of personal, academic, or business reasons.

A sample schedule for a debate tournament, with six preliminary debates and four elimination rounds, might be as follows:

**Friday**

| 10:00 AM – 11:00 AM | Registration |
| 11:00 AM – 11:45 AM | Judge Training and Seminar |
| 12:00 PM – 1:30PM | Round 1 |
| 1:45 PM – 3:15 PM | Round 2 |
| 3:30 PM – 5:00 PM | Round 3 |
| 6:30 PM – 8:00 PM | Round 4 |

**Saturday**

| 8:30 AM – 10:00 AM | Round 5 |
| 10:30 AM – 12:00 PM | Round 6 |
| 12:30 PM – 12:45 PM | Announcements, Awards, and Elimination Rounds |
| 1:00 PM – 2:15 PM | Octofinals |
| 2:30 PM – 3:45 PM | Quarterfinals |
| 4:00 PM – 5:15 PM | Semifinals |
| 5:30 PM – 7:00 PM | Finals |

This schedule, designed for a two-team parliamentary debate format, allows approximately 90 minutes for each round. It would be difficult for the tournament to fail to meet this schedule for events. For example, a tournament debate would require 15 to 20 minutes for preparation time and 40 minutes for actual competition. The schedule includes an additional 30 minutes for judge deliberation, disclosure of the decision, and supplemental constructive commentary, including oral discussion with debaters and the completion of a written ballot. A tournament design for a four-team inter-varsity tournament with nearly 60 minutes of competition time might eliminate a preliminary debate and one or more elimination debates. The schedule might be:

**Friday**

| | |
|---|---|
| 3:00 PM – 4:00 PM | Registration |
| 4:00 PM – 4:45 PM | Judge Training and Seminar |
| 5:00 PM – 7:00 PM | Round 1 |
| 7:15 PM – 9:15 PM | Round 2 |

**Saturday**

| | |
|---|---|
| 9:00 AM – 11:00 AM | Round 3 |
| 11:30 AM – 1:30 PM | Round 4 |
| 2:30 PM – 4:30 PM | Round 5 |
| 5:00 PM – 7:00 PM | Semifinals |
| 7:30 PM – 9:30 PM | Finals |

Some directors host instructional seminars or an educational tournament, which often include some competitive debates. A schedule for such an event, typically offered in a single day, might be the following:

**Saturday**

| | |
|---|---|
| 8:30 AM – 9:00 AM | Registration |
| 9:30 AM – 10:30 AM | Demonstration Debate and Evaluation |
| 10:45 AM – 11:30 AM | Instructional Small Group Session 1 |
| 11:30 AM – 1:00 PM | Lunch |
| 1:00 PM – 2:30 PM | Round 1 |
| 2:45 AM – 3:30 PM | Instructional Small Group |

| 4:00 PM – 5:30 PM | Session 2 |
| 6:00 PM – 6:30 PM | Round 2 |
| | Summation and Awards |

In addition to schedule information, travelers will need to have information regarding any arrangements for transportation, lodging, and meals. Tournament directors need to inform guests of the proximity of airports, train, and bus stations, as well as the cost and preferred method of public transportation or taxi service from such locations to the tournament site. They also must provide walking, driving, and parking directions for those commuting to the site. If tournament hosts are able to arrange for discounted travel options (e.g., group airline discounts), they should include the necessary information, such as an airline or rail service discount code, in the tournament invitation.

Many debate events negotiate a discounted rate for conference guests with one or more local hotels. Special lodging offers should be included in the invitation. Tournament directors should make arrangements for special rates for dates prior to and after the tournament competition dates for those who need to stay extra days because of their travel arrangements. Tournaments may also offer provide "crash," or free, housing for guests. Guests do not expect much when accepting free accommodations – it may be a worthwhile gesture to provide them, much appreciated by those traveling a great distance or otherwise expending significant resources to compete.

Tournament hosts should explain what, if any, food service will be available at the tournament site. This information is not simply a courtesy, but a necessity for guests with dietary health concerns. Tournaments that provide meals to participants should consider the needs of all attendees, making an effort to offer vegan, vegetarian, and low-sugar options, as well as the standard full buffet for omnivores.

## TOURNAMENT OPERATIONS

- Tabulating room staff
- Tabulating hardware and software
- Tournament office supplies
- Guest judging

The tournament director should identify experienced personnel to support tournament administrative tasks and debate tabulation. Experienced individuals may be in the hosting institution or organization, but many experienced tournament tabulation staff and administrators are willing to provide advice or volunteer their time to assist at other sites. It is important to have sufficient personnel to manage tournament operations, *but* it is of equal importance to avoid a bloated tabulating room staff. Few things interfere with tab room efficiency more than an unwieldy and unnecessary bureaucracy to ensure a "responsible" job for each staff person. Some tasks are *not* better managed by several individuals when a single, capable person will do. A director should employ the minimum number of experienced or otherwise talented individuals for the tabulating staff.

There is tournament tabulating software for Macintosh and PC computers for two-team events. There is tabulating software for PC computers for four-team events. The software is free and available on the Internet. Tournament directors should acquire the software that is appropriate for their computer system. The software should be downloaded and tested several weeks before the tournament.

Tournament software needs hardware. The tournament must have one or more computers and a printer. The tournament should have access to a photocopier, if this is at all practical. The director will need to purchase office supplies for tournament operations, including large envelopes or folders for registration packets and ballots, pens, paper, tape, and stapler. Depending on the physical layout of the site, the tournament director may want to rent or purchase walkie-talkies (a relatively modest, one-time expense) for communication with tournament staff at other buildings at the tournament site. The director and other designated personnel should have a cellular phone for emergency communication with guests and site personnel.

Each debate requires one or more judges. The host should anticipate the number of judges required for the event and secure guest judges, as many attending teams will not have judges accompanying them to the event. Tournament directors may also choose to limit entries to those teams with accompanying judges, if it is difficult to identify a sufficient number of judges for the event.

## TOURNAMENT MATERIALS

- Registration packet
- Awards
- Ballots
- Instructional information
- Topic writing and selection

Tournaments work best when guests receive enough information to successfully navigate the physical site and the rules of the event. The tournament director should prepare a registration packet, which is a set of materials to deliver to participants at the time of team registration. The registration packet should include a receipt for entry fees and other tournament costs, copies of the tournament schedule, site and area maps, lists of interesting things to do in the area (if applicable), and contact information for the tournament tabulating room and director.

The tournament director should purchase awards for team and individual performers, if the tournament will present such awards. (Most events do.) The director should ensure the arrival of awards several days prior to the date of the event and examine them for defects or missing items.

Debaters expect an accounting of their performances in an oral and written form. The tournament host should purchase or produce ballots for each judge for each round of debate. If the tournament has access to a photocopier, it is more convenient and decidedly less expensive to design and photocopy a tournament ballot. A sample ballot is included in Appendix 2. The tournament produces photocopies of the submitted ballot from each judge for each of the participating teams in the debate.

The host may choose to provide documents with competitor and adjudicator information. This information may include rules for the competition, guidelines for judging, and recommendations for assisting in the efficient operation of the tournament.

There are different kinds of debate motions, often categorized as limited preparation, closed and open. A limited preparation motion is announced from several hours to several weeks prior to a tournament debate on the motion. Debaters are provided with some time to research materials and prepare arguments on the motion. A closed motion is most easily understood as a literal statement, one that should engage debaters in commonly accepted and obvious terms. An open motion describes a motion with more abstract or indirect language.

Limited preparation motion: *This House would limit civil liberties to promote national security.*

Closed motion: *This House supports China's entry in the WTO.*

Open motion: *This House would bury it.*

It is not readily apparent that a resolution might fit one, and only one, topic category. Indeed, we believe that the distinctions among these categories are more artificial than real. They are important, nevertheless, because tournament directors and judges have expectations about proposition team topic interpretations and arguments that are set by these categories. But motions are not so easily limited to a single category. Could the listed limited preparation topic on restrictions on civil liberties be used as a closed motion? Yes. Is the closed motion on China's entry to the WTO a metaphor that might also be an example of an open motion? Yes.

A tournament director must decide which sorts of motions to include in the contest and the manner to position the motions in the tournament. Should the tournament offer a mix of categories? Should the tournament offer a single category, e.g., only closed motions? Should the motions differ from preliminary debates to elimination round debates? Should motion categories vary from round to round?

In a general sense, tournament directors currently try to encourage debate on diverse topics, although this may be accomplished without using more than one category of motions. It is possible, for example, to promote discussions on a broad range of substantive issues and use only closed motions for debate.

A tournament host should consider the skills, experiences, and expectations of participants, as well as the purposes of the event. These factors will influence the selection of the categories of motions, as well as the wording of specific topics for debate. A host may decide to offer a variety of topic categories at the event. The host might, for example, provide six preliminary rounds of debate, selecting two each of limited preparation, closed, and open motions.

The tournament director, in this circumstance, can use the two motions from the same category in following debates, beginning with the odd-numbered debate round. This format is not complicated and is particularly easy to execute in two-team debates. (It is a bit problematic in four-team rounds of debate but by no means impossible.) In tournament contests with an even number of preliminary debates, each team ought to debate the same number of proposition and opposition debates. In a tournament with six preliminary rounds, each debate team would debate three times as the proposition and three times as the opposition. In an odd-numbered debate, a team could debate on the proposition side or the opposition side. For example, in the first round of debating, half the entering teams would be assigned to the proposition and they would be matched with opposition teams. In the even-numbered rounds, the teams switch sides. The opposition teams debate on the proposition and the proposition teams debate on the opposition. This cycle is repeated in each pair of debates in the preliminary debates, beginning with the odd-numbered round of debate.

If the categories of motions are matched to the debate rounds in which each debate team will argue both the proposition and opposition sides, participants are more likely to consider that the contest is fair. Each team, in the example, would appreciate the opportunity to debate both the proposition and opposition sides of limited preparation, closed, and open motions. If the tournament director placed a limited preparation motion in the first and third debates, rather than the first and second debates, it is likely that some teams would debate twice on the proposition or the opposition on this sort of motion. If limited preparation time provides an advantage to one side of the debate, it may be the case that the director's placement of categories of motions in debate rounds has given an unfair advantage to the some teams in the tournament.

Some tournament directors might choose a single motion category for the entire event. A tournament organized at the time of a national election, for example, might select a series of limited preparation topics on election reform or the salient issues of candidates' or political parties' policies.

It may be the case that some tournament hosts might select a certain type of motion for the championship or grand final debate (so selected, for example, for a large public or broadcast audience available to watch the final tournament debate). It may be necessary to promote the event with an announcement of a specific topic or a topic area. In this circumstance, the director might use a limited preparation motion or closed motion. These motions might "preview" the topic for targeted demographic groups likely to attend or view the debate.

There are, of course, a number of debate tournaments with an odd number of preliminary debates. If this is the case, the tournament director should reserve her most equitable or balanced motion for the last debate, as that will be the debate that will create an imbalance of argument sides for the contest. This final preliminary debate, in an odd-numbered round, will mean that teams debate more rounds on either the proposition or the opposition side.

Are there guides to the creation of effective resolutions for debate? Yes and no. There are guides that seem commonsensical. The motion ought to be interesting. It should a matter in controversy (i.e., one should know that the matter is debatable). Participants should have some knowledge of the topic or the ideas and arguments suggested by it. The motion should be clearly worded. In most instances, the topic should be affirmatively, rather than negatively worded. It is better to avoid topics that begin *"This House would not..."* If the tournament includes participants from more than one country, the director should select some topics that transcend or encourage debate about boundaries (geographic, cultural, economic, etc.).

These and similar guides, or aspirations, might be satisfying ("I want topics that produce roughly equal arguments for the adversaries," "I want motions that will inspire an audience or cause it to swoon," "I want topics that will produce rigorous and challenging debate") but these are rather abstract and unhelpful critical guides and almost impossible to consistently use as standards for generating and constructing topic ideas. For example, the more one thinks about the issue of those matters that make a good resolution, the more one produces standards for constructing viable motions. The more standards for topic wording are generated, the more desirable it appears to apply the standards. The more one tries to apply multiple standards for evaluating a topic, the less likely it becomes that any topic will pass muster. It is something of a paradox.

Much of the criticism of debating motions, and much of the admiration for motions, appears as *ex post facto* commentary on debate. If a debate involves sophisticated, challenging argumentation and refutation, expressed in a clever or entertaining manner, the participants and observers construct the topic as "good." If the debate is shallow and unappealing, the motion is to blame – it is a "bad" motion. These claims are self-serving and have little to do with honest assessment of motions. If motions produce debate or should produce debate (and that is all that we can reasonably expect of them), we should consider them satisfactory. If they suspend debate, and a few motions do, they are inappropriate.

We offer a simple guide for writing a motion: ***Regardless of the category of the motion, keep the wording of the topic simple and direct***. There isn't enough preparation time prior to a debate for participants to figure or imagine the inner workings of the topic author's peculiarities and psychoses. Debaters should be able to take any motion and immediately (or within the allotted preparation time) begin to work the idea. In addition, it isn't necessary to force the hand of participants by including complex information in the actual motion for debate. The debaters will generate complex ideas from basically worded motions. They need to do so. This is the way they are more likely to win the debate.

In addition, simply worded motions provide due consideration to those participants debating in a second or third language. They assist novice or speech-apprehensive debaters, who are likely to be anxious about public speaking or the format and do not need to be confounded by the motion.

Crafting a "simply worded motion" still requires time and care. It may not be so simple to design the motion with the quality of "simplicity." (The simple is not so simple. There you have it. A poorly worded motion.) It is in the interest of a tournament director or topic designer to consider, from several perspectives (which may involve speaking to others about these matters, unless one prefers a schizophrenic or intellectually chaotic approach to idea formation), how debates will occur on the finished topics. There is a context for producing debate motions. The purpose of the motion is to promote debate. If experienced practitioners have considerable difficulty understanding the motion or applying interpretations of it to the context of a debate in a few minutes, the care, simplicity, investment of research and time, and other favorable features of the topic design method lose their relevance. The topic does not work and it should not be considered.

This difficulty is not a reason to permanently discard debate on the motion. There are extraordinarily worthwhile ideas that ought to be included in parliamentary debate tournaments that do not fit a ready, one-size-fits-all topic formula. It may be the case that the topic language must be carefully customized prior to its use in tournament debates. It may require testing in public or practice debates to begin working out the difficulties in its construction. The motion could then be used in later events.

Here is an important, perhaps urgent, note: Motions should be designed well in advance of the actual tournament date. Well in advance. They should be shared with other experienced topic authors for critical review and editing. In addition, the director should draft more motions than required by the number of rounds for the event. The director should, quite obviously, draft at least as many motions as the number of rounds of debate. There are circumstances in which fast-changing national and world events may moot selected topics. Other debate tournaments may use some of the topics that you considered. An announced limited preparation topic for a subsequent tournament may affect your decision to use the same idea for extemporaneous argument training. It is sound to have several additional motions in appropriate categories available as substitutes for the ones that might be pre-selected for the tournament.

It can be argued, however, that categories of motions, as well as the wording of the motions themselves, are different from the substance, core elements, or "heart," of the debate. It isn't the case that appreciation of the motion carries the day. Few debates are won or lost when the motion is announced. Rather, debates are won on reasoning, evidence, and the persuasive skills of participants engaged in sophisticated argument on diverse issues related to the topic's interpretation. After all, any topic interpretation begets a host of argument matters for a debate. It is these subsequently revealed issues, not the language of the motion itself, on which the outcome of a debate ultimately rests.

Topic categories and wording choices may influence the outcome of debates and may set performance expectations for the contestants, but the matter of which side does the better debating or convincingly wins the arguments might still be decisively resolved on other issues. Topic selection, wording, and placement of motions in particular rounds of a debate contest are important matters. These issues, however, will not inevitably alter the outcome of the majority of contest debates. The wording of topics is often a source of complaint for participants, but its influence in the outcome of debates is exaggerated. Of more importance is the ability of debaters to craft a discrete, convincing, and reasonable interpretation of a given motion. Interpretive and argument skills matter more than topic language choices by tournament directors.

## ANCILLARY INFORMATION

- Last-minute travel information
- Harassment and legal information
- Videotaping and broadcast preparation
- Confirmations

The host should update travelers with weather and travel information, particularly if transit delays or inclement weather are likely.

The host should provide any organizational legal information regarding access for differently abled people or harassment policy. Tournament hosts should provide access to the site and support services for differently abled individuals (for example, individuals with impaired hearing or in wheelchairs) and, in a number of cases, may be required by law to provide relevant accommodations. The host should have available information regarding sexual and other harassment and should have a policy in place in the event of a harassment report. Once again, this information may be required by national debate organizations, leagues, or by applicable local or national laws.

The tournament director should consider the legal implications of tournament management, including applicable ethics codes for academic institutions and national organizations, tax requirements, and labor policies. For example, some tournament directors accept personal checks, made payable to them as individuals, as payment for registering teams. This may be an acceptable practice if the tournament is a private profit-making operation by the tournament director, for which the tournament director accepts sole liability. If, however, the director is an employee or representative of an institution, the director may have a different relationship with the tournament. When the tournament is sponsored by an academic institution, accepting personal checks may be a violation of university policy. The university hosts and sponsors the event as a university conference program and expects revenue to be directed to the treasurer's office and general fund. Accepting personal checks made payable to the director may require a tournament director to declare the payments as income, subject to local and national taxes. Payments to guest judges and tabulation staff, done privately ("off the books"), may violate tax and labor policy. These issues are important considerations for directors, who may face serious personal and legal liability for failure to manage what may be the equivalent of many thousands of dollars in tournament payments.

The tournament host may choose to arrange to videotape debates or provide live Internet streaming of selected rounds. These plans should be completed well in advance of the tournament and several tests of audio/visual equipment or Internet configurations and connections should be completed by the date of the tournament. If appropriate, the tournament should provide appropriate waivers for individuals appearing on video or in broadcasts.

Prior to the tournament, the director should confirm all arrangements for the event. Guests should receive confirmation of their successful admission. Tournament service and support – room access, dining services, entertainment, etc. – should be confirmed. Efficient and timely planning will not matter much if there is a last minute error or oversight. It is best to check all the elements of successful tournament operations before guests arrive.

## DURING THE TOURNAMENT

The management of a debate tournament is a surprisingly uncomplicated affair if the host has completed the "before the tournament" tasks. Events ought to follow each other according to schedule. Experienced staff ought to be available to assist with difficulties. Tournament directors need to prepare for unlikely or untoward events.

- Opening Events
- Registration
- Instructional sessions

The tournament director should prepare an orientation session to begin the event. This session may consist of documents supplied to participants at tournament registration, a video presentation, or an opening meeting. The orientation should include rules for the event, schedules, maps, and other resources to facilitate participation and avoid tournament delays. The documents or opening session may also include instructional information for debaters and judges.

Instructional information may include demonstration debates, seminars, training sessions, and support materials. Some contestants may have not participated in debates or in the particular debate format prior to the tournament. A seminar is an opportunity to assist participating debaters in understanding the intricacies of the rules and conventions of debate practice. It is also an opportunity to provide judge information, instruction, and testing. This sort of judge training will both inform judges of practice standards for the tournament and also set consistent standards in deliberations and evaluations of debater performances.

## TOURNAMENT OPERATIONS

- Announcements
  - Tabulations
- Services: Meals, lodging, entertainment, awards
- Troubleshooting

The director should select a conveniently located common area for the public distribution of any announcements. Information that will be used throughout the tournament, e.g., an event schedule or directions to debate rooms, should be posted. Contact information for problems, as well as the location of the tabulating room, should be posted. The site should serve as a gathering place for tournament participants. Judges should secure and return ballots to this area.

The director should decide on a manner to announce each motion for debate. There are several popular forms, including a single common announcement, the private announcement by a judge or speaker, and the selection of the motion by the participants.

Many tournaments have a single public announcement of the motion for each round of debate. Tournament participants gather in a common area at an appointed time and the director of the event or a representative of the tournament-tabulating staff makes an announcement of the motion. Typically, participants have approximately 15 to 20 minutes from the time of the announcement to the start of the debate.

Each tournament sets its own policy regarding preparation time between the announcement of the topic and the beginning of each debate. A sensible rule is that each team should have a minimum of 15 minutes to prepare for debates. If it requires five minutes to walk from the common announcement area to the furthest debating room, the tournament should provide 20 minutes of preparation time (15 minutes + a five-minute walk to the debate site). This time frame provides all debaters a satisfactory minimum preparation time.

Other tournaments attach a copy of the motion to the debate ballot that judges receive prior to debates. After the teams and judge arrive at their assigned room, the judge announces the motion and the teams have 15 minutes to prepare for the debate.

Another form of topic announcement, for two-team debates uses a similar ballot attachment.. The attachment to the ballot, however, has three motions for debate. The proposition team is able to strike or delete one of the motions from consideration and the opposition team is permitted to strike a second of the three motions. The remaining motion is the used for the debate. Each team is allowed approximately one minute to make its choice of a topic strike and preparation time begins after the second topic is struck from consideration.

The results of debates are collected by the tournament administration and used to tabulate tournament results on a round-by-round basis. Tabulating software is available to assist this task. There are, in many regions of the world, persons with experience with tabulating software. If the tournament director or selected staff is not familiar with tournament tabulation methods or software, the director should identify one or more individuals to serve as tabulation directors or consultants. This procedure should ensure no problems or unnecessary delays in tournament operations. Quite obviously, accurate recording of the results of a competition is essential to its purpose and of great importance to guests, and the director need to pay considerable attention to this element of tournament administration.

After the announcement of the each preliminary debate, a member of the tournament staff should post the results of the debate tournament to that point. Tabulating software will produce the team records of each team in the contest. An alphabetical or rank order listing of the teams should be posted in a common area.

A public posting of the tournament results allows teams to verify the accuracy of tabulating room results. Debate teams are able to confirm the announced decision at the conclusion of the debate with the posted version by the tournament staff. Publicly posting results decreases the likelihood of tabulating room error and may avoid a serious matter, namely, the inadvertent exclusion of a qualifying team from the elimination round debates. It is also a convenient way to disseminate information to participants. After all, the results of each debate are hardly the proprietary information for the tournament tabulating staff. In fact, there is no reason for the tabulating room to have access to this information, other than to determine the appropriate debate pairings for following round of debate.

The director must coordinate any receptions, meals, awards presentations, or other gatherings during the tournament. The host should prepare any speeches or announcements for these events well in advance. The director must have contact information for caterers, organizers, or other support staff for social events. Tournament staff should be assigned to manage these events, if necessary, as the tournament director may be involved with other matters at the time. All preparations for social and cultural events, awards, guest lodging, etc., should be confirmed with organizers and vendors prior to the date of the tournament.

The best planning will not necessarily guarantee a problem-free tournament. Inclement weather, hotel and catering company errors, locked classrooms or debating chambers, an insufficient number of judges, computer tabulating hardware and software difficulties, and more can disrupt an otherwise well-planned event. We have several suggestions for tournament directors and staff. These suggestions will not necessarily prevent problems but might assist in their amelioration.

In addition to posting event and contact information and providing guests with it in their registration materials, and having cellular telephones for staff communications, as previously suggested, the tournament host should appoint an assistant tournament director, with the full authority to make decisions regarding tournament operations, in the event that serious difficulties occur at the same time and the director must attend to one of them.

The tournament should maintain a troubleshooting desk or make other arrangements for guest services. This part of tournament operations assists participants with legitimate but relatively minor concerns (i.e., those concerns that do not affect overall operations), including directions to debating rooms, lost and found items, schedule information, notes on dining options in the area, etc.

## AFTER THE TOURNAMENT

### DOCUMENTATION

- Ballots and tabulation results
- Tournament Information
- Review and evaluation

The tournament host should collect the ballots from each for the preliminary and elimination round debates. Staff should organize and place ballots for each team or academic institution in folders or envelopes and make them available to guests at the point that guests are eliminated from the event. The tournament director should ensure that complete tabulation and awards results are included in each folder.

The tournament may choose to post the results of the contest on debate listservs and Websites. Full information for individual and team results may be e-mailed to listservs or forwarded to Website administrators. Some debate leagues or national organizations require that tournament results be forwarded to their offices for inclusion in national rankings for annual awards. The tournament director should promptly and completely deliver tournament tabulation results or a list of award recipients, as required.

The director should also post the motions used during the tournament to debate listservs and Websites. A topic list is an outstanding resource for competitors unable to participate in the contest. It provides a set of topics for practice debating. It familiarizes debaters with the issues considered controversial and appropriate for academic debates. It prevents the duplication of motions at subsequent tournaments.

One of the important functions of tournament administration is to establish an institutional history of the event. As a guide for colleagues, an efficient reference for the administration of future events, and a means to coordinate event publicity, a comprehensive tournament evaluation is a valued asset.

The director should prepare a comprehensive review of the tournament, including files of all invitations and announcements, schedules, support documentation, tabulation results, topics, and award recipients. The director should evaluate the event to anticipate her needs for subsequent tournaments and to provide a documentary history of tournament administration that will be available to future directors.

## PUBLICITY AND CONCLUSION

The tournament staff should promote its successful administration. Publicity may include press announcements to local and national media, broadcast of videotaped debates or tournament excerpts on the Internet, and announcements of future events to debate Websites and listservs. The tournament director should contact local media prior to the competition and be ready to provide written promotional materials or conduct interviews during the tournament.

The director has a final task, namely, to thank those individuals and institutions providing tournament support. A personal note, reference letter, Internet announcement, or thank-you on a Website should suffice to graciously commend the efforts of others, many of whom undoubtedly volunteered considerable time and skill to the endeavor.

# APPENDIX 1

# SAMPLE
# PARLIAMENTARY
# TOPICS

All of the topics included below are actual topics that have been used in tournament competitions, both nationally and internationally, over the course of several years. In this list, you will find topics of all kinds. Some topics are better than others, according to the guidelines we set out in Chapter 12. Some of these motions are closed or relatively closed, while some are open or relatively open. Some topics are metaphorical or idiomatic, and may thus be difficult for non-native English speakers. Other topics are specific to the internal affairs of particular nations, but can be easily modified to fit the needs of your nation or community.

This list can be an effective tool for teaching and practice. Debaters should use the topics for preparation – a good exercise would be to pick a few topics at a time and, for each topic, generate case ideas and topic interpretations linking the case to the motion. Teachers, trainers, and coaches should use the list to provide practice topics for their students. They may also choose to use topics from this list for tournaments or other kinds of scrimmages among debaters or debate squads. The most important function of this list, however, is that it serves to show the wide range of parliamentary debate topics.

This House believes that 'the power to tax is the power to destroy.' (Justice John Marshall).

## OPEN MOTIONS

This House would reject consensus.

This House would put pragmatism before its principles.

This House would heal the wound.

This House would rather be in than out.

This House would break the law.

This House supports the strong state.

Resistance is not futile.

This House would contemplate rather than act.

This House would mind the business of others.

The messenger should be shot.

This House believes that the Emperor is wearing no clothes.

This House should investigate the investigators.

This House would milk the cow dry.

This House would catch 'em all!

This House would be apathetic.

This House believes that the buck stops here.

That radical change is superior to incremental change.

This House would send the boy home.

The journey of a thousand miles begins with one step.

This House has got some nerve.

This House would walk the catwalk.

This House believes that once you start you can't stop.

This House believes that peace is undesirable.

This House approves of political inertia.

This House believes in order to get it you have to give it up.

This House believes love is foolish.

This House prefers second place to first.

This House would open its doors.

This House believes that the light at the end of the tunnel is an oncoming train.

This House would stop using cosmetics.

This House would expose the secrets.

This House would pull the plug.

This House would defend elitism.

This House would redistribute the wealth.

This House should recycle.

This House believes that good things come to those who wait.

This House believes that life imitates art.

This House believes you can judge a book by its cover.

This house believes that festivals are superior to competitions.

This House should pull the plug.

This House should teach an old dog a new trick.

This House should consider carefully that which seems initially successful.

This House should announce that the King is naked.

This House should check its messages.

This House should change its locks.

How you play the game ought to be more important than winning the game.

When they say it's not about the money, it's about the money.

The House would still the fires within.

This House would develop a strategy rather than a theory.

This House prefers cooperation to competition.

This House would hunt them down to the ends of the earth.

This House would reject dogma.

This House would rock the boat.

This House would balance the books.

This House believes the customer is always right.

Dramatic failure is more useful than mild success.

This House believes that silence means consent.

This House believes that information wants to be free.

This House believes that the local is preferable to the global.

This House should balance its diet.

This House would lock its doors.

If at first you don't succeed, quit.

This House should embrace

Adults must respect children.

This House believes that it's time for a change.

This House believes in the devolution of power.

This House would remain anonymous.

This House would break the law in the interests of justice.

This House would break a bad law.

This House would let them in.

This House supports civil disobedience.

This House believes that the end justifies the means.

Resolved: Actions speak louder than words.

This House believes in the greatest good for the greatest number.

This House would stick to its principles.

This House believes in Right and Wrong.

This House needs a nanny state.

This House would legislate, not liberate.

This House believes that divided we stand, united we fall.

The carrot is more effective than the stick.

This House would put an "X" in the center square.

This House would meet cruelty with kindness.

This House would reject big government.

This House would rather be public than private.

We don't believe that imitation is flattery.

Only the lives of the mighty have value in this world.

The power of one is stronger than the power of many.

Obedience to authority is an excuse for cowardice.

True courage is demonstrated through passive resistance.

The conflict that occurs within is as complex painful as the conflict that occurs without.

This House would throw caution to the wind.

This House would live outside the law.

This House would privatize it.

This House would rather be beautiful than clever.

This House rejects a cost-benefit analysis.

This House would not vouch for vouchers.

This House doesn't believe these politicians.

Ignoring the fringe is better than engaging it.

This House believes that childhood is more important than adulthood.

This House would remove government from the lives of the people.

This House believes apples and oranges make strange bedfellows.

Be it resolved that needs of the many outweigh the needs of the few.

This House should grease the wheels of justice.

This House believes that there are necessary illusions.

This House would repeat the mistakes of the past.

This House believes that fortune favors the foolish.

This House believes that it is better to be a middle of the roader.

This House believes that the people are wrong.

This House believes that we have never had it so good.

This House would let the majority rule.

This House believes in freedom from fear.

This House prefers justice to popularity.

This House expects the Spanish Inquisition.

This House should be a spiritual House.

This House should be a virtual House.

This House would support gridlock.

This House is in contempt of the court.

This House would assist those who wish to die.

The grass grows greener on the other side.

This House believes in the survival of the fittest.

This House should save the family farm.

This House should resist the tyranny of principle.

Regulate the regulators.

This House should break the law.

This House would encourage saving our green.

This House believes it is better to stand alone.

This House would test its tires.

This House is sad, cold and lonely.

This House calls for grants,

not loans.

This House would bring back the rope.

This House will not survive.

This House would thwart the will of the majority.

This House should hide the truth.

This House would rage against the machine.

This House believes the pen in mightier than the sword.

Be it resolved that might makes right.

This House believes that there ought to be a law.

Corporate power has gone too far.

This House would burn the village to save it.

This House believes that fanaticism works.

This House believes that the truth is out there.

This House believes that old enemies can become new friends.

Resolved: This House believes there is no blank slate.

This House would boldly go where no House has gone before.

This House would rather be a tortoise than a hare.

This House would rather explode than implode.

This House believes that what costs little is of little worth.

This House would root for the underdog.

This House would watch the skies.

This House would watch the watchers.

This House would assassinate

its enemies.

This House would defend elitism.

This House believes in painting the town red.

This House would cry over spilt milk.

This House would return the relics.

This House would repair the damage.

This House would not stand by her man.

This House would centralize.

This House would steal the beggar's tin cup.

This House would check it out.

This House believes that progress is a myth.

This House would blame society.

This House would do the salsa.

This House should be forced to give up its vices.

This House would find the truth.

This House should forgive and forget.

This House would rather be East than West.

## TAXATION

Wealthy people's taxes should be raised and poor people's taxes should be lowered.

This House would use taxation to regulate behavior.

This House should replace the federal income tax with a federal sales tax.

Citizens should not be forced to pay taxes to finance

Social Security.

The government should be financed exclusively by voluntary contributions.

Citizens should be taxed to finance public education.

You can spend your own money more wisely than the government.

This House would give substantial tax relief to prevent a recession.

This House supports a flat tax.

This House would cut taxes.

In certain circumstances, a conscientious objection to paying taxes is justified.

This House would abolish direct taxation.

This House believes that taxation is theft.

This House believes that a fairer society needs higher taxation.

This House believes that low taxes are preferable to extensive government service.

## CRIMINAL AND CIVIL JUSTICE

A victim's deliberate use of deadly force is justified as a response to domestic abuse.

In the criminal justice system, truth-seeking ought to take precedence over the rights of the accused.

This House believes in trial by jury.

The rights of the victim ought to take precedence over the rights of the accused.

This House would legalize

its feminine side.

This House believes that it is more important to give than it is to receive.

This House would give it up.

This House would eliminate the subsidy.

Be it resolved that it is better to lead than to follow.

The loophole should be closed.

You don't need a weatherman to know which way the wind blows.

This House believes in competition.

This House believes that the whole is greater than the sum of its parts.

This House would make it up as we go along.

The ray of hope is a blinding light.

Just chill.

It is time to fish, or cut bait.

This House would upset the balance.

This House would turn the tables.

This House would follow them to the ends of the earth.

This House would unhitch the trailer.

This house would gamble on a dark horse.

This House would blow it up.

This House believes in the survival of the fittest.

People should be accountable for their own rescues.

Apathy is more problematic than obedience.

This House believes that we should merge into one lane.

This House would repudiate patriotism.

This House would repudiate history.

This House would free the prisoners.

This House believes that deception is necessary.

This House would let the people decide.

This House would fail until it succeeds.

It is better to be safe than to be sorry.

This House believes there are no boundaries but our own.

This House would sell to the highest bidder.

This House would blow stuff up.

This House would spend it.

Bury it.

This house would raise the bar.

This House believes that those who destroy should rebuild.

This House would trade swords for plowshares.

Resolved: that payments are always unbalanced.

You should build a fence around your house.

This House believes that it is best to stay parked than to jump on the accelerator.

This House would seek a simpler way.

No justice, no peace...

This House would seek a sinister way.

This House would hold its horses.

This House would go to the other extreme.

This House would come out of the closet.

This House would add fuel to the fire.

Embarrassment is the best teacher.

Freedom from is better than freedom to.

There is no place for personal privilege.

Good riddance to the second millennium.

Railings only stop the foolish.

Resolved: You sell the sizzle not the steak.

This House would be guided by the youth.

This House prefers restraint to activism.

Resolved: Love is over-rated.

This House would bring back the boot camp.

Resolved: Silence is violence.

Resolved: that what goes up must come down.

Resolved: that the secret of success is that there is no secret of success.

This House would break the glass ceiling.

This house believes that 9 out of 10 doctors are wrong.

High fences make good neighbors.

This House believes that the ends do not justify the means.

This House believes that the blind are leading the blind.

This House believes that the end is near.

Justice delayed is justice denied.

This House believes that gold

is not cold.

This House believes in magic.

This House would comfort the afflicted and afflict the comfortable.

This House believes that a zebra doesn't change its spots.

This House would rather be poor than rich.

Cleanliness is not next to godliness

This House would plan the perfect wedding.

This House supports the culture of openness.

This House would name them but not shame them.

This House would walk in a sacred manner.

This House would become a great mountain.

This House should increase access to information.

This House regrets devolution.

This House would uproot the cedar.

This House would rebalance the powers.

Speed bumps are a failure of road planning.

Liberty is more precious than law.

This House would put out the fire.

This House believes you can't handle the truth.

This House believes that well done is better than well said.

This House would heed its priests.

Science fiction will become

science fact.

This House would take a walk on the wild side.

Resolved: If the thunder doesn't get you, the lightning will.

This House needs a miracle.

This House should break the silence.

This House would respond.

This House would get down and dirty.

This House would embrace the contradiction

This House would put the fat cats on a diet.

This House would have zero tolerance.

This House would rage against the machine.

This House would drop out.

This House believes that charity begins at home.

This House says "Anarchy rules."

When in conflict, this house would rather be cheap than easy.

This House believes in playing favorites.

This House would go home.

Finish the job.

Give legitimacy to the union.

Our trust is misplaced.

Oops, this House did it again.

This House would sleep with the enemy.

This House would revisit the 1970's.

This House would reach for the stars.

This House would remove government from the lives of the people.

This House would repudiate

history.

The fact that most people think something is true, makes it true.

Something can be true in theory but not in practice

Sometimes it is morally correct to be dishonest.

This House should spoil its children.

This House would smoke a cigar.

Resolved: The trend toward centrist politics is desirable.

This House would reveal its secrets.

This House believes that God is a comedian.

This House would shred its documents.

In this instance, family members should exercise tough love.

This House believes that Shakespeare was right.

Resolved: Let it be.

This House believes that change is not progress.

This House will seek forgiveness later rather than permission now.

This House respects its elders.

This House believes in traditions.

This house prefers great taste to less filling.

This house would push the button.

This house believes that greed is good.

It is time to throw off the shackles of tradition.

This House would look to the past, not to the future.

prostitution.

The system of justice, in this House, should be retributive, not distributive.

This House would impose mandatory sentences for repeat offenders.

This House believes in "Three strikes and you're out"

This House would lock 'em up and throw away the key.

This House believes that the Japanese government should allow trials to be broadcast on television.

This House opposes the death penalty.

A swifter and more probable punishment of crime would reduce crime rates.

Sodomy and prostitution between consenting adults should be legal.

It should be legal to require criminal defendants to testify in their trials.

This House believes that crimes should have victims.

This House would eliminate due process of law.

This House believes that civil litigation should have the same requirements as criminal litigation.

That the means of police interrogation are less important that the ends.

This House should limit the type of evidence admissible in courts.

This House would discontinue federal control of state prisons.

Resolved: This House believes rewards work better than punishments.

Be it resolved: Due process is

overrated.

This House believes that convicted rapists are as bad as murderers and should be sent to prison for life.

Illegally obtained evidence should not be admissible in a criminal trial.

This House favors retribution over rehabilitation.

This House would limit the option of litigation.

This House believes that judges should be elected.

This House would chemically castrate sex offenders.

This House would publicize the whereabouts of sex offenders.

This House would put cameras in the courtroom.

Resolved: That law enforcement agencies should be given greater freedom in the investigation and prosecution of crime.

This House would televise criminal trials.

Resolved: That the federal government should substantially change rules and/or statues governing criminal procedure in

federal courts in one or more of the following areas: pretrial detention, sentencing.

This House believes that justice should be blind.

Resolved: Violent juvenile offenders ought to be treated as adults in the criminal justice system.

This House would crack down on petty crimes.

This House would extradite criminals to face the death penalty

This House believes that rape victims' sexual history should be admissible in court

This House wouldn't trust a jury.

This House should alter the system of jury selection.

This House should take a tougher stance toward criminals.

DRUG POLICY

This House would legalize all drugs.

This House believes that the drug war is a civil war.

This House believes that the war on drugs is inadvisable in a free society.

This House would legalize soft drugs.

This House would legalize hard drugs.

This House believes that the war on drugs is misdirected.

This House would ban all alcoholic drinks.

RELIGION

This House believes in the separation of church and state.

This House would ordain homosexuals.

This House would tax religious institutions.

This House believes that religion is, and should be, a political force.

This House believes that religion and politics don't mix.

This House calls for a representative clergy.

Resolved: that God isn't playing an important enough role in modern life.

This House believes religion is the opiate of the masses.

This House believes in the existence of God.


POLITICAL SYSTEMS AND PHILOSOPHIES

This House believes that only the elite can truly successfully manage national affairs.

This House believes in pacifism.

This House would use proportional representation to decide national elections.

This House would use force to make peace.

This House believes that democracy is a sham.

This House believes a businessman makes a good President.

Resident non-citizens should be given the right to vote.

Special interest groups have too much influence in elections.

The government should take one or more actions to make it easier for citizens to vote.

The voting age should be set at 16.

This House would require that all candidates participate in mandatory, nationally televised debates in presidential elections.

This House would adopt s system of compulsory voting for all citizens.

This House prefers meritocracy to democracy.

Public campaign tactics should be limited in one or more ways.

This House believes that there are better alternatives to democracy.

This House believes that politicians have come nowhere since Machiavelli.

This House believes that politics is inherently dishonorable.

This House believes state power is more important than federal power.

This House would prefer anarchy to oppression.

This House believes that the state has a duty to protect individuals from themselves.

This House would be communist.

This House would give Marxism another try.

This House favors a parliamentary form of government.

This House believes that strong dictatorship is better than weak democracy.

This House would reform the present system of checks and balances.

This House believes that one man's terrorist is another man's freedom fighter.

This House believes that the right wing is dead wrong.

This House would support a six-year presidential term of office.

This House believes that the President was a victim.

This House believes a constitution is only as good as those who enforce it.

This House believes that there can be no justice where laws are absolute.

This House believes an unjust government is better than no government at all.

Resolved: That politicians should be forgiven when leaving office.

This House has high hopes for third parties.

Be it resolved that the government that governs least governs best.

This House would reform the national campaign process.

This House believes the decisions of the court should reflect the values of the people.

This House prefers honest representation to pure democracy.

This House believes that the judiciary should be popularly elected.

Resolved: That the power of the Presidency should be significantly curtailed.

The only proper function of government is to defend the individual rights of its citizens.

Resolved: that politics should be about the citizens and not the parties.

This House regards royalty as irrelevant.

This House believes that the government has forgotten its role.

This House supports campaign finance reform.

This House demands fully representative government.

This House would rather have a president than a monarch.

This House believes that the state should fund all political parties.

This House would ban all private donations to political parties.

This House calls for more use of the referendum.

This House believes that true democracy is direct democracy.

This House believes that negative political advertising is significantly detrimental to the democratic process.

This House believes that the public deserves the politicians it elects.

This House regrets the rise of career politicians.

This House believes that voting should be compulsory.

This House believes that it's a crime not to vote.

This House believes in libertarian government.

This House believes that violence by the people is the result of oppression by the state.

This House supports political advertising.

This House would reject the professional politician.

This House believes that there is a better way to elect the president.

This House opposes patriotism.

This House believes in term limits for federal officials.

This House believes in direct democracy.

This House should reform the political process.

This House would limit the cost of election campaigns.

This House believes in the two-party system.

## PRIVACY AND INDIVIDUAL RIGHTS

This House believes danger is the price of liberty.

This House believes that the right to die is the ultimate personal freedom.

This House believes that the right to privacy is more important than the freedom of the press.

This House demands a bill of rights.

This House would codify its rights.

This House believes in the concept of intellectual property.

The public's right to know outweighs the individual's right to privacy.

This House believes that freedom has been taken too far in the western world.

Resolved: That greater controls should be imposed on the gathering and utilization of information about citizens by government agencies.

This House believes in the right to die.

This House would introduce a National Identity Card.

This House believes the right to privacy has gone too far.

This House believes that the rights of the oppressed should be less important than the rights of the oppressors.

This House believes that security is more important than freedom.

This House believes that personal liberty must be restricted to reduce the threat of domestic terrorism.

The protection of public safety justifies random drug testing.

The public's right to know is of greater value than a candidate's right of privacy.

Resolved: that drug testing in the workplace should be abolished.

This House believes that press freedom should be restricted to protect the privacy of public figures.

This House would restrict the liberty of people in order to prevent harm to their health.

## PHILOSOPHY

Freedom of the individual is a myth.

Resolved: This House believes dualism should be broken down.

It is possible to identify truths.

This House rejects all forms of violence.

Human beings' interests are necessarily in conflict.

This House believes that it is never right to take a life.

This House believes there is no such thing as a winnable war.

This House believes in absolute Truth.

This House deplores utilitarianism.

This House rejects *a priori* truth.

This House believes that conventionality is not morality.

This House values life over liberty.

When in conflict, individual rights take precedence over government rights.

Materialism will lead to the downfall of humanity.

This House believes that the ends do not justify the means.

Violence is an appropriate expression for the silenced.

This House believes that substance is more important than philosophy.

Human beings are fundamentally good.

Natural instincts prevail over intellectual actions.

Humans have no free will.

This House believes that skepticism has replaced ideology.

This House believes that humanity was born for cooperation, not competition.

This House believes that Plato was right.

The fact that most people believe something is good makes it good.

Moral principles should be based on the requirements of human life, not commandments.

This House would re-think postmodernism.

This House believes that collectivism is better than individualism.

This House believes that there is no justice without retribution.

When called upon by one's government, individuals are morally obligated to risk their lives.

Community standards are of greater value than individual liberty.

Laws that protect individuals from themselves are justified.

Reality is a linguistic construction.

This House supports radical feminism.

This House believes that the good life is best measured by aesthetics.

This House regrets the decline of conventional morality.

EQUALITY AND SOCIAL JUSTICE

This House would require prospective human parents to be licensed before having children.

This House would privatize the pension problem.

This House would address the concerns of an aging population.

The government should make reparations to black people, and other abused minorities.

This House believes that feminism has devalued parenthood.

This House believes that the battle of the sexes is far from over.

This House would allow homosexual couples to adopt children.

_____ is the best way to protect rights of homosexuals.

The state should make inroads into parental rights.

This House would give money to beggars.

This House believes that charity begins with the homeless.

This House would help beggars become choosers.

Be it resolved that welfare be available only to persons over the age of 21.

Be it resolved that community service be a requirement of welfare payment.

This House would support positive discrimination.

Social responsibility should be compulsory.

Housing should be a basic human right.

That the courts and legislature have overreacted to sexual harassment in the workplace.

The government should more actively protect the rights of persons with disabilities.

This House would end the war on poverty.

Be it resolved: The federal government ought to enact a policy to promote multiculturalism.

This House would reform the welfare system.

This House would support radical redistribution.

This House would give the young a voice.

This House believes that there is no such thing as universal human rights.

This House believes that social injustice justifies political violence.

This House believes that a

common culture is of greater value than a pluralistic culture.

The Women's Movement has done more harm than good.

This House supports same-sex marriage.

This nation should pay reparations for violating the human rights of its people.

This House would relax immigration laws.

This House would introduce hiring quotas.

This House believes that capitalism is detrimental to social justice.

This House believes that the 'melting pot' has failed.

This House would hold the military to a stricter standard on sexual harassment.

This House would put those on welfare to work.

This House would ration the old to nurture the young.

This House believes that racists should be accountable for the consequences of their doctrines.

This House would spend less on the police and more on the people.

The west should treat state-sponsored sexism as apartheid.

This House believes that the government must place the human interest above the national interest.

This House believes that special interests have ruined democracy.

This House believes that compassion should be bounded by fiscal necessity.

This House would end all clas-sification by race.

This House would speak English.

This House would allow same-sex couples to adopt children.

This House would advocate color-blind justice.

The federal government should enact a policy to restrict entitlement programs.

This House deplores class warfare.

This House believes that the community is more important than the individual.

This House would pay a parent for staying home.

This House would reframe the urban future.

This House would establish a youth policy.

This House would place privilege before merit.

This House would restrict the rights of immigrants.

Resolved: that peace and justice are two sides of the same coin.

That violence and progressive dissent ought to be mutually exclusive.

The safety net should be mended.

This House would support expanded legal protections for homosexuals.

This House believes in social unity over cultural diversity.

This House would adopt a superior alternative to affirmative action.

This House would adopt quotas.

This House believes that

social welfare is the responsibility of local governments.

That political and legal equivocation of Judeo Christian marriage with civil marriage is unjustified.

This House believes that equality is the benchmark of society.

This House would politely say "No" to reparations.

This House should close its borders.

This House supports open borders.

This House believes that good health is a human right.

This House believes that the best man for the job is a woman.

All citizens should be treated equally by the law regardless of race; affirmative action is wrong.

The government should redistribute wealth by taxing some citizens in order to provide goods or services to others.

The law discriminates against women and treats them worse than men.

This House believes that family values are over-rated.

Resolved: that affirmative action should focus on class, not race.

This House opposes affirmative action.

This House believes that the scales of justice are tilted.

This House would support exceptions to gender equality in the workplace.

This House supports discrimination.

Women have fewer legal and

cultural advantages than men in our society.

This House would soak the rich.

This House would hold people responsible for the actions of their ancestors.

This House would open the gates to immigrants.

This House believes that humanity is created equal.

Peaceful and healthy immigrants should be allowed to cross the border freely.

Toleration is a virtue.

This House believes that racism can be controlled by legislation.

This House believes special protection creates special problems.

This House would means-test state benefits.

This House would abolish the welfare state.

This House believes the welfare state is a right, not a safety net.

Affirmative action should be used to even out differences between the sexes.

This House believes that minority privileges deny equality.

LABOR AND ECONOMIC POLICY

This House believes that renewed strength of labor organizations is necessary for a progressive economy.

This House calls for a mandatory retirement age.

This House believes in the restraint of commerce.

This House believes that the government should regulate the economy.

This House would increase consumer protection.

This House believes that accountants are to blame.

It is better to stimulate the economy through tax cuts than through increased spending.

That House believes that we should subsidize traditional industries.

This House believes that multinationals are the new imperialists.

Capitalism is an immoral economic system.

Reducing federal spending relative to GDP would create more prosperity.

This House would stabilize gas prices.

The government should subsidize some businesses and farms.

This House hates capitalism.

This House would increase partnerships between government and private enterprise.

This House would establish a living wage.

Capitalism is the only ethical economic system.

This House would increase the minimum wage.

This House would promote infrastructure development.

Resolved: That the government should nationalize the basic nonagricultural industries.

The recent mega-mergers of media companies will help

competition more than they will hinder it.

This House would return to an unregulated free market.

This House regrets globalization.

This House supports the right to work.

Resolved: That the federal government should significantly strengthen the guarantee of consumer product safety required

of manufacturers.

This House believes that global capitalism degrades community.

This House believes that the right to strike should be given to all employees.

Wages should be raised 15 percent.

Small organizations are able to adapt to today's business environment better than large organizations.

This House believes you should invest in foreign markets.

That the work week should be shortened to 30 hours.

Enron reveals capitalism's moral bankruptcy.

This House believes in economic competition.

This House would end corporate welfare.

This House would re-nationalize the public utilities.

This House would increase taxes on the rich.

Resolved: That the federal government should establish a national program of public work for the unemployed.

Resolved: That the federal government should guarantee a minimum annual cash income to all citizens.

Resolved: That the federal government should adopt a program of compulsory wage and price controls.

This House would break up economic power.

This House would resurrect communism.

This House would increase consumer protections.

The significance of consumer confidence has been overrated.

This House would stop the free exchange of currencies.

This House would get out of the stock market.

This House believes that equality and capitalism are incompatible.

This House would save the surplus.

Resolved: That the federal government should adopt a permanent program of wage and price control.

Resolved: That the federal government should implement a program guaranteeing employment opportunities for all citizens in the labor force.

Resolved: That the federal government should significantly curtail the powers of the labor unions.

Resolved: That the nonagricultural industries should guarantee their employees an annual wage.

Resolved: That the requirement of membership in a labor organization as a condition of employment should

be illegal.

Resolved: That labor organizations should be under the jurisdiction of anti-trust legislation.

This House would hold tobacco companies liable for the consequences of their products.

This House would set a maximum limit on salaries.

This House would bail out failing industries.

This House believes that trade unions must modernize or die.

This House believes in supply-side economics.

Resolved: Labor should be given a direct share in the management of industry.

This House believes that the right to strike should be given to all employees.

This House supports the power of labor unions.

This House believes that labor unions have outlived their usefulness.

## ARTS AND LITERATURE

This House believes that public monies should not finance art.

This House believes art is the essence of a nation's character.

Art is unnecessary for human progress.

This House believes in poetic license.

This House would let the language die.

This House would pay to go to a museum.

This House would allow the depiction of erect penises in art and film.

This House would abolish state funding of the arts.

Art is like a shark, it must move forward or it will die.

This nation should have an official language.

Art is permitted, but nature is forbidden..

This House would establish English as the official language.

## FREE SPEECH

Political correctness is the new McCarthyism.

This House believes any book worth banning is a book worth reading.

Communities ought to have the right to suppress pornography.

This House believes that censorship can never be justified.

This House would ban prisoners publishing accounts of their crimes.

This House supports Larry Flynt.

Be it resolved: Hate speech ought to be banned.

This House believes that money is speech.

This House would give racists a platform.

This House would support a constitutional amendment to protect the flag from desecration.

The protection of domestic order justifies restrictions on free speech.

This House believes the press is too free.

Be it resolved that censorship of television, film and video materials be increased.

This House believes that obscenity is expression.

This House believes that political correctness has gone too far.

This House believes that political correctness is necessary to achieve social justice.

This House would be politically correct.

This House would legalize all adult pornography.

This House believes that a ban on flag burning better serves fascism than freedom.

Resolved: that the government should take a more active stance protecting free speech.

Resolved: When they conflict, respect for cultural sensitivity ought to be valued above commercial use of free speech.

Resolved: A journalist's right to shield confidential sources ought to be protected by the First Amendment.

This House would restrict free speech.

## TRADE POLICY

Be it resolved that the GATT system of international governance should be significantly revised.

The West will regret free trade.

This House will regret the trade bloc.

This House believes the WTO is a friend of the developing world.

This House believes that trade rights should be linked to human rights.

This House would expand NAFTA.

This House believes that NAFTA is a mistake.

That on balance, free trade benefits more than it costs.

This House would restrict non-tariff barriers.

This House would pass fast-track authority.

Resolved: Something needs to be done about the WTO.

People are better off with tariffs than with complete free-trade today.

This House rejects the multilateral agreement on investment.

## INTERNATIONAL AFFAIRS AND POLICIES

This House would test nuclear weapons.

This House believes that industrialization assures progress in the developing world.

In international relations, economic power is preferred to military power.

This House would rebuild the Berlin Wall.

This House should adopt a more moderate stance toward Iran.

Resolved: That the government should substantially increase its security assistance to one or more of the following: Egypt, Israel, Jordan, Palestinian National Authority, Syria.

Resolved: That this nation's foreign policy toward one or more African nations should be substantially changed.

This House should apologize for its imperialistic past.

This House should end its foreign military operations.

This House believes that developing nations need strong dictatorship.

That supporting indigenous efforts at independence is more important than respecting state sovereignty.

This House would expand population control measures in India

This House would be more realistic about humanitarian intervention by our military forces.

Let the world police itself.

Test nuclear weapons.

This House would end the embargo with Cuba.

This House supports a Palestinian state.

This House would end unconditional aid to Israel.

This House would substantially reduce IMF and World Bank lending programs.

The debt of the third world should be forgiven.

This House believes that the poverty of the Third World is the fault of the First World.

This House has no business in Bosnia.

This House believes that the UN has failed.

India should engage in political discourse rather than increasing their weaponry.

This House would eliminate the veto power of the United Nations Security Council.

It is time to shun Arafat. Iran should not be considered part of the "Axis of Evil." Tony Blair should receive the Nobel Peace Prize.

This House believes we don't need Europe.

This House believes that the UN is a toothless watchdog.

This House would give the UN a standing army.

This House would reject a united Europe.

This House would give land for peace.

This House believes that the international community should start a dialogue with the Front for the Islamic Salvation of Algeria.

The Chemical Weapons Convention should not be ratified.

All foreign aid should be privately funded.

This House should enact a more aggressive foreign policy.

This House regrets humanitarian intervention.

This House fears China.

This House would end the arms trade.

This House believes that democracy is so good, everyone should be made to have it.

This House believes that child labor is justifiable in the developing world.

This House would invade in the interests of democracy.

This House believes that the assassination of dictators is justifiable.

Resolved: The possession of nuclear weapons is immoral.

Resolved: The intervention of one nation in the domestic affairs of another nation is morally justified.

This House fears Islamic fundamentalism.

Romania should b admitted to the European Union.

Romania should be admitted to NATO.

Protection of human rights justifies the use of military force.

This House supports the establishment of an international criminal court.

This House would ban all nuclear weapons.

This House believes in the right of any country to defend itself with nuclear weapons.

This House believes that economic sanctions do more harm than good.

This House would always prefer sanctions to war.

This House believes that terrorism is sometimes justifiable.

This House would take steps to substantially reduce nuclear proliferation.

Further debt relief for developing nations is needed

This House would negotiate with terrorists.

What steps should the UN take to stop civil unrest in Africa?

This House believes war to be an unjustified response to aggression.

Yugoslavia is not dead.

This House condemns the UN embargo of Iraq.

This House would make amends for the legacy of colonialism.

Sweden should abolish its monarchy and become a republic.

This House prefers isolationism to interventionism.

Resolved: That the further development of nuclear weapons should be prohibited by international agreement.

Resolved: That the non-communist nations of the world should establish an economic community.

This House believes that making Arafat a partner in peace was a mistake

This House believes political assassinations are a legitimate tool of foreign policy.

This house favors limiting our support of Israel.

This house would shift its foreign policy focus to the western hemisphere.

This House would override national sovereignty to protect human rights.

This House should significantly curtail military aid to Israel.

The United Nations Charter should be substantially changed.

This House would expand NATO.

Resolved: The federal government should substantially increase its security assistance to one or more of the following Southeast Asian nations: Brunei, Burma(Myanmar), Cambodia, Indonesia, Laos, Malaysia, Philippines, Singapore, Thailand, Vietnam.

Resolved: That the federal government should substantially increase its development assistance, including increasing government to government assistance, within the Greater Horn of Africa.

Be it resolved that a permanent United Nations military force be established.

Be it resolved that international sanctions against Serbia be lifted.

Be it resolved that all east European countries be admitted into NATO.

Be it resolved that the Organization of American States should establish a regional drug interdiction military force to halt

the flow of drugs in the Western Hemisphere.

On to Baghdad.

Adios, Latin America.

The United Nations should mandate and enforce an Israeli-Palestinian settlement.

This House would substantially increase population assistance in foreign aid programs.

This House would end financial aid to foreign nations.

This House would support a Pax Americana.

Nationalism stands in the way of peace.

That carrots are better than sticks in foreign policy.

Resolved: A federal world government should be established.

Resolved: That the non-communist nations should form a new international organization.

Globalization is a masquerade for cultural imperialism.

This House would support the independence of Quebec.

This House should act against political oppression in the People's Republic of China.

Sanctions will help the peace.

This House would eliminate slavery in Africa.

This House believes that the first world owes more to the third world than the third world owes to the first world.

This House believes that increased relations with China would be detrimental.

This House would intervene in Chechnya.

This House believes that international conflict is desirable.

It is immoral to use economic sanctions to achieve foreign policy goals.

This House would use economic sanctions to enforce a ban on nuclear weapons testing.

This House believes that the UN is dysfunctional.

The possession of nuclear weapons is immoral.

This House welcomes a borderless world.

This House calls for a New World Order.

This House believes in the right of indigenous peoples to self-determination.

This House would rather live on a desert island than in the global village.

This House believes that human rights are a tool of Western foreign policy.

This House believes that aid to the Third World should be tied to human rights.

This House would manage ethnic conflict in Central Asia.

This House values human rights over state sovereignty.

This House would take policy action to support Kurdish self-determination.

Interference in the internal affairs of other countries is justified.

This House believes that Okinawa should be independent.

This House would increase support for the developing world.

This House would unite Ireland.


ENVIRONMENTAL POLICY AND PHILOSOPHY

This House would substantially restrict visitors to the National Parks.

This House believes that the value of natural resources can be found only in their exploitation.

Be it resolved that the use of

animals for public entertainment (zoos, circus acts, etc.) be illegal.

This House would restrict private car ownership.

Old growth forests should be logged.

This House believes that the lives of animals should not be subordinate to the rights of humankind.

Be it resolved that all forest land that currently exists as natural habitat remain so.

This House would ban all experimentation on animals.

This House believes that meat is murder.

Resolved: That the federal government should adopt a comprehensive program to control land use.

Resolved: That the federal government should control the supply and utilization of energy.

This House would free the animals.

This House believes that we have no more right to risk the health of animals than of humans.

This House believes that animals have rights too.

This House would break the law to protect the rights of animals.

This House would ban hunting with hounds.

Privatizing all unused federal public land is a good protection for the environment.

Technology should be utilized to solve ecological problems.

This House believes that the value of natural resources is

found in their exploitation.

When in conflict, This House values environmental protection over economic growth.

High petrol prices are a good thing.

Sustainability is just a concept that assuages our consciences while we continue consuming at the same rate.

Sustainability is not an achievable goal.

Sustainable development means a decrease in our standard of living.

This House would act decisively to stop global warming.

This House believes that the government should take measures to substantially improve natural disaster relief.

This House believes that the exploitation of animals is immoral.

Resolved: that vast areas of western lands currently under the jurisdiction of the Bureau of Land Management (and administered as "multiple use" areas) be reclassified as "wilderness areas" in which mining, grazing, etc. would not be permitted.

Resolved: that the federal government allocate public monies to protect or purchase sufficient lands in the midwestern region of the U.S.A. to ensure the survival of all forest-nesting songbird populations.

Resolved: that genetic material from other subspecies or

even other species should be used to save endangered populations like Red Wolves and Florida Panthers.

Resolved: that the federal government should greatly reduce the land area available for livestock grazing in the western states, and instead manage such lands for native species.

Resolved: that the federal government should develop a plan to restore patterns of water flow in the Colorado River to more closely approximate those that occurred before construction of the Glen Canyon, Hoover, Davis, Parker, Imperial, and Laguna Dams, and to implement that plan by 2050.

Resolved: that the U.S. should begin immediately to phase-in measures to reduce the rate of increase in atmospheric $CO_2$ concentration.

Resolved: that populations of Gray Wolves established by recent introduction into Yellowstone National Park and central Idaho be removed on the justification that they are genetically distinct from populations natural there and therefore not protected under the Endangered Species Act.

Resolved: that the federal and Florida state governments should act to restore the water flow pattern to the everglades ecosystem that was characteristic before modern water diversion projects began.

Resolved: that the federal government should develop and implement a plan to reestablish the native fish fauna of the Great Lakes, including the removal of exotic species (e.g., Zebra Mussels, Sea Lampreys and Round Gobies) currently established in the lakes.

The government should substantially reduce oil imports.

Resolved: that the importation, breeding, cultivation, and sale of all exotic organisms be prohibited in the United States of America, including those not native to the United States of America overall as well as those not native in a particular area of the country. Exemptions could be allowed for particular species necessary for biological control of already-established exotics, or for other human uses deemed to be of critical importance.

Rolling blackouts are preferable to environmental degradation.

This House supports the international trading of pollution permits.

Resolved: that the National Park Service should develop and implement a policy of limiting visitors to National Parks at a level consistent with maintaining the integrity of the parks' natural communities and critical ecosystem functions.

Resolved: that the federal government take all necessary steps to prevent the introduction of the brown tree snake (Boiga) to the Hawaiian Islands, including strict inspection of all ship-

ping, passenger luggage, etc.

Non-human species deserve greater protection.

This House would grant personhood rights to primates.

Resolved: that the development of all commercial products that make use of biological resources originating on public lands will include negotiations with the appropriate government agency for payment of reasonable royalties to the public. Biological resources shall include all organisms, parts of organisms, and specific products of those organisms, including enzymes, hormones, etc.

Environmental pollution demands a truly global response.

This house would save the dams, not the salmon.

Resolved: that the federal government should redirect its protection efforts to focus on areas identified as unprotected biodiversity "hotspots" by GAP analysis.

This House would save the tropics.

This House would substantially reform farming.

This house believes anthropocentrism is necessary.

Resolved: that the federal government act immediately to consolidate former President Clinton's designation of 58.5 million acres of National Forest lands as roadless areas off-limits to logging and mining, and not to reverse that designation. Resolved: that the federal

government act to prohibit the killing of bison that leave Yellowstone National Park and enter private lands.

Federal courts should grant standing to animals to pursue their rights.

This House believes the environment can hold its own.

This House believes that nature is more important than unemployment.

This House would go forth and stop multiplying.

This House calls for increased population control.

Resolved: That the federal government should increase regulations requiring industries to substantially

decrease the domestic emission and/or production of environmental pollutants.

This House would subsidize agriculture.

Overpopulation is the world's greatest threat.

This House believes that the Kyoto Summit didn't go far enough.

This House believes that global warming is the biggest international crisis.

This House would put the environment before economics.

This House would recycle environmentalists.

This House would protect the lesser species.

This House believes spaceship earth is crashing.

Global warming will create catastrophic effects within 30 years.

This House would privatize national parks.

## POPULAR CULTURE

This House believes American culture places too great an emphasis on athletic success.

This House has an unhealthy obsession with sport.

Baseball is better than soccer.

This nation has sacrificed aesthetics for convenience.

This House should oppose the Olympics.

This House is resolved that there should be integration of the sexes in professional sports.

This House believes that we resemble the Simpsons more then the Waltons.

This House believes that dogs are better pets for humankind than cats.

This House believes our obsession with celebrities is harmful.

The piercing of body parts (except earlobes) should be prohibited for anyone under 18.

This house would save the Twins.

This House believes that it is better for athletes to retire at the peak of their careers.

This House believes that there is too much money in sport.

This House applauds the Olympic ideal.

This House believes that international sport is warfare without weapons.

This House would blame Hollywood for the ills of society.

This House supports a national lottery.

This House would ban boxing.

This House would ban all blood sports.

This house believes the Super Bowl ain't that super.

This House condemns gambling of all forms.

This House believes that beauty pageants for children should be banned.

This House believes that fashion enslaves and oppresses women.

This House would restrict the movement of professional sports franchises.

This House laments the dedicated follower of fashion.

This House believes that the advertising industry causes body fascism.

This House believes that advertising is poison to society.

This House condemns the paparazzi.

Be it resolved that drug testing be compulsory for all athletes involved in national and international competition.

This House would ban all tobacco advertising.

This House prefers Sega to Shakespeare.

This House believes that public funding of sports facilities is immoral.

Parents ought not purchase war toys for their children.

This House believes that music is more influential than literature.

This House would pay its college athletes.

State-run lotteries are undesirable.

This House believes that motion pictures are a reflection of society norms.

This House prefers country music to classical music.

This House believes that violence has no place in entertainment.

This House would end its participation in the Olympic Games.

This House would shut down Hollywood.

This House believes that professional athletes are paid too much.

This House believes that it is acceptable to "out" gay celebrities.

This House believes that commercialism has gone too far.

This House believes that the continued production of sport utility vehicles is undesirable.

This House believes that advertising degrades the quality of life.

## MEDIA AND TELEVISION

This House believes that television destroys lives.

This House believes that journalistic integrity is dead.

This House believes that television is more significant than the computer.

This House believes that the media has gone too far.

The media are corrupt.

This House believes that the news should be interesting rather than important.

This House supports domestic content quotas in broadcasting.

This House believes that the media has become too powerful.

Resolved: That the federal government should significantly strengthen the regulation of mass media communication.

Be it resolved that television is the major cause of increased violence in our society.

This House believes reporters should report not affect the news.

This House would hold the media responsible.

It is proper for the government to own the TV and radio airwaves.

This House would televise executions.

This House believes that the state should have no role in broadcasting.

This House would turn off the TV.

Resolved: that, on balance, television has done more harm than good.

This House believes the media should tone it down.

SCIENCE AND TECHNOLOGY

This House would leave the planet.

This House thinks that Internet "junk mail" should be illegal.

The ethical cost of selling human eggs outweigh the potential benefits.

When in conflict, this House values scientific discovery over the welfare of animals.

Science is more dangerous than religion.

This House would censor the Internet.

This House calls for further use of nuclear power.

This House believes that science is a menace to civilization.

This House believes that the march of science has gone too far.

This House believes that science has nothing to regret, not even the ruins of Hiroshima.

This House fears the Information Age.

This House believes that medical technology has outstripped morality.

Resolved that alternative energy sources replace nuclear power.

Resolved that the use of antibiotics should be significantly limited.

Resolved that genetic testing on human fetuses should be prohibited.

The federal government should significantly restrict research and development of one or more technologies.

This house would clone humans.

This House believes that research should be restrained by morality.

This House believes that space travel should be privatized.

This House believes that you

should keep your genes to yourself.

This House should regulate on-line gambling.

This House would fear technology.

Resolved: Technology dehumanizes.

This House would ban genetic cloning.

This House believes computers are the answer.

This House would go to space.

This House would delete Microsoft.

This House ought to put its designer genes back in the closet.

That on balance, resources spent on space exploration would be better used if directed toward the exploration of earth.

This House would let the information superhighway run free.

This House calls for universal genetic screening.

This House would expand stem cell research.

This House would choose its babies.

This House believes that the benefits of genetic engineering outweighs its risks.

This House believes that the internet is the new opiate of the masses.

All software must be shipped with the source code.

This House would reduce applied research for basic research.

This House would ban genetic screening.

This House would test everyone for HIV.

This House would patrol the information superhighway.

Computers contribute to society's moral decline.

Internet e-commerce will ultimately fail.

Space research and development should be significantly curtailed.

This House believes that technology is killing our work ethic.

Resolved: The Internet should be funded by government subsidies, as opposed to private investment.

Resolved: The growth of e-business is a benefit to the average small company.

Resolved: The benefits of telecommuting outweigh the negatives.

Resolved: It is unethical for companies to track individuals' use of the Web without their knowledge.

That schools should use filtering software to prevent children from viewing restricted material on the Internet.

Genetically engineered food is the answer to feeding the world.

Xenotransplantation is the solution to the shortage of organs for transplantation.

Opposition to human cloning is based on ignorance rather than insight.

This House would buy every child a computer.

The Internet needs to be regulated.

Engineering is an art, not a science.

Internet security is an oxymoron.

Planned obsolescence is necessary for technological progress.

This House believes that space exploration and development should be an international priority.


EDUCATION POLICY

This House believes that the students should run the school.

This House believes that public schools should forego freedom for safety.

This House rejects distance learning in higher education.

This House believes that physically challenged people should not be separated in schools.

This House would eliminate letter grades.

This House believes that everyone should attend college.

Public education is necessary.

The government should institute mandatory arts education.

Resolved: Colleges and universities have a moral obligation to prohibit the public expression of hate speech on their campuses.

This House believes that vocational training is more important than liberal arts education.

Resolved: That more rigorous academic standards should be established for all public elementary and/or secondary schools

in one or more of the following areas: language arts, mathematics, natural sciences.

Resolved: that charter schools erode public education.

This House would judge schools by their examination results.

This House would put Latin and Greek on the national curriculum.

This House would always educate boys and girls together.

Resolved: The use of grades in schools should be abandoned

This House would make the student pay back his debt to society.

This House believes that private schools are not in the public interest.

This House believes that religion has no place in schools.

This House would reform education.

This House would make school sport voluntary.

Resolved: That the federal government should guarantee an opportunity for higher education to all qualified high school graduates.

This House rejects military recruiters at educational institutions.

Uniformity in education leads to mediocrity.

This House would revolutionize the educational system.

This House believes that every citizen has a right to a college education.

This House would keep the bedroom out of the classroom.

This House believes that women's studies should not include men.

This House would accept advertising in public schools.

This House would change its policy on funding education.

Resolved that Norplant be available to all females students enrolled in public secondary schools.

This House supports prayer in public schools.

Resolved that the federal government should deny public education to illegal immigrants.

Teachers' salaries should be based on students' academic performance.

This House believes that it's better for the Japanese people to learn world history than Japanese history.

Tenure should be abolished in universities.

Public education ought to be a right, not a privilege.

This House believes that schools should not prepare students for work.

This House believes that computers are the demise of education.

This House supports single-sex education.

This House would pass legislation to post the Ten Commandments in public school classrooms.

This House rejects the business model for institutions of higher education.

This House believes that nursery education is a right, not a privilege.

This House would be allowed

to leave school at 14.

This House would charge tuition fees for university students.

This House believes that a degree is a privilege, not a right.

This House would report violations by college students to their parents.

Institutional censorship of academic material is harmful to the educational process.

This House believes that universities should report all assaults to the police, even without the consent of the victim.

Access to higher education should be a right.

This House believes that to improve education, it is more important to raise salaries than standards.

Limitations on the content of secondary school publications are unjustifiable.

Resolved: The government should adopt a policy of equalizing educational opportunity in tax-supported schools by means of annual grants.

This House believes that higher education was intended for the intellectual elite.

THE UNITED STATES OF AMERICA

This House believes that the USA is more sinned against than sinning.

This House would denuclearize the USA.

Resolved: The Supreme Court of the USA should uphold

substantive due process.

This House should honor its treaties with one or more Native American nations.

This House believes that "Homeland Security" should not be a cabinet level position.

This House rejects the American way of life.

This House would have a new song for America.

This House believes that the USA should repay its debt to the United Nations.

Resolved: That the USA should reduce substantially its military commitments to NATO member states.

Be it resolved that the USA should significantly increase its role in Russia's financial future.

Resolved: That the federal government should adopt an energy policy that substantially reduces nonmilitary consumption of

fossil fuels in the United States of America.

This House believes that justice in America can be bought.

This House believes that America's right is wrong.

This house regrets the American response to September 11.

Bush and Cheney are an axis of evil.

Resolved: The USA should move toward protectionism in foreign trade.

The USA should not abandon National Missile Defense.

A fully insured America is unrealistic.

This House wishes Plymouth Rock had landed on the pilgrims.

Resolved: that the Rehnquist court made the wrong decision.

Resolved: that the Supreme Court of the United States erred in awarding Bush the presidency.

Racism contributes to United States' policy toward Africa.

The U.S.A. should change its foreign policy.

The Democratic Party is moribund.

The U.S. electorate is jaded by campaigning via television.

Dick Cheney should not have to reveal confidential information relating to the Enron scandal.

The Federal Communications Commission should restrict the use of wireless communication in spectrum designated for digital television.

This House would maintain United States military bases in Asia.

This House would curtail corporate puppetry of U. S. politics.

The United States has responded inappropriately to terrorist attacks.

The United States is a terrorist network.

This House believes that the American dream has become a nightmare.

This House believes that, if America is the world's policeman, then the world is America's Rodney King.

This House regrets the influence of the USA.

Jesse Helms is right.

Americans have too many rights and not enough responsibilities.

The USA ought to increase access to the political system.

The federal government of the United States has responded appropriately to the attack on America.

The United States of America has overemphasized individual rights.

The USA should support bilingualism.

This House believes that the USA is a racist society.

Resolved: That all military intervention by the United States of America into the internal affairs of any foreign nation or nations in the Western Hemisphere should be prohibited.

Resolved: That any and all injury resulting from the disposal of hazardous waste in the United States of America should be the legal responsibility of the producer of that waste.

This House believes that America's constitutional rights are being too harshly infringed.

This House believes Bush's education plan is an improvement.

This House believes that the US should take a tougher stance toward Israel.

The USA should significantly increase military spending.

Resolved: That the Congress of the USA should enact a compulsory fair employment practices law.

Resolved: That the USA should adopt a policy of free trade.

Resolved: That the USA should significantly increase its foreign military commitments.

Resolved: That the USA should discontinue direct economic aid to foreign countries.

Resolved: That the Congress of the USA should be given the power to reverse decisions of the Supreme Court.

The USA should punish China for its human rights abuses

This House believes the Electoral College is still necessary.

Resolved: The United States of America is a terrorist state.

Resolved that the U.S. has overplayed the sanction card.

This House believes that America is blinded by the light.

Resolved: That the United States of America should substantially change its trade policy toward one or more of the following: China, Hong Kong, Japan, South Korea, Taiwan.

Resolved: That one or more U.S. Supreme Court decisions that recognize a federal Constitutional right to privacy should be overruled.

Resolved: That the United States of America should substantially change its development and assistance policies toward one or more of the following nations: Afghanistan, Bangladesh,

**323**

Burma, Bhutan, India, Nepal, Pakistan, Sri Lanka.

This House believes that the foreign policy of the USA is responsible for Sept. 11

Resolved: That the Commander-in-Chief power of the President of the USA should be substantially curtailed.

Resolved: That the federal government of the United States of America should amend Title VII of the Civil Rights Act of 1964, through legislation, to create additional protections against racial and/or gender discrimination.

Resolved: That the federal government of the United States should adopt a policy of constructive engagement, including the immediate removal of all or nearly all economic sanctions, with the government(s) of one or more of the following nation-states: Cuba, Iran, Iraq, Syria, North Korea.

Be it resolved that the U.S.A. should significantly increase its aid to Russia.

Be it resolved that the U.S.A. should significantly reduce its superpower role.

Be it resolved that the U.S.A. should withdraw from NAFTA.

Be it resolved that the U.S.A. should significantly revise its trade status with Japan.

The government of the United States of America should reduce due process protections in one or more areas.

This house believes the Supreme Court has gone too far.

Be it resolved that the U.S.A. should stop all aid to Islamic Fundamentalist governments.

Be it resolved that the U.S.A. should take a greater role in the Israelis/Palestinian peace process.

Be it resolved that the U.S.A. should significantly increase its ties to China.

Be it resolved that the U.S.A. should lift the embargo against Cuba.

Be it resolved that the federal government of the USA should expand its role in educating America's youth.

Be it Resolved that the federal government of the United States of America should fund the relief efforts of faith-based organizations.

This House believes that the First Amendment applies to the Internet.

Jesse Ventura is right.

Be it resolved that hegemony by the USA is detrimental to world stability.

American sexual mores are ridiculous.

This House believes you can go to the mall and see America.

This House thinks the USA is the Titanic.

This House believes that the USA should be less involved in world affairs.

The American media works against the best interests of the public.

The American criminal justice system ought to place a higher priority on retribution than deterrence.

This House would dramatically

increase funding for the National Endowment for the Arts.

This House is resolved that President Bush should sign the Ottawa Treaty to ban the production and export of land mines.

This House would treat America's youth like adults.

We believe that America's safety net catches more than it misses.

Be it Resolved: That the federal government should substantially increase its support to the arts of America.

The USA should build a missile defense system.

This House would abolish "Don't ask, don't tell" policies.

This House is resolved that a global marketplace is good for the USA.

Resolved: that President Clinton did more harm than good.

This House would not have named Washington National Airport after Ronald Reagan.

The Supreme Court should expand executive privilege.

This House would eliminate the Department of Education.

This House would induct the 51$^{st}$ state.

This House believes that Miranda rights favor the guilty.

This House believes in the fall of the American empire.

The Supreme Court ought to interpret the Constitution more strictly.

The United States of America

should mind its own business.

This House believes that the U.S. government should stop subsidizing farmers.

Resolved: The presidential pardon procedure needs to be restructured.

The federal government of the United States of America should increase its military aid to one or more East Asian nations.

This House would grant political independence to Washington, D. C.

This House would repeal Title IX.

The federal government of the United States of America should substantially change its nuclear waste policy.

The USA should increase its trade agreements with Africa.

The USA should surrender in the war on drugs.

There should be additions to Mount Rushmore.

Resolved that the juvenile court system be abolished in Illinois.

Resolved that University Laboratory High School adopt block scheduling.

Resolved that parental notification of abortions by minors be mandatory in the USA.

Resolved that testing for performance-enhancing drugs be implemented in all NCAA Division I sports.

Resolved that all cars produced in the USA after January 1, 2008 be electric or hybrid-electric.

Resolved that California reinstate affirmative action in all public universities.

The government of the USA should significantly curtail access to public parks in America.

The USA should approve an Equal Rights Amendment.

Litigation has replaced legislation in America.

This House believes that country music reflects a decline in American culture.

Point Loma Nazarene University should kill its Crusader mascot.

Be it resolved that the United States of America should adopt the Nuclear Test-Ban Treaty.

The United States of America should reform Social Security.

The Congress of the USA should enact reparations for descendants of slaves.

This House would eliminate the CIA.

The Helms-Burton Act should be enforced.

Resolved: that Medicare is worse than no care at all.

This House believes that the USA should apologize to Latin America.

This House believes that the IRS needs to be abolished.

This House believes that American automobiles are a better bargain than European automobiles.

## THE EUROPEAN UNION

This House believes that the European Community ought to expand now.

Europe should take deliberate steps to stop Russia's siege of Chechnya.

This House believes that the single European currency will fail.

This House believes that Europe should be the next USA.

This House would join a European defense alliance.

This House welcomes European federalism.

This House believes that a wider Europe is not in Britain's interest.

This House welcomes the Euro.

This House believes that Eurovision song contest is the role-model.

## HEALTH CARE

This House believes that basic medical care is a privilege, not a right.

Be it resolved that national comprehensive health care would fail.

The government should provide universal health care.

Capitalism impairs health delivery systems.

This House would significantly reform the health care system.

This house would standardize health care.

This House would protect the patient.

This House would force feed anorexics

This House believes that the markets and health make poor bedfellows.

# ART, ARGUMENT AND ADVOCACY

Resolved: That the nation should significantly reform its system of health care.

Modern medicine over-emphasizes prolonging life.

The rich will always be healthier than the poor.

## UNITED KINGDOM

This House is resolved that the British monarchy is the best system of government the world has ever known.

This House would tax the monarchy.

This House says, "God save the Queen."

This House would give Britain a written constitution.

This House would limit the terms of MPs.

Resolved: That the government should adopt a program of compulsory health insurance for all citizens.

This House would tear up the Act of Union.

This House calls for the disestablishment of the Church of England.

This House would allow 18 year-olds to be MPs.

This House believes that MPs should represent their constituents, not lobby groups.

This House would introduce proportional representation in Britain.

This House has no confidence in Her Majesty's Government.

This House would provide complementary medicine on the NHS.

This House believes that

Britain's licensing laws are outdated and draconian.

This House believes that New Labor is Old Tory.

This House believes that the "first past the post" system is undemocratic.

This House would privatize the BBC.

This House believes that Britain has failed its responsibilities to refugees.

This House would privatize the NHS.

This House would buy British.

This House would abolish the Commonwealth.

This House believes that the Commonwealth has outlived its usefulness.

This House believes that, if the Commonwealth didn't exist, no one would think of mentioning it.

This House would dissolve the House of Lords.

This House would abolish the A-level.

This House would allow queens to fight for Queen and country.

This House would remove the privileges of Oxbridge students.

## FORMER SOVIET UNION

This House is resolved that communism was better than capitalism for Russia.

This House mourns the demise of the Soviet Union.

## MILITARY AFFAIRS

Military conscription is superior to a volunteer army.

The military limits freedom of expression too much.

This House believes that military justice is an oxymoron.

This House believes that military spending is detrimental to society.

This House would lift the ban on gays in the military.

## GUN CONTROL

Resolved: That the government should adopt a policy of mandatory background checks for the purchasers of firearms.

That possession of handguns should be made illegal.

This House should increase regulation of firearms.

This House believes in the right to bear arms.

Gun manufacturers should be held liable for gun-related deaths.

This House would mandate gun safety education in all schools.

Resolved: The government should substantially increase restrictions on gun manufacturers.

Citizens should have the right to carry concealed guns.

Be it resolved that an armed society is a polite society.

## REPRODUCTIVE RIGHTS

This House believes that the unborn child has no rights.

That public money should not

326

be used to pay for abortions.

This House supports surrgacy for profit

Women should have the right to have an abortion if they so choose.

This House believes that a woman's body is her temple.

This House believes that abortion is justifiable.

This House would allow surrogate motherhood.

Abortion must be outlawed.

This House believes that contraception for teenagers encourages promiscuity.

## OTHER PUBLIC POLICY ISSUES

This House would re-introduce National Service.

This House would continue to prosecute World War II criminals.

This House would legalize voluntary euthanasia.

That the draft should be abolished and replaced by professional military forces.

This House would impose a curfew on children under 10.

This House will support students' mobility

This House would make tobacco companies pay compensation to the individual.

This house would put limits on the issuance of credit cards to anyone less than 25 years old.

Be it resolved that new drivers will be issued a restricted license, and that these restrictions will apply for one year.

This House would ban smoking.

This House would ban smoking in public places.

Public transport is more convenient than cars.

Emergency action for earthquakes and typhoons should be improved.

The automobile is the ultimate cause of urban decline.

## FAMILY MATTERS

This House would make divorce easier.

This House demands new family values.

This House believes that marriage is an outdated institution.

Marriage and government should be divorced.

This House would get married for the sake of the children.

## AUSTRALIA

Australia is an old economy country.

It is morally justifiable to bury nuclear waste in Western Australia.

Australian foreign policy has contributed to Indonesia's unrest.

## CANADA

Be it resolved that native Canadians be given the right to self-government.

Be it resolved that it is essential for Canada to maintain its military presence in Somalia.

Be it resolved that spraying for mosquitoes in Winnipeg is in the best interest of the public.

Be it resolved that capital punishment be reinstated for premeditated murder.

Be it resolved that the burning of stubble by Manitoba farmers be restricted.

Be it resolved that the trial period for Sunday shopping be extended.

Be it resolved that gambling be illegal in Manitoba.

Be it resolved that the City of Winnipeg take the responsibility of financing a new arena, to be located within the city limits.

Be it resolved that Quebec should separate from Canada.

Be it resolved that Canada's military role shall be only in self -defense.

Be it resolved that Canada shall privatize its medical system.

Be it resolved that taxpayer money no longer be used for the support of the Winnipeg Jets.

## TOPICS ABOUT DEBATE

This house would run a value case

NPDA should embrace one or more of the following format changes: A.Include an additional rebuttal on each

**327**

side;B. Add cross-examination time after each con-
structive speech; C. Adopt
the Worlds 4-team format

Parliamentary debate should
permit quoted evidence to
be used in debates

Debate, by its very nature,
teaches unethical practices.

# APPENDIX II

# RESOURCES

## SAMPLE AMERICAN PARLIAMENTARY DEBATE BALLOT

## NAME OF TOURNAMENT

MOTION:_____

## PROPOSITION

Team Name or Code _____

Speaker 1_____    Points _____    Rank _____

Speaker 2_____    Points _____    Rank _____

## OPPOSITION

Team Name or Code _____

Speaker 1_____    Points _____    Rank _____

Speaker 2_____    Points _____    Rank _____

## THE DECISION

The Decision is awarded to the (prop/opp) _____.

*Indicate low-point win _____.*

*Judge's Name and Affiliation _____*

_____

**Reason for Decision**

# SAMPLE BRITISH PARLIAMENTARY DEBATE BALLOT

## NAME OF TOURNAMENT

MOTION: _____

---

**FIRST PROPOSITION TEAM:**

Rank: 1st   2nd   3rd   4th
     (circle)

Speaker 1:      Score:

Speaker 2:      Score:

---

**FIRST OPPOSITION TEAM:**

Rank: 1st   2nd   3rd   4th
     (circle)

Speaker 1:      Score:

Speaker 2:      Score:

---

**SECOND PROPOSITION TEAM:**

Rank: 1st   2nd   3rd   4th
     (circle)

Speaker 1:      Score:

Speaker 2:      Score:

---

**SECOND OPPOSITION TEAM:**

Rank: 1st   2nd   3rd   4th
     (circle)

Speaker 1:      Score:

Speaker 2:      Score:

---

*Judges Names* _____

# TOURNAMENT DIRECTOR'S RESPONSIBILITIES

## BEFORE THE TOURNAMENT

### ANNOUNCING THE TOURNAMENT
- Acquire contact information
- Arrange for a date and site
- Draft an invitation

### INFORMATION FOR TOURNAMENT GUESTS
- Schedule
- Transportation information
- Lodging information
- Meal information

### TOURNAMENT OPERATIONS
- Tabulating Room Staff
- Tabulating Hardware and Software
- Tournament Office Supplies
- Guest judging

### TOURNAMENT MATERIALS
- Registration packet
- Awards
- Ballots
- Instructional Information
- Topic Writing and Selection

### ANCILLARY INFORMATION
- Last Minute Travel Information
- Harassment and Legal Information
- Videotaping and Broadcast Preparation
- Confirmations

## DURING THE TOURNAMENT

### OPENING EVENTS
- Registration
- Instructional Sessions

### TOURNAMENT OPERATIONS
- Announcements
- Tabulations
- Services: Meals, Lodging, Entertainment, Awards
- Troubleshooting

## AFTER THE TOURNAMENT

### DOCUMENTATION
- Ballots and Tabulation Results
- Tournament Information
- Review and Evaluation

### PUBLICITY AND CONCLUSION

## WEBSITES (DEBATE SITES)

American Parliamentary Debate Association
http://www.apdaweb.org/

Associacion Nacional De Debate Politico (Spanish language, Mexico)
http://simarro.net/asociacion.nacional/ASOCIACIONNACIONALDEDEBATEPOLITICO.html

Australasian Intervarsity Debating Association
http://www.debating.net/aida/

British Debate (English Speaking Union)
http://www.britishdebate.com/

Canadian University Society for Intercollegiate Debate
http://www.cusid.ca/

Debate Central
http://debate.uvm.edu/

English-Speaking Union
http://www.esu.org/

Estonian Debate Society
http://www.debate.ee/English/EngIndex.html

European Debating Council
http://www.debating.net/EUCouncil/

International Debate Education Association
http://www.idebate.org/

Japan Parliamentary Debate Association
http://www.asahi-net.or.jp/~cj3m-lbky/parlidebate.html

Latvian Universities Debating Center
http://www.debating.net/ludc/

National Parliamentary Debate Association
http://www.bethel.edu/Majors/Communication/npda/home.html

Slovakian Debate Association
http://www.sda.sk/

South African National Debating Council
http://www.debating.org.za/

Spanish Universities Debate League
http://www.debating.net/flynn/spain.HTM

World Debating Web page
http://www.debating.net/flynn/colmmain.htm

## WEBSITES (DEBATE SUPPORT)

Understanding USA:
www.ted.com

Encyclopedia of World Problems and Human Potential:
www.uia.org

UN Human Rights Web site:
www.unchr.org

Human Rights Watch:
www.hrw.org

Lawyers Committee for Human Rights:
www.lchr.org

Amnesty International:
www.amnesty.org

Belfer Center for Science and International Affairs
www.ksgnotes1.harvard.edu.bcsia

Institute for Policy Studies:
www.ips-dc.org

Peace and Conflict Resolution Gateway:
www.csf.colorado.edu/peace

PeaceNet/EcoNet/WomensNet/AntiRacismNet:
www.igc.org

International Peace Research Institute, Oslo:
www.prio.org

World Health Organization:
www.who.int

Medicins Sans Frontieres:
www.doctorswithoutborders.org

Physicians for Social Responsibility:
www.psr.org

American Public Health Association:
www.apha.org

National Council on Science and the Environment:
www.cnie.org

Feminist Gateway:
www.feminist.org/gateway

Queer Resources Directory:
www.qrd.org

Planned Parenthood Federation of America:
www.plannedparenthood.org

US Federal Government Resources:
www.fedworld.gov

National Archives:
www.nara.gov/research

Legal Resources:
www.findlaw.com

Legal Information Institute:
www.law.cornell.edu

Justice Information Center:
www.ncjrs.org

National Bureau of Economic Research:
www.nber.org

Education World:
www.education-world.com/research

Environmental Research Foundation:
www.rachel.org

US Institute for Peace:
www.usip.org

Federation of American Scientists:
www.fas.org

National Security Archive:
www.gwu.edu/~nsarchiv

# APPENDIX III

# ARGUMENTATION
# AND DEBATE
# GLOSSARY

**act utilitarianism** A theory of ethics that says our duty is to act in the way that produces actual overall consequences better than, or at least as good as, those that any other act open to us would produce.

**action theory** A methodology for critical examination that dictates that the social investigator should not be indifferent to the object of study. This theory argues that because individuals are both the subjects and objects of study, any investigation should involve principled stands on the problems studied and intentions of changing these circumstances.

**actualization theory** A theory of human behavior, based on the work of Abraham Maslow, that claims that individuals will strive toward becoming everything they can be, given the psychological need for self-fulfillment. Maslow proposed a hierarchy of needs: physiological, safety, belongingness, esteem, and self-actualization, with final achievement possible after lower-order needs are fulfilled.

**ad hominem** An attack on the advocate of an argument rather than on the content of the argument itself.

**Ad populum** An appeal to the people or other majoritarian sentiment as the basis for a claim.

**add-on** An advantage of the affirmative plan. Usually presented in the 2nd affirmative constructive and independent of whatever advantages were presented in the 1st affirmative constructive.

**advantage** The claimed benefits of the affirmative plan.

**affirmative** The side in a debate that supports the resolution.

**agent counterplan** A counterplan that argues that the plan the affirmative implements through one agent of change should instead be implemented through another agent of change.

**agent of action** The persons or institutions responsible for implementation of policy directives.

**alternate causality** A circumstance in which more than a single cause may result in a particular effect.

**analogy** A similarity or likeness between things in some circumstances or effects, when the things are otherwise entirely different.

**anarchism** A theory advocating social relations without coercive government that holds that society should be held together and progress by the natural harmony of decentralized voluntary associations.

**appeal to tradition** A fallacy of reasoning; an appeal to historical behavior as the basis for continuing to act in a certain manner.

**apriorism** The claim of a presumptive truth or condition.

**argument** A reason or reasons offered for or against a proposition or measure.

**as-if hypothesis** A method of thinking in which one formulates a coherent conjecture and proceeds to critically examine an issue on the basis that this conjecture is probably true.

**assertion** An unsupported statement; a conclusion that lacks evidence for support.

**attitudinal inherency** A type of inherency that identifies an unwillingness of those in power in the present system to take corrective measures to solve the affirmative's harm.

**audience** The listening, reading, or viewing individual or group reached by a performative or communicative act.

**authority** A position of power, credibility, or special function, attained by qualities of experience, insight, and skill.

**backlash** A response to progressive campaigns for marginalized or powerless social groups, involving efforts to discredit and undermine social advances.

**ballot:** 1) Literally, the piece of paper filled out at the end of a debate by a judge that says who won, who lost, and who got what speaker points. 2) Figuratively, what debaters are trying to win in each debate, so that they can be said to "collect" ballots through the course of a tournament, i.e., "We have three ballots, so I think we're going to clear."

**begging the question** An argumentative fallacy offering repetition of a claim as a proof for a claim.

**better definition standard** Proofs used to establish a hierarchical ranking system for the definitions of terms for a proposition.

**bias** A prejudiced attitude on the part of the source of evidence quoted in a debate. It is often argued that when sources are biased, their testimony is questionable and sometimes unacceptable.

**bibliographical criticism** Criticism of texts that pays close attention to format and the circumstances of publication as factors influencing meaning.

**bracket** The arrangement of teams in elimination rounds whereby teams debate each other according to seeding.

**break** To advance to the elimination rounds of a tournament. (See also clear.)

**break rounds** Preliminary rounds in which a team's ability to clear and advance to elimination rounds is at stake. At most tournaments, teams will need a certain record to advance to the elimination rounds, such as 3-2 or 5-3.

**brief** The outline of an argument, including claims, supportive reasoning, and evidence.

**brink** An element of a disadvantage which claims that the policy action of the affirmative plan is a sufficient condition to alter current institutions in a way to produce a dangerous or counterproductive consequence. A brink is the point at which a disadvantage begins to happen: It may be said that the plan would push us "over the brink" into the abyss of the impact.

**burden of proof** The responsibility of the person, upon introducing an argument, to provide sufficient reasoning and detail for the argument that the opponent is obliged to take the issue into consideration.

**canon** A set of works described as essential for the national literary culture.

**capital theory** Differing economic analyses of the theories of production, growth, value, and distribution.

**cards** Evidentiary quotations used to support arguments.

**case** The affirmative argument for the resolution; usually a reference to the arguments presented in the opening constructive speech by the affirmative side.

**case list** A list kept by a squad and by individual teams that tracks what plans and advantages are being run by other teams.

**case-side** Issues that relate to the stock or core issues of an affirmative case, including the demonstration of the ongoing nature of a problem (inherency), the qualitative and/or quantitative measure of a problem (significance), and the availability of a potential remedy for a problem (solvency). Also referred to as "on-case" arguments.

**categorical imperative** From the German philosopher Immanuel Kant, the general claim that one should not act in ways that one cannot, without inconsistency, will that everyone else should act as well.

**causal principles** An expression of multiple principles, such as that every event has a cause, that the same cause must have the same effect, and that the cause must have at least as much reality as the effect.

**chaos theory** The study of phenomena that appear to be random, but actually have an element or regularity that can be described mathematically.

**citation** The identifying, bibliographical reference material for evidence used in a speech. At a minimum, the citation for expert testimony must include the author's name and qualifications, the publication's title and date, and the page number for the specified quotation. Also known as the "cite."

**civil society** The nongovernmental aspects of modern society, e.g., religious, economic, and voluntary associational relations.

**clash** The direct and indirect opposition of the arguments of another person or side in a debate.

**clear** Slang. "to clear" To advance to the elimination rounds of a tournament. (See also break.)

**closure** A sense of formal completeness or clear outcome.

**collectivism** A theory of social and political organization, based on common or collective action, rather than individual action. The most general form of collective action is the state.

**comparative advantage** An argument, usually employed by the affirmative, that says that even if the affirmative does not completely solve the harm, it is still advantageous compared to the status quo.

**competitiveness** An argument for evaluating the legitimacy of a counterplan in formal debate. The presence of the counterplan should force a choice for the decision maker between the policies advocated by the affirmative plan and the counterplan. Competition is the quality of a policy that makes it a reason to reject another policy. Classically, competition was measured solely by means of mutual exclusivity. Now, however, competition is largely defined in terms of net benefits so that when we say a counterplan is competitive or net beneficial, we mean that it is better alone than the plan or any combination of the whole plan and all or part of the counterplan. (See also permutations, net benefits, counterplan, mutual exclusivity.)

**concede** To admit that an opponent is right about a certain argument or set of arguments. (See also grant.)

**conditional** Arguments advanced in debates that may be dropped at any time without repercussion to their advocates. Usually this phrase is used in the context of conditional counterplans, which can be dropped if undesirable without forfeiture of the debate.

**consequentialism** A doctrine that the moral rightness of an act or policy depends entirely on its outcome or consequences.

**constructive speeches** The foundational, opening speeches of a formal debate, in which the participants establish the major arguments that will be subject to analysis, refutation, and revision in the debate's subsequent stages.

**consultation counterplan** A counterplan that argues that we should consult another relevant actor as to whether or not the proposition team's plan should be implemented. That alternate actor is therefore given a kind of veto power over the adoption of the proposition team's plan. If the alternate actor says yes, the plan is adopted. If, on the other hand, the alternate actor says no, the plan is not adopted.

**contentions** The outlined arguments of the opening affirmative constructive speech.

**contextual definitions** A defining interpretation of the resolution that incorporates many or all of the terms of the topic.

**cooption** The influence of outside parties hampering an agency's [[agent's??]] efforts to carry out his instructions.

**counterplan:** 1) Noun A policy proposed by the opposition. The policy must offer a reason to reject the affirmative plan in the debate. Generally, the counterplan will either try to solve the affirmative's harms in a more beneficial way, e.g., by "avoiding" (not linking to) disadvantages accrued by the affirmative plan. Traditionally, it was thought that counterplans had to be both non-topical and competitive. These days, topical counterplans are more accepted as the emphasis shifts to net benefits and policy comparison and away from abstract theoretical concerns. Counterplans may also have advantages, which are similar to affirmative advantages in that they are benefits accrued by the counterplan. 2) Verb To run a counterplan.

**counterposition** See counterplan.

**criteria** Methods of decision making in a debate.

**critical linguistics** A method of analyzing the structure of language, presuming an encoded system of beliefs and ideologies in the use of social and political language and texts.

**criticism** Any or all of the activities of evaluation, description, classification, or interpretation of language and text.

**cross-examination** The question-and-answer period following constructive speeches in formal policy debates.

**debatability** A standard, usually found in topicality debates, that says that as long as a definition provides fair grounds for debate, it should be accepted.

**debate format** The order of speeches and the speaking time limits for each speech.

**decentering** A tool of deconstruction involving the denial, dissemination, or deferral of central meanings, particularly authoritarian Western concepts.

**decision-making theory** The investigation of the rational decision processes of persons and institutions in government and politics.

**deconstruction** A strategic textual analysis demonstrating a profound skepticism concerning the stability of meaning in language, based on the questioning methods of French philosopher Jacques Derrida.

**deductive reasoning** The act of reasoning from known principle to an unknown, from the general to the specific.

**delay counterplan** A counterplan that suggests that the judge or audience withhold implementation of the proposition team's plan until a specific time or condition named by the opposition team.

**deontology** The view that duty is a primary moral notion and that at least some of our duties do not depend on any value that may result in fulfilling them. In some circumstances, the justification of duties is an appeal to absolute rule, e.g., an opposition to the taking of life.

**dialectic theory** The investigation of the complex and sophisticated approaches to conflict or dialogue in which the generation, interpretation, and clash of opposing ideas leads to a fuller mode of thought.

**dialogism** The underlying assumptions of the Russian philosopher Mikhail Bakhtin, that argue that all utterances are dialogic in that they anticipate the response of the audience. In speech, therefore, we "define ourselves" by our relationships to others.

**difference principle** A proposal by political philosopher John Rawls that argues that unequal treatment is only justified if, by so doing, the least advantaged members of a society are made better off.

**disadvantage** (also known as a "DA" or "dis-ad") The bad thing that will happen when a plan goes into effect. In formal debates, opposition teams run disadvantages when they want to show that adoption of the government's plan will lead to far greater undesirable than desirable consequences. To win a debate on a disadvantage, the opposition team must generally prove at least three basic things: that the disadvantage links to the affirmative plan; that it is unique to the affirmative plan; and that the impact of the disadvantage is sufficiently undesirable to outweigh the affirmative advantages.

**disco** A charming, somewhat old-fashioned term used to describe a debate strategy where a team takes advantage of the interrelationship among arguments in the debate. Usually, one team will strategically concede large portions of their opponents' arguments, hoping that this tactic will allow the debate to re-focus favorably on their arguments. Often this strategy is used to capitalize on mistakes or contradictory arguments made by the other team.

**discourse analysis** An approach to language analysis, emphasizing action and interaction in texts and speeches.

**dispositional counterplan** A counterplan which, if proven disadvantageous or non-competitive, can be dismissed from consideration.

**double turn** In answering a disadvantage, a double turn takes place when a team argues a link turn ("We solve that problem") AND an impact turn ("That problem is actually a benefit") on the same disadvantage. When this happens, the affirmative is saying that they stop a good thing from happening; in essence, running a new disadvantage against themselves.

**effects topicality** A type of topicality standard that contends that the government's case is only topical by effect rather than by mandate. In these debates, it is often said that the government has failed to present a prima facie case or that they have mixed burdens – in this case, the burdens of solvency and topicality.

**elimination rounds** The single-elimination rounds that occur after the preliminary rounds at most tournaments. These rounds are usually seeded, using a bracket whereby the top seed (the team with the highest preliminary record) debates the bottom seed, etc.

**empirical evidence** Evidence or proof that is based on past examples or statistical studies.

**empiricism** Any theory emphasizing experience rather than reason as the basis for justifiable decision making.

**essentialism** The belief that there are essential features, or universal foundations, of human nature.

**ethnography** The study of expression and speech from culture to culture.

**evidence** Expert testimony, in the form of quotations from literature, broadcasts, the Internet, etc., used to support a debater's reasoning. Broadly, evidence is also reasoning used to prove a point.

**example** A sample that is selected to show the qualities or characteristics of a larger group.

**existential inherency** A kind of inherency that argues that if the affirmative can demonstrate a massive problem exists, then they have met their burden of inherency by showing that the present system is not solving it.

**extensions** Arguments that occur in response to opponents' arguments that extend and develop the original arguments.

**externalities** The costs and benefits of economic activity that are not incurred or enjoyed by the person or group performing it.

**extra-topicality** Government plans that contain planks or actions not specifically called for by the resolution.

**fallacy** A mistaken inference or an erroneous conclusion based on faulty reasoning.

**false dichotomy** Also known as a false dilemma, an argument fallacy that falsely analyzes a circumstance as a choice between only two possible alternatives.

**federalism** 1) A political concept, critical in the framing of the Constitution of the USA and elsewhere, that divides labor between the states and the federal government. 2) A disadvantage, sometimes run in conjunction with the states counterplan, which usually argues that the affirmative plan is an abuse of federal power, i.e., it violates the federalist doctrine, and that is bad.

**feminism** Any of the varieties of analysis of the exploitation and manipulation of women; some of these analyses provide proposals for social reform and transformation.

**fiat** A term used to describe the process that allows debate of the affirmative plan as if it were already adopted.

**field definition** An interpretation of individual terms or phrases of a debate proposition from an academic discipline or scholarly "field."

**flow** A system of note taking for debates that includes systematized guides for multiple speakers and tracking multiple issues.

**flow sheet** Also known as flow, the transcription of a debate; the notes used by debate participants to track arguments from speech to speech.

**funding plank** The part of the plan naming or listing those sources from which the plan will receive its funding.

**games theory** In debate, a paradigm that holds that debate is a kind of academic game and should thus be fair and competitive for its participants

**generic arguments** Arguments, usually used by the opposition, that are general and can be made to apply to a wide range of affirmative cases or plans.

**grant out of** To concede some of the opposition's arguments in order to back off of a position a debater had previously taken. For example, the speaker might concede the affirmative's "no link" argument to render the opponent's disadvantage irrelevant.

**hasty generalization** A claim that an example, or set of examples, is insufficient to prove a more generalized proposition.

**hermeneutics** The study of interpretation.

**hypothesis testing** A paradigm whereby the resolution is considered to be like a scientific hypothesis. The debate is said to test the truth of the resolutional statement ("This House should..."). Many people characterize this paradigm as implying that the resolution should be the focus of the debate, as opposed to policy making, which implies that the plan should be the focus of the debate.

**ideology** An investigation of the general science of ideas, knowledge, and values. The historical development of ideology understands individual perception and value as shaped by the social and economic situation of a person.

**impact** Most generally, the consequence of an idea that is presented in a debate. The consequence may be expressed in terms of the qualitative or quantitative significance of an issue or the role that an idea will play in the outcome of the debate. Typically, impacts are the bad or good events that happen as a result of an affirmative case, counterplan, or disadvantages.

**indeterminacy** The assumption that texts have gaps and inconsistencies built into them and that they are open to multiple possibilities for interpretation. The reader is thus obliged to revise the text with her or his own knowledge, identity, and experience.

**individualism** An understanding of human social life through the behavior of individuals. As the basic unit of society, individuals (not groups or nations) have rights that serve as the basis for moral reasoning.

**inductive reasoning** The act of reasoning from the specific to the general.

**inherency** 1) An explanation of the reason or reasons for the failure of current decision makers to make policy moves in the direction of implementation of the affirmative plan. In formal debates, the issue of inherency functions to establish the probability of unique advantages for the affirmative. 2) The thing or reason why someone is not doing something about a plan right now; the cause of a problem's existence.

**intertextuality** A concept that suggests that texts are not autonomous objects with clearly defined boundaries but are involved in a web of references to other textual material through allusion, quotation, style, assumption, etc.

**intrinsic** A description of a situation in which a disadvantage is a necessary result of the affirmative plan and cannot be prevented in another way. Sometimes government teams may argue that the opposition's disadvantages are "not intrinsic" to their plan, i.e., they could be prevented by other means.

**invisible hand** An expression by Scot economist Adam Smith to describe his belief that the actions of individuals in a free marketplace taken for their own economic benefit are guided in a manner to provide benefits for the society as a whole.

**irony** A mode of expression in which one thing is said and the opposite is meant.

**jargon** Specialized or technical language. In formal debate, jargon describes the use of terms not readily discernible to a lay audience, e.g., "fiat," "competitiveness," "effects topicality," "off-case," "permutation," etc.

**judging philosophy** A method or practice a judge uses to decide the outcome of a round. Although few judges have explicit philosophies or ironclad paradigms anymore, it is possible to guess their judging philosophy through careful observation and experience.

**jurisdiction** An argument often used in topicality debates that assumes the resolution provides limits on the judge's power. This argument states that if the plan is not topical, the judge has no power to fiat the plan and it is said to be outside her or his jurisdiction.

**kritiking** Otherwise known as "critiquing," this is a method of criticism in formal debate that focuses on the language, reasoning, underlying assumptions, expert testimony, interpretations, and proofs of the opponent. The argument form is often referred to as a "critique" or "kritik", meaning a type of argument that uncovers the fundamental assumptions of a team, case, word, or argument, and uses criticism of those fundamental assumptions to win the debate.

**lay judge** A term applied to persons who judge debates but who are not formally trained in policy debate (i.e., are not coaches or debaters or former debaters). Treat with respect.

**legislative intent** Part of a plan that provides that future judgments about the meaning of the plan will be based on its advocates' speeches.

**limiting standards** Any of the evaluations of the definitions of the terms of a formal debate proposition that establish a hierarchical system and demonstrate a preference for precise, conservative, and "limited" interpretations of the terms.

**Lincoln-Douglas debate** A debate format in which two individuals debate each other, using a time format of 6-3-7-3-4-6-3 (six minute opening affirmative constructive speech, three minute cross-examination, seven minute negative constructive speech, three minute cross-examination, four minute affirmative rebuttal, six minute negative rebuttal, three minute closing affirmative rebuttal).

**linearity** A ratio of the degree of policy action to a degree of beneficial or undesirable consequences.

**linguistic competence** An idealization of the knowledge rather than the use of language.

**linguistic criticism** An investigation of a text that considers its cultural and historical setting.

**link** A causal relationship. In formal debates, the relationship of one's argument to the opponent's position and the internal chain of reasoning in a complex argument. More specifically, links are how disadvantages or advantages apply to a proposition team's case. Note: Since disadvantages often employ chains of causal reasoning, we may speak of different levels of link. An "initial link" is the one that applies directly to the proposition team's plan or advantages, while the "internal links" are links in reasoning or causality that bridge the gap between the initial link and the impact.

**iterary theory** The assumptions and methods of textual analysis, including the application of a text to external analysis (e.g., Marxism, feminism, anarchism, psychoanalysis, linguistics, sociology, etc.).

**Marxist criticism** An approach to textual criticism that relates the literature to the political, economic, and social circumstances of its production.

**metaphor** A reference to one object in terms of another, so that the features of the second are transferred to the first. Metaphor is claimed to be the central process by which humans construct the world through language.

**mixing burdens** A term from the antiquated concept of stock issues, that describes when a proposition team uses one stock issue to prove another. This tactic is said to be unfair because the proposition team has to prove each issue independently. The only way this term is currently used is in debates about effects topicality, where the opposition may argue that a government team is using their solvency to prove they are topical. This is said to be bad because the government's case should have to be a topical example in order to allow the opposition a fair chance to clash with the affirmative.

**multiple causations** The claim that no one factor can account for the outcome of a particular event and that there are many factors that lead to its occurrence; these factors interact and cannot be considered independently in assessing the outcome of a behavior.

**mutual exclusivity** A claim that it is impossible for the proposition team's plan and the counterplan to coexist and an historical test for the competitiveness of a counterplan in formal debates. For example, an affirmative plan that calls for the USA to increase and modernize its NATO forces and a counterplan that calls for the USA to withdraw from NATO are said to be "mutually exclusive."

**narrative** A presentation that has the qualities and form of a story.

**narrative fidelity** The plausibility or credibility of a story, how likely the elements of a story are true.

**Nash equilibrium** Named after mathematician John Nash, the concept refers to a situation in which individuals participating in a game (a central concept of gaming theory and its application to debate as a "game") pursue the best possible strategy while possessing knowledge of the other players' strategies. The principle works on the premise that any individual cannot improve her or his opportunities given the other players' strategies.

**natural justice** Generalist legal principles that are independent of the conventions or formal practices of particular legal systems.

**natural law** A foundation for human law, natural law refers to embedded principles in human society or the rules of conduct or innate moral sense inherent in the relations of human beings and discoverable by reason or recognized by historical developments. It is contrasted with statutory or common law.

**natural rights** A theory of human rights that argues that rights arise from the nature of human and social existence.

**negative** The side of a formal debate that opposes the affirmative's proofs for the resolution.

**negative utilitarianism** A version of utilitarianism that substitutes the reduction of harmful or undesirable consequences for the provision of goods or benefits. The purpose of the theory is to avoid the disadvantages of utopianist criticism, namely, that there are dangers inherent in the design and implementation of a "perfect" world. The principle of negative utilitarianism attempts to avoid those costs by re-framing the discussion to focus on the elimination of evil.

**net benefits** One standard of counterplan competition. A counterplan is said to be "net beneficial" when it alone is a policy option superior to the whole plan and all or any part of the counterplan; in other words, the counterplan forces a choice between the policies advanced by the affirmative and negative teams in the debate.

**nihilism** A theory that rejects traditional values, such as the belief in knowledge, metaphysical truth, and the foundation of ethical principles.

**normal means** A term usually applied to proposition team plans used to describe the specifics of how the plan might be funded, implemented, or enforced. For example, a team's plan might say at the end: "Funding and enforcement through normal means." Often what is meant is: "However a plan like ours might normally be done, that is how this plan will be done." Proposition teams usually say they employ this phrase to avoid confusion; however, it serves a strategic purpose in plan design. Do not assume that there is general agreement over what "normal means" means. In the case of funding, for example, there are many ways that governments fund their programs (borrowing, re-allocation, new spending, etc.).

**objectivism** One or more theories that claim that a given subject matter contains objects existing independently of human beliefs and attitudes.

**off-case** In a formal debate, the opposition argumentation (in limited circumstances, supplemental proposition team argumentation) that does not directly refute the foundational arguments of the case proper, i.e., the first affirmative constructive arguments. "Off-case" generally refers to the forms of indirect refutation by the negative, e.g., topicality arguments, counterplans, disadvantages, and critiques. This term used to mean the arguments made in a debate that linked to the plan, as opposed to those that linked to the case. These days, it refers to arguments that are being debated on pieces of paper other than those devoted to the affirmative case. These arguments should be labeled as "off-case" arguments in the opposition speaker's roadmap, where she or he will say something like "I'm going to present two 'off-case' arguments, and then I'll be debating the proposition team's advantage and solvency."

**off-case flow** The notes transcribing the off-case arguments.

**on-case** In a formal debate, the argumentation by the affirmative and negative sides that is directed to the foundational or stock issues of the affirmative case, i.e., the issues of inherency, significance, and solvency. (See also case-side.)

**opportunity cost** The sacrifice made when selecting one policy over another.

**paradigm** A systematic and rational appraisal of debate that identifies the preferred features of the event and suggests models of analysis and deliberation. In contemporary policy debate, the most common paradigmatic approaches have included policy making, hypothesis testing, gaming, and performance. Although paradigms are usually conflated with judging philosophies, debaters can and often do have paradigms. (See also judging philosophies.)

**paradox** A contradictory statement from which a valid inference may be drawn.

**parliamentary debate** A format for extemporaneous debate. Parliamentary debate involves two-person or three-person teams. Formats include two or four competing teams in a single debate. Debate is on a topic announced some 15 to 20 minutes before each debate. Limited parliamentary procedures (points of information, points of personal privilege, points of order) are used in the contests, varying by tournament guideline.

**parsimony principle** A claim that one should pursue the simplest hypothesis; also known as Ockham's Razor, the principle suggests that one should not make assumptions that are not essential to a proof and that one should not make extended, contrived, and artificial relations between concepts.

**permutation** A test of the competitiveness of a counterplan or counterposition, it is an argument that explains how the functions of the plan and counterplan are complementary and mutually supportive. More practically, a permutation is a type of argument used by affirmatives to illustrate the noncompetitiveness of counterplans. Affirmatives argue that if it is possible to imagine the coexistence of the plan and the counterplan, and if such an imagined example would be net beneficial, then the counterplan does not provide a reason to reject the affirmative. (See also net beneficial.)

**philosophical competition** A now-defunct standard of competition for counterplans that argues that since the two plans are philosophically different, they are exclusive of one another.

**plan spike** A part of the plan designed to improve its workability or diminish its disadvantages.

**policy debate** A format of formal debate that calls for implementation of a policy directive or course of action. The common format for policy debate involves team debate with constructive speeches of eight or nine minutes and rebuttal speeches of five or six minutes for each of the participants. There is usually a three-minute cross-examination period following each of the constructive speeches.

**policy making** A paradigm that says debate rounds should be evaluated from the perspective of a pseudo-legislator weighing the advantages and disadvantages of two conflicting policy systems. (See also paradigm.)

**post hoc ergo propter hoc**: Literally, "after the fact, therefore because of the fact." A fallacy of reasoning that presumes a specific causal relation for two or more conditions because one of the events followed the other event.

**post-modernism** Theories of culture and politics that claim that the values and assumptions of modernism no longer hold and a reassessment is in order, based on alterior perspectives of a number of individuals and groups.

**pragmatism** The claim that the meanings of propositions lay in their possible effects on our experiences; a test of the validity of concepts by their practical effects.

**preemption or preempt** An argument designed to respond to another argument that has not been made, but which is anticipated.

**preparation time** Also known as "prep time," a period of time given to individuals or teams to prepare their speeches during a debate.

**present system** A description of current governmental, corporate, educational, and cultural institutions or policies.

**presumption** A corollary of burden of proof, the argument that accords an advantage to the attitudes, institutions, and practices that currently exist. In other words, "presumption" is the assumption that a system should be kept unless there is a clear reason to change it. Although this term comes from law, in debate it is usually understood to mean that the judge should presume for the status quo unless the affirmative or government team provides a clear and convincing reason to change. (See also burden of proof, status quo.)

**prima facie** Literally, "on its face," the responsibility of the advocate of a debate resolution to offer a proof for the proposition in the opening presentation, such that an opponent is obliged to answer the major elements of the case proper.

**procedural arguments** The arguments that establish the way the elements of a debate will be conducted; determinative issues that are contested in a debate regarding debate practice and the method of appropriate decision making and distinguished from the substantive issues of the proposition.

**proof** That which reduces uncertainty and increases the probable truth of a claim. Evidence is transformed into proof through the use of reasoning, which demonstrates how and to what extent the claim is believable. Proof is, of course, a relative concept, ranging from probability to certainty.

**proposition** Also known as a "topic" or a "resolution," a subject to be discussed or a statement to be upheld. Usually, a proposition is of fact, value, or policy that the affirmative is obligated to support. The resolution is generally understood to focus debate by dividing argument ground on any given topic.

**rationalism** A theory advancing reasoning as the basis for making moral judgments and acquiring knowledge.

**reasonability** A topicality standard that says the affirmative only need offer a definition that is not excessively broad and would appear legitimate at first glance.

**rebuttal** Refutation of an opponent's argument; also, the summary speeches of a debate.

**reductio ad absurdum** Literally, a "reduction to absurdity," a proof of a proposition by showing that its opposite is absurd or a disproof of a proposition by showing that its logical conclusion is impossible or absurd.

**refutation** The overthrowing of an argument, opinion, testimony, etc. Refutation is a direct and specific response to an opponent's argument.

**resolution** See proposition.

**reverse voting issue** An argument that suggests that the presentation of a frivolous or unfair issue in a debate should subject the advocate of the argument to a loss.

**rule utilitarianism** A version of utilitarianism that suggests that one should not seek the best possible outcome but one that is generally satisfactory.

**sandbag** To preserve important parts of an argument for use in a later speech.

**Sapir-Whorf hypothesis** The thesis that languages vary substantially and unpredictably and that these differences in languages construct different perspectives and realities.

**scarecrow** Formerly known as a "straw man," this is a fallacious argument that identifies a weak argument of an opponent and falsely characterizes all of the opponent's arguments as equally deficient.

**scenario** An outline of a real or imagined case study of a proposed course of action. Usually, a scenario is a picture, explained through specific examples, of what would occur if an advantage or disadvantage were to happen. (See also story.)

**scouting** The practice of knowing what arguments are being made by other teams, scouting is necessary for adequate preparation. Scouting includes, but is not limited to, keeping a case list. (See also case list.)

**second line** Additional evidence for presentation in rebuttals or constructive extensions.

**self-fulfilling prophecy** The principle that events occur as anticipated, not because one is able to predict a potential effect, but rather because one will behave in a manner that will inexorably produce the effect.

**self-serving bias** The claim that people will tend to deny responsibility for failure and take credit for success.

**semantics** The scientific study of the nature, structure, and meanings of speech forms.

**semiotics** A study of the science of signs or codes (oral, textual, artistic, etc.) in society.

**severance permutation** A permutation that contains only part of (rather than all of) the proposition team's plan.

**shift** To abandon an original position and take up a different one.

**shotgun** A strategy of presenting a profusion of unrelated, scattered attacks against an opponent's case. Usually considered to be tacky.

**significance** An expression of qualitative or quantitative dimension of a problem or condition; often listed as a "stock issue" in formal debate. Traditionally used as a measure of the need claimed by the affirmative or proposition team.

**slippery slope** Widely recognized as a logical fallacy, this type of argument says that a particular course of action sets in motion an unstoppable chain of events whereby an undesirable result becomes inevitable. One example of this argument is often made in debates about assisted suicide – "If we allow some so-called mercy killings, what's to stop the state from calling other bigoted policies mercy killings as well?" (See also fallacy.)

**snowball** An argument very similar to the slippery slope, which states that a small action can become much bigger through time: Imagine a snowball rolling downhill, collecting more snow as it goes.

**social contract** The duty to obey the government and the law and the right of the government to make the law arises from the contractual relationship, explicit or implied, of the government and the governed.

**socialism** A variety of theories emphasizing that the social or collective nature of economic production serves as the justification for public action regarding the distribution of economic goods and services.

**solipsism** A claim that nothing exists beyond one's immediate experiences.

**solvency** A stock issue that expresses the ability to successfully implement a suggested policy directive. Solvency is the ability of the affirmative plan or negative counterplan to solve the problem.

**speech act theory** Developed by John Rogers Searle, the claim that when one is saying something, one is simultaneously doing something.

**spread** The rapid introduction of multiple arguments in a formal debate.

**standards** A hierarchy or ranking system to evaluate arguments presented in a debate, usually an evaluation of the merit of definitions of key terms of the resolution in a topicality argument. A set of rules that allows the judge to decide which argument is better. Usually employed in topicality debates or counterplan competition discussions.

**states counterplan** A specific type of counterplan. Opposition teams often counterplan with sub-federal action, saying the 50 states (in the USA) or other provincial, decentralized governments would be a superior policy option. This counterplan is often run with net benefits such as the federalism disadvantage. These disadvantages, in order to be considered net benefits, would have to argue that federal action in the area of the plan was bad. Frequently, opposition teams running this counterplan will also claim that their policy is better suited to solve the affirmative harm area because states are better positioned (via efficiency, experimentation, enforcement, or whatever) than the federal government. (See also counterplan, federalism, net benefits.)

**status quo** Literally, "the way things are." An understanding of current institutions and policies; the current state of affairs. Usually, the proposition team tries to prove that a world with their plan would be better than the status quo.

**stock issues** The core elements of a logical proof of an affirmative case, including the key elements inherency, significance, and solvency.

**story** Debaters often use stories to prove their points. When a debater tells a link story, she or he is using narrative to explain how a link might play itself out in real life. In debate, stories and scenarios are concrete examples of more abstract concepts and arguments. Stories and scenarios make arguments specific and tangible. (See also scenario.)

**study counterplan** A variety of generic counterplan that says that instead of acting in the specified area of the proposition or the proposition team's case, we should instead study the problem to find the most desirable course of action.

**subpoints** Supporting points of arguments, often used to structure larger arguments.

**subjectivism** Any of a number of theories that identify material subjects as dependent on human beliefs and attitudes.

**sufficiency principle** Also known as a "sufficient condition," a circumstance in which a cause is sufficient, in and of itself, to produce a particular effect.

**take out** Any argument in refutation that undermines, or "takes out," an opponent's position; usually refers to an argument that eliminates the link or relevance of an opponent's argument.

**text** Anything that signifies in any medium.

**threshold** The degree of change necessary to precipitate a particular outcome; usually, the degree of change of an affirmative plan from current policy that will trigger undesirable consequences (disadvantages).

**time frame** The amount of time it takes for a particular condition, usually impacts, to occur.

**topicality** The issue that establishes the relation of the affirmative plan to the language of the topic; the proof that the affirmative argument is a representation of the resolution. Also known as "T."

**turn** An argument that reverses the position of an opponent. Turns usually come in two kinds: link turns and impact turns. Link turns are arguments that attempt to reverse a link established by the other team. For example, a negative team might run a disadvantage that said the plan hurt economic growth. The affirmative might argue a link turn by saying that the affirmative actually helped economic growth. An impact turn is an argument that tries to reverse an established impact. In this same example, the affirmative might argue that economic growth is actually bad, thereby turning the impact of the disadvantage. Also known as a "turnaround," or, historically, as "turning the tables."

**uniqueness** The claim that any benefit or cost is relevant to the advocacy of one side of a debate and can be used to decide favorably for that side or unfavorably against the other side. Uniqueness is the part of a disadvantage that proves that your plan and only your plan could trigger the impacts. Affirmative advantages can also have a burden of uniqueness: If their harm is being solved now, then there is no unique need for the plan.

**utilitarianism** Any of a variety of consequentialist views that claim to maximize good or minimize evil.

**vacuum test** A versatile, if often silly, argument employed in topicality and link debates that asks the hypothetical question: "If we looked at the plan in a vacuum, would it fulfill _____ condition?" In effects topicality, a vacuum test is used to determine if the plan is topical in itself.

**values** Principles, acts, customs, and qualities regarded as desirable by individuals or groups.

**voting issues** The arguments in a formal debate that are used to decide the ultimate outcome of the debate.

**weighing the issues** A comparative analysis of all the issues in a debate; an evaluation of their relative probability and impact conducted in order to determine which are most important, and thus, who wins. Rebuttalists usually weigh the issues, saying things like "Well, the plan may increase crime a little bit, but that's a small price to pay to safeguard our constitutional rights," thereby comparing the impact of the negative's crime disadvantage to the impact of their racial profiling advantage.

**whole resolution** An argument in formal debate suggesting that the proposition side must responsibly maintain a proof for all the possible interpretations, not a single instance or set of examples of the proposition.

**workability** A condition whereby a proposal could actually operate to solve a problem if implemented as legislation.

**zero-sum** Circumstances in which the interests of one or more parties are advanced at the direct and reciprocal expense of the interests of one or more other parties.

# APPENDIX IV

# SAMPLE DEBATE
# TRANSCRIPTS

The following is a sample of the opening speeches of the first proposition and first opposition speeches in a British format debate. The speeches are annotated to identify successful strategies, reveal omissions and missed opportunities, find strategic agreement, and critically investigate the debate's substantive material, including argument examples. The beginning of the second proposition team's case is also included as a model of argument extension of the opening proposition speech. Points of information are included and evaluated. The annotations are bulleted and italicized.

The motion for the debate is "This House believes in affirmative action."

> First Speaker, First Proposition: "Mr. Chairman, adjudicators, ladies and gentlemen: hi. You may remember me better from such films as *Surf Nazis Must Die* and *The Return of the Italian Stallion, Part 2*. Ladies and gentlemen, I've been called out of retirement to try and demonstrate to all of the people at this table how to debate. If you listen carefully, the motion for debate is quite simply that this House believes in affirmative action.

> - *A brief and entertaining introduction can be effective. This is brief.*

Myself and my disheveled-looking partner want to define the motion in very clear terms. Ladies and gentlemen, we want to see the introduction of affirmative action to eradicate the inequality between the sexes, and in particular we want to see the introduction of legislation to permit government and public agencies to require the imposition and the introduction of quotas in training and employment in the private and the public sector only where there is clear, recurring, and evident statistical evidence that great inequality exists in the particular areas where quotas are going to be introduced. And to further clarify, we're not necessarily and automatically talking about the introduction of a 50 percent quota. The exact quota for each individual sector, for each individual employment body, or each individual state body will be decided according to the circumstances. Quotas of 20 percent may be necessary; quotas of 50 percent may occasionally be necessary. In other words, it's an open-ended process."

- *This is a clear definition of the motion, with sufficient exposition for the opposition teams, judges, and audience to understand both the identified problem and its solution. The proposed plan of action is a bit ambiguous, which almost always succeeds in assisting the proposition debates. Opposition teams should take care to insist on further clarification of "open-ended processes," as they are likely to change throughout a debate, typically at the expense of the opposition.*

"We believe that legislation has to be introduced to give the state the power and the authority to introduce this quota system. Norway, Sweden and the German Republic have already done this. The UK refuses to do so. The European Union refuses to do so. Many other countries such as the USA operate half-hearted affirmative action policies. We're going whole hog. We say: Give the government this power. The reason why we're doing this is quite simple: Equality legislation, which has been in the Western world for 30 years, has simply failed to produce a satisfactory income and a satisfactory level of success. We don't disagree that at low levels, there is generally a progressive movement towards equality in the Western world. At high levels, there are enormous, built-in levels of inequality. Equality legislation is not working."

- *This passage demonstrates that the problem is ongoing and significant. This portion of the opening speech offers numerous examples of the need for policy reform. In addition, several examples of successful implementation of the suggested affirmative action policy are included ("Norway, Sweden, and the German Republic") as expressions of solvency arguments.*
  *The speaker's rhetoric is quite strong, with effective summaries for major points.*

Opposition speaker [rising]: "Point of information."

First Speaker, First Proposition: "No thank you. Equality legislation is not producing the results that we are looking for. As a consequence,"

Opposition speaker [rising]: "Point of information."

First Speaker, First Proposition: "In a moment. As a consequence, we think aggressive action needs to be taken. We need to drive the process forward, and my partner and I are arguing that we think quotas are the way to go."

Opposition speaker: "Well, what happens if there aren't that many women applying for the certain jobs?"

First Speaker, First Proposition: "Exactly. Thank you. That's what's known in theatrical terms, being an actor, ladies and gentlemen, as feeding a cue. You see, the entire point is that there is deeply embedded cultural deterrence to equality. People are being deterred for applying for certain posts. People are being deterred from moving towards certain positions. We think the classic example, ladies and gentlemen..."

- *This is an outstanding reply to a well-articulated point. Not only does the speaker provide a reasonable answer to a question that is, more likely than not, on the minds of the judges and audience, but the first proposition speaker does so in a manner that makes the opponent's position seem trite and predictable (i.e., "feeding a cue").*

Opposition speaker [rises]: "Point of information."

First Speaker, First Proposition: "No, thank you, sir. The classic example lies in the political process. We see a situation where, to a large extent, representation of women in Western democracies is down to around a level of 20 percent. In France, 11 percent, in the UK, 22 percent. Ridiculous, given the 50-50 split between men and women in the population. What's happening is that there is a glass ceiling, ladies and gentlemen – a system of values that acts as a deterrent. There is a culture in place that acts as a deterrent towards people applying, to answer our opponent's point. It acts as a deterrent for people being promoted – it creates problems of perception. And this is our key first argument, ladies and gentlemen. We are going to develop this further, but what we're arguing is that you have a problem with value perception. The way to alter the value perception is to put the people in place. If you put the people in place, ladies and gentlemen, if you push women, if you require certain a proportion of women running for political parties, a certain proportion of women at a high level of judicial office, at high level political offices, then change will follow."

- *The use of statistical information effectively provides evidence to support a well-reasoned point.*

"We've seen the classic case in the British Parliament, ladies and gentlemen. For the first time in 150 years, there's been an attempt to rein back the old-boy all-night work and drink culture of the British Parliament. Only since, in the last two years, have you had a high proportion of a female intake. Quite simply: You change the values, you provide role models. In other words, ladies and gentlemen, [opposition speaker rises] you start challenging the culture. You see the people in place and change follows."

- *This is a good example of the use of an analogy to prove that a plan of action would work in a different public policy sphere.*

Opposition speaker: "But what you also see, for example, is an example where in the Scottish Parliament, the Labor Party adopted an affirmative action policy for their candidates. As you see people being able to put forward the backlash of 'Here are women who aren't here because they're good enough.'"

First Speaker, First Proposition: "Thank you. This is the 'backlash' argument. What's fascinating about the 'backlash' argument is that in 1968, when the Equal Pay and Race Relations legislation was introduced in Britain, the first thing they said was: 'Oh no, if you legislate for equality, the white males will be really annoyed.' It happens every single time. The backlash argument, ladies and gentlemen, is classic nonsense. We've never seen a backlash in these circumstances, ladies and gentlemen. What we're arguing is that you need something to change perceptions and change values. People need to be shown that women can do politics. Women can do politics equally well. It's very, very important to realize that we've seen the introduction over many years of a gradualist approach, where it'll be all right in the end, and you'll have a gradual moving up of women through the process. Ladies and gentlemen, this is a key argument: I do not see why this generation of female graduates or the next three, four, or five generations of women need to labor under a disadvantage caused by perception. I don't see why our female opponent and other people like her have to suffer from perceptions and disadvantages that I don't have to suffer. That's the problem with the gradualist approach. There's a price to be paid. Ladies and gentlemen, Norway and Sweden quit quota policies in the parliamentary process. But quotas for selection have the highest proportion of women in Parliament – over 50 percent – in Norway. They had the only female Prime Minister for a very, very long time. The first three female leaders were from Scandinavia. This is tangible evidence that these policies can work. And on those grounds, ladies and gentlemen, we urge you to support the motion."

- *Here is more "tangible evidence" that the proposed plan would work. At three distinct points in the opening address, the first speaker for the proposition is able to provide examples or analogies to bolster the claim that a workable solution to a serious social injustice is readily available. This is a fine presentation, with considerable evidence to support artfully executed points.*

---

First Speaker, First Opposition: "Thank you very much, ladies and gentlemen. It's a pleasure to be representing the New World in this debate here today. Maybe I'll bring some new ideas, some fresh ideas, to one that was very lacking on the government side here today – a case that was basically substantiated with examples from Norway, and offered very little about how changing numbers with their convoluted scheme will actually change perceptions in British society. That is what really has to be looked at today. I want to deal, first of all, with this point he brought up about the failure of British society to produce results."

- *It is important to establish your own claim in the debate before reacting to the points of the opposing side. A brief introduction from the first speaker for the opposition would make for considerably stronger presence in the debate. The judges and audience have listened to the opening proposition speaker for seven minutes. That person had an opportunity to develop a rapport with them. If you attack before making your own connection with the judges and audience, you are likely to subtly antagonize them. You are still an unknown quantity and you will be assaulting a familiar.*

  *Debaters need to accurately represent the positions of the other side of the motion or risk losing their credibility. The opposition speaker is duly interested in undermining the claims of the opening proposition speaker. Unfortunately, his inaccurate characterization of the first proposition speaker's examples will hurt his own cause with judges paying attention to the debate. The opening proposition speaker had considerably more to say than an argument "basically substantiated with examples from Norway."*

"He says that the system is not working. He comes before us with a convoluted plan that says: 'Well, basically, um, 50 percent is good enough in some areas and not good in other areas,' and the question I have to ask is: Why is less parity in some areas better than in other ones?' He has given us very little evidence on that point."

- *This is the beginning of an effective rejoinder but the speaker does not commit a sufficient amount of time to fully analyze the proposition plan.*

"What we should ask this House is: Why, in fact, are women being dissuaded from these jobs? What he is trying to have us believe on the government side of this House is that this is some sort of culture of misogyny, some sort of culture where women are traditionally shuffled out of places of prominent work within many industries. What we're going to decide upon, here on the opposition side, is that this is *not* the deterrent for women going into these areas. In fact, a lot of other areas have to be looked at, and the government should have looked at. The first is the issue of child care, and how in fact a lot of women..."

- *The speaker for the opposition argues an alternatecausality. It is not discrimination in hiring and promotion but discrimination in services that is the cause of the problem. Affirmative action programs, dedicated to employment hiring and promotion matters, would be of little consequence if there are other significant barriers to women's employment.*

Three government speakers [rising, raising hands in various manners]: "Point of information."

First Speaker, First Opposition: "Don't have it, while in countries like Japan, women do have avenues to take proper child care, and when they can..."

Fourth government speaker [rising to join the other three]: "Point of information."

First Speaker, First Opposition: "Yes, one point."

Government speaker: "You mentioned Japan, which of course has the worst equality record of any industrialized nation. The whole point is that things like child care will follow when the women are in place through quotas."

First Speaker, First Opposition: "We found that in areas like the metropolitan police in London, quota systems reduce the quality and reduce the ability of people to do their jobs properly."

Two government speakers [rising]: "Point of information."

First Speaker, First Opposition: "No, sit down. The second point that was brought up was this idea of backlash. He says there's no backlash. But there is a backlash, I'm going to argue, on the quality of services..."

Government speaker [rising]: 'Point of information."

First Speaker, First Opposition: "which are provided to people in areas. I'm going to give you an example. He brought up the example of Norway, with its 50 percent parity. Not at this time. In a little bit. I'm going to give you the example of the Indian Parliament – another part of the world where people are fighting for the better treatment of women. There was a 50 percent gender parity proposal that was put forth. And what happened? There were inferior candidates put forth, there was..."

- *At this stage of the debate the first speaker for the opposition is barraged with points of information and, to a significant degree, the speaker loses control of the floor. The fatal error? In replying to points of information, the opposition speaker says, "Not at this time." In fact, the same line is delivered seven times. The speaker less frequently says "No," or "No, thank you." The problem is that no one on the opposing side knows which later time is acceptable. The opposing speakers continue to rise to a point of information, only to be repeatedly told "Not at this time." But every subsequent moment of the speech is a different time.*

*If speakers want to control the floor, they must say "No" to points of information and avoid saying "Not at this time."*

Government speaker [rising]: "Point of information."

First Speaker, First Opposition: "Not at this time. There was voter backlash, voter apathy. There was a rolling back of the gains..."

Government speaker [rising]: "On this point, sir."

First Speaker, First Opposition: "...that women had gained in India simply because these things..."

[A second government speaker rises, reaches out hand.]

First Speaker, First Opposition: "...weren't allowed to be done incrementally. No, not at this time. Legitimacy in liberal democracy is fundamental, and to assault that fundamental principle of legitimacy in liberal democracy by giving an uneven playing field..."

Two government speakers [rising, hands outstretched]: "Sir."

First Speaker, First Opposition: "...to level the playing field is fundamentally offensive."

[A third government speaker rises]

First Speaker, First Opposition: "I'll take your point."

Government speaker: "Do you accept, sir, that the very backlash you talk about comes from the very people who try to keep women out of the workplace to begin with? What we're trying to do is challenge that."

First Speaker, First Opposition: "What you can do is you can challenge it, but you have to ask yourself what the best way is to challenge it. By simply saying to a Parliament that you can't have the best people doing their jobs, that you can't have the best people changing values incrementally, that is fundamentally wrong and that is what we stand against. What I want to explore, and what my partner and I are going to explore on the first opposition side here today, is the fundamental offensiveness of fighting discrimination with discrimination. Pardon the rather clichéd example here, but if Martin Luther King were here in this debate today, he'd be rolling in his grave while he was watching the debate." [general laughter]

Government speaker [rising]: "Point of information, sir."

First Speaker, First Opposition: "No, no, no. What I want to deal with here is the fact that many organizations, especially in North America, such as the American Civil Liberties Union, and the Jesse Jackson-led Rainbow Coalition, have in fact stood against the fundamentally offensive principle that in a race case..."

Government speaker [rising]: "Point of information, sir."

First Speaker, First Opposition: "No, I know your case centers on gender, but.... No, not at this time."

Government speaker [rising]: "Point of..."

First Speaker, First Opposition: "No, not at this time. What they are saying is that it should be based not on the content of one's character but instead on the content of one's trousers, or..."

Government speaker [rising]: "Sir?"

First Speaker, First Opposition: "...the content of one's

skin, and we fundamentally stand against this. Not at this time. Because what it does, in sociological terms, is pigeon-hole members of society."

Government speaker [rising]: "Point of information, sir."

First Speaker, First Opposition: "Not at this time. It defines members of society by the color of their skin, by what sex they are..."

Government speaker [rising]: "Sir?"

First Speaker, First Opposition: "...and not by their abilities to do their job."

Government speaker [rising]: "Point of information, sir?"

First Speaker, First Opposition: "No. And if you want to build a society in which women, or blacks, or any other group is looked upon on even grounds, you have to do that without putting them in a pigeonhole."

Government speaker [rising]: "Point of information, sir."

First Speaker, First Opposition: "Surely we've had enough of that in society. What it does is impede integration and proper community-building. On that point, madam?"

Government speaker: "Sir, are we not pigeonholing at present when we say that men can do certain jobs and women can do certain other jobs, and we're not going to do anything about it?"

First Speaker, First Opposition: "Society's not saying that. It's saying that women can do the jobs. They're invited to, but society is not striving and should not be striving to have the constructs in place to allow that to be attainable. You cannot come up and tell me that people who seek office, who are working these long hours, jogging between Westminster and Edinburgh, have the proper kind of child care services to allow for that."

Government speaker: "On that point."

First Speaker, First Opposition: "You have to see that in fact a community is built not by putting people into categories but is based upon leveling the playing field, incrementally offering the right kind of ways of getting people involved in the public sector. On that point?"

- *This is a potentially dangerous position for the opposition. The speaker seems to support an incremental movement in the direction of that which the proposition has advocated in the debate, in other words, a slow-motion version of the case. This claim seems to accept the underlying principles of the proposition case but, with incremental rather than systemic change, will take decades to achieve the same goal.*

Government speaker: "What you seem to be saying, sir, is that women can't go into work because there are inadequacies in things like child care. Who's pigeonholing now?"

First Speaker, First Opposition: "I'm not pigeonholing anyone. I'm just identifying one of the realities out there for women. It's fundamentally different, I think, to offer women child care than to say: 'You know what? We're going to allow you a position in government because you happen to fit one of our number categories.' And we're not so sure what those number categories are…"

Government speaker [rising]: "Sir?"

First Speaker, First Opposition: "…on this government side, because they say: 'You know what? For politics, 50 percent might be good enough in Norway, but for a police force or for firefighters, they might not be able to make the physical requirements, so we might have to have a ten percent quota there.' What they're doing is not only pigeonholing. They're pigeonholing within different professions. I'd ask why it isn't 50 percent for everything. Can they answer that?"

Government speaker [rising]: "Point of information."

First Speaker, First Opposition: "Yes?"

Government speaker: "Sir, you talk about number categories. Is it just a coincidence that 78 percent of British MPs
at the moment are men? This is a *de facto* number category
working at the moment. You've got to change the factual circumstances, sir."

First Speaker, First Opposition: "Yes. But changing the factual circumstances while compromising the fundamental
principles of liberal democracy is not the right way to go
about it. Margaret Thatcher, believe it or not, for all of the
glory that she brought to Britain, showed that women can
assume positions of leadership, that women do not have to
fight a numbered quota system to get there, but can achieve
based on the fact of their leadership abilities. And that's
what we stand for on the opposition side here today. This
kind of wishy-washy, let's bend the numbers to suit our purposes, is fundamentally wrong. Fighting discrimination
through discrimination is not the way to solve our problems.
Society needs fewer categories, not more. We can achieve
progress by allowing people to work out things on their own
terms. Thus we fundamentally oppose this case. Thank you
very much."

- *The first speaker for the opposition ends the speech with a powerful
  conclusion. This is quite necessary here, as too many of the good
  opposition points were lost or made incoherent in a maelstrom of
  points of information.*

---

First Speaker, Second Proposition: "I find it quite bizarre
that this side's case is accused of being simplistic when –
let's face it, the only real explanation by the opposition of
why women are not favored in employment is that there
isn't adequate child care. I've been writing down everything

they've said, Mr. Speaker, and that's about all they've said in terms of explaining the employment gap between male and female. What we've identified is a realistic problem which they've then taken and said: 'Well, we have to oppose you because we're the opposition' without actually giving us any substantive arguments that show why our system doesn't work. What I'm going to try and do is this speech extending the debate into the second half is, first of all, go back over the whole idea of how you challenge the existing discrimination. Do you do it from the inside or from the outside? I'll give you my perspective on that. Secondly, this whole backlash argument – I'm just going to clear that up. Then thirdly, I'm going to move the debate on to look at the whole concept of the meritocracy, because we think that's what they think it should be all about. What we're going to show is that the meritocracy doesn't exist. It doesn't evolve naturally. You have to put means in place to allow that meritocracy to flourish."

- *The first speaker for the second proposition establishes a clear organizational structure for the speech, indicating that there will be an extension of the opening proposition case (fulfilling one of this speaker's responsibilities in the debate) as well as seriously engaging the two main points of refutation from the first opposition team's stand on the floor. This is an effective tactic, as it educates judges about your role in the debate and **frames** the presentation (it sets expectations for the performance that the speaker will undoubtedly meet).*

Opposition speaker [rising]: "Point of information."

First Speaker, Second Proposition: "No, thank you. So, first of all, the whole concept of pigeonholing, they are arguing on this side of the House that the best way to change problems within an employment environment is from the outside. They specifically said that you don't get any benefits from aggressively fighting for social change from within. The point of information that I gave earlier was from last week where a group of female speech therapists were given 2.5 billion pounds because they aggressively fought from the inside. Had they not been in the profession, there would have been no challenge to the current system. That's the argument we use on this side of the House."

Opposition speaker [rising]: "Point of information."

First Speaker, Second Proposition; "Can I go for a bit longer? Then I'll take your point. So what we say is that you can't just say that ours is a bad system without telling us why. The rebuttal of the Norwegian example was: 'Well, who likes Norway? They've got a crap football team, and the Eurovision song contest isn't going to go that well for them.' Well, ladies and gentlemen, it's just not deep enough on this side of the House. So we say challenging from within gets results, and they're not providing us with any results from their approach. Ms. Roach?"

Opposition speaker: "You're totally contradicting your own policy here. What you're doing is not proposing to change a profession from within, but to impose restrictions on it from the outside. How is that change from within?"

First Speaker, Second Proposition: "Because it challenges two levels. The first point is that people refuse to apply because of the male yahoo atmosphere that they don't feel comfortable with. You say that there is another issue of no child-care availability. We say that you can do both with this system because it gets women into the workplace who will fight for the next round of changes that they acquire to then allow further women to get into that same workplace. The second point is their whole issue of the backlash. Who is the backlash, ladies and gentlemen? These white, angry men? Who are they? They are the very people who want women kicked out of the workplace. They are the very people who want blacks kicked out of the workplace."

Opposition speaker [rising]: "Point."

First Speaker, Second Proposition: "No, thank you."

- *The opposition side may be correct here. The argument from the second proposition team's opening speaker seems to contradict some of the basic principles of the opening proposition team and, paradoxically, support the claims of the opening opposition speaker. The argument that inside movement of affirmative action may be appropriate does not seem to extend the original proposition case. An extension in the second proposition presentation should be consistent with the first proposition interpretation of the motion. And it should not be conflated with either the rhetoric or substance of the opening team for the opposition.*

---

What follows are the first two speeches from an American parliamentary debate on the motion "This House should return the goods."

1.

**Prime Minister Constructive:** "Thank you very much. I believe that debate is a vigorous discourse in which we should discuss important and controversial issues. Keeping that in mind we turn to the topic: "This House should return the goods." We're talking about return of stolen cultural artifacts – art objects. We have a worldwide phenomenon of systematic theft by imperialist nations of cultural artifacts, and they are now being held with impunity. What we would advocate, on the side of the government, is that these artifacts should be returned when we can identify the rightful owners. And so, there are several reasons why we would advocate this issue. The first one is that we need to move beyond Western conceptions of law, because the current way the legal system works is that we allow countries to act tyrannically. We allow them to steal cultural artifacts, to use their political or physical power to prevent their return, and then, after a certain period of time, then they just say 'Well, now the statute of limitations gives us immunity on this issue, and we're no longer liable, and you can't have them back now.' So what we need to do is create a specific exemption to the statute of limitations that would allow for the return of cultural artifacts. We've had this tyrannical action with the stealing of the Parthenon frieze, with Nazi art, with Native American artifacts, and we would advocate the return of these as well as other stolen cultural artifacts.

"It goes beyond that. What we also need to do is establish an appropriate relationship between states. The theft of cultural artifacts is a way to assert cultural dominance by one country over another country. In fact, this is what the British Museum is. The British Empire went out around the world and collected ... well, collected is a nice way to say it. One might aptly say that they stole cultural artifacts from around the world and now their culture is able to subsume all other cultures – within their culture, they subsume all other cultures and that makes them the superior culture. And only with the return of these artifacts..." [Opposition speaker rises]

Opposition speaker: "Point of information."

Prime Minister: "Hold on, I'll get to you in one second. Only with the return of these artifacts can we start down the path of an equitable relationship between states. Yes?"

Opposition speaker: "What about cases where the rightful owner is unclear?"

Prime Minister: "Well, it's unclear, Andrea. It's unclear. As I said, we needed to return these when the rightful owner could be determined. Now, if the rightful owner can be determined, then it wouldn't be unclear. I think in the examples that I've given, such as the case of the Parthenon frieze, the ownership is very clear. There is historical record establishing what happened. In fact, Lord Elgin *sold* the Parthenon frieze to the British Museum. In the case of Nazi art, the Nazis were very organized. This caused many deaths, but also resulted in specific records about who stole what art. These records are just now becoming available.

That's why we need to provide for an exemption within the statute of limitations to allow for the return of these artifacts. When we cannot establish a rightful owner we will, of course, not return them. That's an interesting point you bring up.

"Before I got off on that tangent of Andrea's very pointed question, I was talking about why we need to establish an equitable relationship between states. The reason why is if we can establish an equitable relationship between states, we can increase peace, stability, and harmony between nations. Just as if you can establish a more equitable relationship with your brother, you start fighting less if he gives you back all of the toys he has stolen. It's the same sort of idea on a larger and more important scale.

"The last important reason for the return of cultural artifacts is that we need to move beyond our own ideas about what the role of cultural artifacts actually is. What we need to do is look at an example of one cultural artifact in the USA, which would be the Declaration of Independence. What do we do with the Declaration of Independence?"

[Opposition speaker rises, crosses arms]

"We stick it under a piece of plastic laminate, we enclose it in gas, we put two armed guards beside it, and then we install a three million dollar video camera created by NASA's Jet Propulsion Laboratory to make sure that no one steals it. It must, by the way, be one hell of a camera for that price. In any case [gestures to standing opposition speaker], and you're going to get called on any minute now, so you can stop shifting around…"

[Standing opposition speaker appears to jog, almost imperceptibly, in place]

"We come to believe that anyone who *fails* to take these kinds of precautions is failing in their duty to respect cultural artifacts, just as [gestures to standing opposition speaker again] Nate is failing in his duty to respect me as a speaker by doing this sort of little dance [turns to opposition speaker]. But I'll take your question anyway."

Opposition speaker: "So what should we do with the Declaration of Independence? Everyone should be able to touch it and fold it and write on it? Tell me: What should we do?"

Prime Minister: "No, I'm saying that what we do with the Declaration of Independence is fine, but we should recognize, in fact, that this treatment frequently destroys the religious, cultural, or political significance that other, distinct cultures place upon their cultural perspective. Look at the Igbu tribe, who deliberately allow their objects to decay because they need to preserve the desire to re-create. In fact, they value deterioration as an aesthetic virtue. There's nothing wrong with our aesthetic perspective, that we want to preserve this from decay, but we should also respect other aesthetic perspectives because your aesthetic perspective dictates how you view yourself and how you view others. It goes down to the fundamental consideration of what you view as beautiful. Once you allow people to co-opt the abilities of other people to make these critical determinations, once you take an Igbu artifact and place it under a glass case and destroy that distinct aesthetic perspective, you strike at the very heart of what it means to be human. So to prevent that and to correct for that, I would urge a proposition ballot. Thank you very much."

—————————

First Opposition Speaker: "I'd like to thank everyone for coming. Let's talk about the ridiculous assumptions behind this case. First of all, they say that we're only interested in returning these things, quote, 'when the rightful owner can be determined.' We ask them 'When can that happen?' They say: 'We provide very good examples of that. We've provided the example of the Parthenon frieze and the example of

Nazi art.' Well, the Parthenon frieze was built using stolen funds and marble that Athens actually appropriated from other countries in the year circa 400 B.C. So who owns the Parthenon frieze? Is it the people who actually owned the objects that were amalgamated into the Parthenon? Or is it the Greeks, who stole those things and used them to build the Parthenon? Let's look at the example of Nazi art. Let's say that the Nazis are stealing several things from the museums of the Vichy government in France. Which were, in turn, stolen from the Germans during the wars over the French Revolution. Who owns those pieces of art?"

Government speaker, rising: "Will you take a point?"

Opposition speaker: "The simple fact is that it's not as simple as looking at the last time an artifact was stolen because the history of cultural artifacts is one of theft, and you can't avoid this. There is no clear-cut case, as Judd would have you believe, in any situation where the rightful owner can be determined. It's never like their example of some kid stealing another kid's shoes. On that point?"

Government speaker: "So do you deny that there are explicit records of Nazi art that trace back the legitimate owners?"

Opposition speaker: "No, I'm not denying that. I'm saying that there are legitimate records tracing back legitimate ownership in the sense that that legitimate ownership was, in fact, still a stolen cultural artifact. There is never any art artifact that is produced without theft. If you think about even the most basic art artifact, it is produced using the labor of a lower class in order to sustain a class of elite intellectuals and artists who then use that elitism to create these art objects. Art is a world of theft, and it's implicated in theft, and you cannot blindly assume, as the government has, that this does not happen."

[Government speaker rises]

Opposition speaker: "Sit down, please. Now, then they say: 'Well, we're viewing art wrongly.' We ask for an example of this. They offer the example of the Declaration of Independence. We say: 'What should we do with the Declaration of Independence?' They say: 'Well, actually, that's fine, but the problem is the Igbu tribe.' Let's look at the Igbu tribe. Now, I don't know too much about them, but just based on what the speaker said, if the Igbu tribe creates things and they like those things to decay, then why are they objecting to us taking those things and putting them into our museums?"

Government speaker, rising with hand outstretched: "On that point."

Opposition speaker: "Clearly, they have no investment in having these things for their own personal use because they want them to decay. Please sit down. Now, here are two questions. Number one: Are they talking about art? Are they interested in the benefits of art? If they are, they need to realize that there's no one context to art. Art can mean many different things to many different people. Just because you don't belong to the Igbu tribe doesn't mean that you can't appreciate them from your own aesthetic perspective."

Government speaker: "Point of information."

Opposition speaker: "No, thank you. Sit down."

Government speaker, taking his seat: "You don't have to get so upset."

Opposition speaker: "Okay, I know I don't have to get upset, but how about you stay sitting for more than 30 seconds?"

[Government speakers both stand up]

Opposition speaker: "That's great. Please, both of you, sit

down. Secondly, they say: 'Well, we need to move beyond Western conceptions of law.' But where have they gotten these very mystical and Eastern conceptions? From the involvement with and investigation of these art artifacts. That's what gives them these other perspectives. That's what allows them to make these arguments. Additionally, you need to consider the care of this art. It's a simple fact that most of these societies do not have the ability to maintain this art because they are developing societies and, quite frankly, they have other priorities. Look at the Parthenon frieze. The two marbles that have been left on the Parthenon frieze are in a state of extreme decay, whereas the Parthenon marbles that are in the British Museum are in a state of remarkable artistic effectiveness. Or, they could be talking about the people. They may not want to help the art: They may instead want to help the people."

[Government speaker rises]

Opposition speaker: "Please sit down. Let's talk about reparations in terms of war. They say that when there's a war and people steal art, we have an obligation to return that art. But there's a limited amount of political capital in terms of reparations. It's not like everyone in Germany is running around stumbling all over themselves to pay billions of dollars back to the French. That's not a movement in Germany. In fact, it happens only with great amounts of political capital and at a tremendous political expense. You need to ask yourself: What is the most effective use of that political capital? Is it to restore art objects, something that the top one percent of the top one percent of the people use, create, and experience? Or is it in industrial, environmental, and medical reparations – things that affect the lives of the vast majority of these countries?

"All that their proposal does is extinguish these symbols of imperialism. They say, and this is a quote: 'We need to establish an appropriate relationship between states.' I agree. But you don't simply do that by closing your eyes and erasing all of the history of imperialism. There is a system

ART, ARGUMENT AND ADVOCACY

that exists right now whereby certain countries, most notably Western countries, are far more powerful than countries around the world. One of the major signs of that power disparity is the fact that these artifacts exist in locations other than where they were produced. When you move those artifacts back, you don't change the situation. You don't make those countries equal. Don't let them fool you into believing that. What you do is just eliminate the *sign* of that inequality. You eliminate the fact that all of us can, for example, talk about this. Why is this a debatable issue? Because we have been made aware that there is inequality in international relations through the existence of these art objects in disparate locations. When you move the art objects back, you will deny the same lesson to other people. After the objects are returned there will be no sign of inequality, no sign for us to determine whether we should be changing our policies as they relate to the rest of the world.

For all these reasons, we beg to oppose."

# INDEX